ORGANIZATIONAL
—LAW—

THE **A-Z** OF INDIAN CORPORATE LAW

ORGANIZATIONAL LAW

THE **A-Z** OF INDIAN CORPORATE LAW

DR. REENA LENKA

White Falcon Publishing

www.whitefalconpublishing.com

Organizational Law: The A-Z of Indian Corporate Law
Dr. Reena Lenka

www.whitefalconpublishing.com

ISBN - 978-1-63640-353-3

Self Introduction

Hello everyone. This is Dr. Reena Lenka, Founder/Director of RL Consultancy and Training Institute, Pune, India. Today I would like to give you my small introduction. I am an MBA in HR, PHD in HR, and Postgraduate Diploma in Business Management as well. I have 10 years of work experience as a corporate HR trainer for corporates like IABM, Pune, India; India Com, Pune, India; and ICICI Prudential, Pune, India. I have 10 years of work experience as an HR faculty in various management institutions, like Symbiosis College of Management Pune, India; Ness Wadia College of Commerce, Pune, India; Neville Wadia College of Management, Pune, India; Tilak Maharashtra Vidyapeeth, Pune, India; and MIT College of Management, Pune, India. I have 10 publications to my credit in various international journals, as well as 5 Scopus publication in HR in various international journals.

Thank you and God bless you.

Contents

The Indian Contract Act, 1872

❖ *It is the most important and first topic of business law*

What do you mean by a contract?

- An agreement based by law, between two or more people, could be a written or oral agreement, it is not mandatory that it should be in written format. Anything that can give proof when there is a requirement and is agreed on the willingness of two or more people for the similar terms and conditions is known as a contract. At the same time, it has legal backing. If someone is not following the contract then, the other person can sue that person.

Contract is an agreement based on law.

❖ **PROPOSAL**

- When one person signifies to another his willingness to do or to abstain from doing anything, with a view to obtain the assent of the other to such acts or abstinence, he is said to make a proposal- when the person is willing to do something or to abstain himself from doing something. For example, I am a faculty and if a parent comes to me and requests me to take home tuition for their son, who is in class 10. And I agree to that and I say okay fine I will be taking your tuition for class 10th but there is a clause there if I am taking tuitions for the particular boy I am not supposed to take any other tuition for anyone, this is asking someone to abstaining himself from doing something and if I accept this willingly and then it becomes a proposal.

❖ <u>PROMISE</u>

- When the person to whom the proposal is made signifies his assent too, the proposal is said to be accepted. A proposal, when accepted, becomes a promise. - when going for a contract, a proposal is made, a promise is made by a person who is giving you the proposal. If it is accepted by the other person then it becomes a promise. For example – if you want to take a house on rent, suppose I Professor Reana Lenka having a house and I want to give the house on rent, its is a two-bedroom flat, per month I am asking the person who is taking on the rent Rs.20,000, this is the proposal I am making to people who are ready to take the house on rent for 20,000rs. per month this is the proposal and this is what I have given to the public if my friend comes to me and says Reana I am ready to take your house and I am ready to pay 20,000. And this becomes a promise.
- The person making the proposal is called the "promisor" and the person accepting the proposal is called the "promisee".

❖ <u>CONSIDERATION</u>

- When at the desire of the promisor, the promise or any other person has done or abstained from doing, such act or abstinence or promise called a consideration for the promise.

Consideration is the desire of the promisor, while I am giving the proposal, whatever terms and conditions I have put in the proposal. For example – if I have a car, a Maruti 800 and I want to sell it to someone for the price of two lakhs rupees, I give this offer and I promise to do that, I would be selling it. At the same time, I have mentioned certain clauses. Whoever wants to purchase the Maruti 800 for 2 lakhs of rupees That, person has to give me instant cash. I won't be accepting cheques these are the clauses I have made. Based on this offers, terms and conditions I have put for this particular transaction if it is accepted by the other person without saying anything that becomes a consideration. Simply put- What the other person is ready to get in lieu of certain kinds of conditions is consideration. For example, you doing a job, you're getting a job and getting a pay of Rs.20,000 it's a consideration why because you have accepted the job and for that, you need to give them eight hours of your day, and for that, they would be paying you Rs.20,000. This is a consideration. What a person wants to forego, to get something that is known as consideration. A contract cannot be made without a consideration.

❖ AGREEMENT

- Every promise and every set of promises, forming the consideration for each other, compose an agreement. It is a promise made by the promisor and accepted by the promisee without any counter clause. If it is not willingly accepted, then it is not an agreement.
- An agreement not enforceable by law is said to be void. agreement is not enforced by a law it is not considered as an agreement for example there is a birthday party, you invite your friend for a birthday party and your friend has accepted the invitation Saying I am ready to come for the birthday party, but the friend doesn't turn up, then you cannot take the person to court, because it is not an agreement but if I have a flat, I want to sell the flat for 50 lakhs of rupees which is a two-bedroom flat. My customer wants to take my flat for 50 lakhs of rupees and I do the transaction, I handover the flat but my client doesn't want to pay 50 lakhs of rupees and now wants to pay only 20 lakhs of rupees this is an agreement and it is backed by law, and this cannot be a void one. This is an agreement which can be taken to court and the person can be sued. But in the previous example, we cannot sue the person if he doesn't want to come to the birthday party that cannot be an agreement.

❖ CONTRACT

- An agreement enforceable by law is a contract. It is an agreement by two or more parties willingly agreed upon and enforceable by law. It means that if any of the parties are not fulfilling the terms and conditions of the contract, then the other party can be sued.

❖ STEPS INVOLVED IN THE CONTRACT

- Proposal and its communication – When thinking about making a contract, first you need to make a proposal. Whatever we want to give becomes a proposal.

- Acceptance of proposal and its communication – Once the proposal is accepted, it has to be communicated. For example, my friend is having a bike, and he wants to sell the bike for 30,000 rupees and has given an offer to everyone I want the bike, I think I will pay 30,000 and go for the bike I don't communicate this to my friend, after 2 or 3 days I reach my friend's place with Rs.30,000 and say that I want to purchase your bike. And my friend says that I have already sold the bike. And I cannot fight with my friend Because I have accepted, I need to be communicative, and my friend is not a God that he will come to know or understand what is happening in my mind. In every contract, everything needs to be communicated, whether it is a proposal, an acceptance, or anything else.
- Agreement by mutual promises – It refers to the agreement where parties are agreeing to the terms and conditions mutually.
- Contract – A written document
- Performance of a contract – It refers to how are you fulfilling the terms and conditions of the contract. For example, I go to a vegetable vendor, I want to purchase one KG of mangoes and the vegetable vendor has one KG of mango I am ready to pay, I am ready to pay Rs.130 for the Mango, I pay Rs.130, and I am taking the mangoes this is a performance of the contract. The term was that I go to the market like the Mango, and the vendor would be quoting the price, I paid the price and I got the mangoes. This is the performance of the contract in this respect. If it is for renting a flat, The performance of the contract would be signing of the contract and giving the money, deposit, the advance, this would be the performance of the contract. Being a student if you're taking admission in the college, there the performance of the contract would be full of filling the form, money or instalments maybe the fee would 50,000; 60,000 or 1 lakh, whatever it is, get the receipt from the accounts department, giving a proof that you already paid the money and then you get the admission. And it is a performance of a contract in terms of college admission.

These are important steps of a contract.

Essential requirements of a valid contract or the features of the contract

- Offer and its acceptance by both parties - When giving an offer, accepting the fact that it should be free, that is, no one is forcing anyone for anything, then it becomes a feature of a contract.
- Mutual and lawful consideration for agreement - It should be mutual and lawful, it shouldn't be anything unlawful. For example –(for the unlawful) the owner of the company wants to give you the job, I am in a need of a job and I need to get in a very good position, a position as a senior finance manager, you got the position, the owner says I am ready to give you the job if you want a job you need to kill the person who is already in that position, and you accept it. And this will not be in a contract, This cannot be a lawful Consideration. Lawful consideration is whatever you are doing should be legal. You shouldn't be going against any law.
- It should be enforced by law. Hence intention should be to create a legal relationship. Agreements are social or domestic in nature and not contracts. There shouldn't be any kind of ulterior motive to the contract. Whatever you are going for should be legal, And it should be fulfilled, when you're going for any kind of social or domestic nature, for example, are going to an NGO to sign a contract or as COVID-19 is going on, you want to help the government by Contributing to the fund care, this is not an agreement this is out of on your own will, you are doing it no one is forcing you to do it this cannot be an agreement and this is not a part of a contract. Contract as a give and take. Here it is not a give-and-take it is just a social gesture, a global gesture and this cannot be a agreement.
- Party should be competent to contract. It should be eligible enough for a contract. For instance, you should be a major not a minor, of sound mind, matured enough, and in a position to think, A person who is mentally unstable, suffering from mental illness, drunken, or idiot cannot be competent enough for the contract. Also, you need to be an Indian citizen and more than 18 years old to be competent to contract.

- The object should be lawful - The very base of the contract should be lawful. You cannot go and sign a contract with a terrorist.
- Certainty and possibility of performance - Whatever the terms and conditions of the contract, it should be feasible enough for a human being to fulfill the terms and conditions of the contract. for example – most of the people are scared of death, some person wants to get a feel of the heaven without dying and one of your friends said that okay you could do that with the help of a Baba, you go to a Baba and you say the Baba that I am ready to go to heaven and I want to go to heaven, Baba say that for that you need to pay me five lakhs of rupees, and I'll send you to heaven. In this example, I am giving you because do you think this is possible being a human being like a baba who can send you to heaven without you dying. So this cannot be the base of a contract. Anything which you are doing should be possible for a human being. If you're entering a contract for selling a car or a bike, taking admission in college all these things are possible and are in the preview of human beings Capabilities. And this becomes a feature for a contract.
- The contract should not have been declared as void under the Contract Act or any other law - Void means something that doesn't exist. In law, if you're entering into a contract with a minor (who is less than 18 years old), it is considered as a void act. Because you should be entering into contract with someone who is mature enough to think and understand the terms and conditions of the contract.

❖ *OFFER*

When going for a contract, you need to make an offer.

- May be express or implied - Express means whatever you're saying, other people would understand. For example, if I am giving an offer for selling my book for 500rs. I get the offer and I need to say to the people that yes I have a HR book which is costing Rs.500 which I need to sell-off. And the people would be taking that as an offer. Until and unless I don't express or say no one would be understanding it and it cannot be an offer. Imply means by default you have to take it no one is going say it or it is your responsibility to accept those terms and conditions, for example, I have a laptop which I want to sell for Rs.20,000, and I get this offer to my friends and colleagues, one of my colleagues comes to my house and he wants to take it and I said go ahead take the laptop, he or she takes the laptop and doesn't offer me the price and is ready to take off with that laptop. This is what implied is all about no one is going to teach you that once you're taking a good means you need to pay what is the same and this becomes the implied one.

- May be positive or negative - An offer can be a positive one. You may be selling or giving rent and the person is taking your offer, so it becomes a positive offer. An offer can also be a negative one, where you are expecting someone to do something or, more accurately, not to do something, that is, you're stopping someone from doing something. For example, suppose you are given an offer to join a company as an HR manager and every month you would be paid Rs.70-Rs.80,000 and you are also being told during the appointment letter that along with this, you are not supposed to do any kind of other business apart from doing this job. This becomes a negative offer where you are being stopped from doing something else along with what you are doing.

- Must intend to create a legal relationship - Whatever offer you are giving, it should be fulfilled by you. Both parties should be accepting it and going the legal way, while maintaining a good and legal relationship.

- Terms of the offer must be certain - You should be giving your offers in certain ways and terms and conditions that are understandable by other people. For example, if you are selling flower vase for Rs.1000, a crystal flower vase is very beautiful, And you're making your offer as certain, whereas if you say the price range of this flower vase is Between Rs.500-Rs.1000 means the offer is not certain. Whenever you're making an offer you should be certain and the terms and conditions should be certain.

- May be made to a specific person or class of persons or anyone in the world at large - offer can be to a specific person, for example, I want to sell pen drive to my friend so I would be only giving the offer to my close friend whom I know would be taking it that becomes a specific person or a class of person. During Diwali or

Dussehra so many sales goes on in pantaloons, Amazon is also giving, everyone is going for a sale, these are the international level sale it would be at a large scale and for everyone Class of person, if this sale is only for India, pantaloon India it would Be for a class of persons in India.

- Must be communicated to the offeree - Whatever were you thinking, I want to give my house and every month Rs.30,000 and deposit should be Rs.35,000 these terms and conditions should be communicated to the offeree then only it can become an offer.

- Must be made with a view to obtain the assent - Whatever you are giving, it should be offered in such a way that people are ready to take that offer. For example, I am selling a laptop, A second-hand laptop for five crores of rupees, it is not possible for anyone to take the laptop or that offer, after all, it is a second-hand one It is not an Antique one where people would be interested why they should go for this offer but if I want to sell my laptop say for 30,000 or 40,000 people can go for it and this becomes a offer.

- May be conditional - The terms and conditions mentioned, for example, I will sell my laptop but you for that you need to pay Rs.30,000 in cash and it is a condition in which you are putting if it is so that can be the offer.

Termination of the offer - *How an offer can be terminated?*

- By notice of revocation - Revocation means you are putting in certain terms or conditions apart from what it was there. For example – if you're selling your car for 2 lakhs of rupees and your friend was ready but suddenly you need more money. what are you do is you call up your friend and saying I'm not ready to sell my car for two lakhs of rupees you can take it for, you now have to pay three lakhs of rupees and that becomes a revocation, the previous contract which your friend was ready to pay for, it would become null and void it would be cancelled and it would be a termination of offer previously the offer was something now it has changed and the price has increased so it can come to termination of the offer. The revocation can take place before your friend gives you the money and before the contract comes to an end. Any changes can happen before The contract takes place.

- By lapse of time - Within a time frame, if you're not taking the offer, it leads to a termination of the offer. For example, if LG is going on sale and they're saying, till next Monday 13th of April the sale would be going on and the price of the refrigerator and washing machine and every products the LG have it would be on 50% reduction, I see the offer and I Feel that it's a very good offer I should go and get myself something I was in a need of microwave and I want to purchase it, I don't turn up to LG by 13th, I go to LG on 15th and I demand a 50% discount on the price of LG microwave then it is not an offer the offer has already been terminated because it was for a specific time and since I didn't turn up means the Offer comes to an end.
- By failure of the acceptance to fulfill a condition precedent to acceptance - Acceptor is the one who would be taking up your offer, and he is not able to fulfill a condition before the acceptances need. For example – I have a second-hand leather bag and I want to sell it off, the condition was the leather bag I was selling off for Rs.3000 and my condition was my friend was supposed to give me at least 1500 before it takes the bag and after he takes the bag after one day can give me another 1500. 1500 was already given to me, but the next day. I haven't got the other 1500 that means the offer is terminated because the person my friend hasn't fulfilled the condition Which is already put when the offer was made.
- By failure to accept according to the mode prescribed - If an offeree is not accepting the offer in prescribed format, then the offer comes to a termination. For example suppose my friend has a car, and he wants to sell it off for three lakhs of rupees. But what I have already conveyed to my friend is that the car, the seat cover should be changed. But that was my condition since I am making an offer I cannot make a counter condition, that is what my friend has already given and that becomes the termination of the offer. My friend has already given an offer to sell the car for three lakhs of rupees without him putting any kind of conditions, But when I am accepting the offer and I am putting this condition means that the offer comes to an end.
- By death or insanity of the offeror - Suppose there is a house and the owner of the house wants to sell that house for 50 lakhs of rupees and he has already given the advertisement and people are

ready to purchase the house. But the day the people are coming due to certain reason the person has lost his mental balance or has met with an accident and he is seriously injured and is almost on the verge of death then the offer comes to an end.

- By rejection - When the offer is made and is rejected by the offeror, then the offer comes to an end.

Essentials of a valid acceptance

While making an offer acceptance is important, if the acceptance is not there, then it is not a valid contract.

- Acceptance must be absolute and unconditional - Whatever conditions given it has to be accepted in that format. For example suppose you're taking admission in MBA college and the fee is four lakhs of rupees for two years, when you're taking an admission it would be two lakhs in a year, one lakh per six months, this is the condition which is being put by the college, you being a student when you are accepting that and paying one lakh of rupees within six months taking admission and that becomes an acceptance. If you say you cannot pay one lakh of rupees and you can only pay Rs.30,000 initially so that cannot be an acceptance.
- Acceptance by usual mode as desired by the offeror - The acceptance format given has to be accepted by the offeror. For example, if you're getting a job, and you got an appointment as a marketing manager in a company like reliance, there is a prescribed format which you need to fill up, they will be giving your offer letter which you need to sign and accept it. So it should be in that accepted format. Whatever terms and conditions are there in the offer letter when you're accepting and signing it that becomes an acceptance.
- Acceptance cannot precede the offer - suppose today I am giving an offer to the public, I want to sell bedsheets, and I have 1000 bedsheets, good quality Jaipuri cotton style bed sheets but I want to sell it off. Per bed sheet I want to sell for 500 or 600 this is what I have decided, and this I was discussing with my friend. Before I give the offer my friend says I want to purchase 10 of

your bedsheets. This cannot be an acceptance, because I have just decided, I haven't given the offer before I give the offer, the acceptance cannot be made. And this cannot be an acceptance.

- Acceptance may be express or implied - whatever is expressed whatever I am saying like I am selling off a brand new boss music system that is expressed for Rs.50,000 or one lakh of rupees that means this is expressed then only you can understand and when you accepting after that the acceptance happens. Implied means when you purchase the system it is but obvious that you have to pay for it.

- Acceptance must be given within a reasonable time - When you are accepting, it should be in a prescribed time. When you're getting a job and you have been appointed as a software programmer In IBMI. You haven't given a offer letter and management says you decide and you tell me, you have been selected but you have other offers in hand and you disclose the same to the management and the management say is that okay fine you take your time and you need to inform us within a week and you say okay. If you didn't convey your acceptance of this offer within a week, it does not stay valid, because it was not accepted within the prescribed time.

- Acceptance must be by an ascertained person (offeree) - Acceptance must be done by the same person who has been given the offer. Today if, I being a faculty is giving an offer to the student, whoever is interested can come and take tuitions from me, and that to a specific class like BBA or MBA students are accepted then that becomes an acceptance. If engineering students are coming to me it will not be an acceptance. Because this offer has not been given to the engineering students.

- Offer cannot be accepted after it was rejected unless it is renewed - Once the offer is made, it has to be accepted there. But if you're rejecting it, then it cannot be an acceptance. You can only accept it if it is renewed. For example – I have been given a position as an assessment officer at IBS College of management it is a very good college but the problem is I being working with some where else I cannot take offer immediately and the criteria was I am supposed to join by tomorrow but I am working as a full-time faculty in some other college, it is not possible for me. I can't join the college the next day, I need one month so I can put down my papers and inform the management and then I can go if this thing is happening to me then what I will do I will reject the offer and I will say not possible for me, I need one month other than that I cannot accept the offer. This rejection happens and then acceptance cannot happen. If this offer is renewed further and they like me very much and they really want me to join the job and they say we will give you one month where you can join then a new appointment letter has to come to me and then I accept it and it would be considered as an acceptance.

- Silence does not imply acceptance - If I don't say anything, how can the other person know if I have accepted anything. For example- i want to Sell my laptop, to my friend for Rs.30,000, I convey this to her and she is interested but she doesn't say anything, she just thinks that the laptop is in good condition I should be taking it but she doesn't say anything then what happened it is not an acceptance how am I supposed to know that my friend is interested in that laptop so I go ahead and sell the laptop to someone else who would be accepting it and conveying the same that I am interested and I am ready to take.

- Acceptance must be made before the lapse or revocation of the offer - before the time gets over because for everything there is a specific time if I am not acting on the specific time then it is not an acceptance, acceptance beyond a specific time is not acceptance or any terms and conditions if it has changed it is not an acceptance revocation mean you are changing The terms and conditions. Like the previous example I gave you of the job, that would be a revocation. And this revocation will start with the new contract.

- Acceptance of offer means acceptance of all terms attached to the offer - If I am accepting, it means I am not supposed to put any other condition. For example I have a Samsung cell phone, I want to sell it, so that, with that money I can get a new cell phone I start advertising for the same, people who are interested in my cell phone, as it is in very good condition and I said I want to sell it off for 20,000, and this is the offer which has been made this has to be accepted as it is one or two people come, they say that it is in a very good condition but we cannot pay Rs.20,000 I will only pay 10,000 this is not an acceptance. Since my terms and conditions are for 20,000 it is in good condition, good brand cell phone I am ready to sell it all for 20,000 only and those are my terms and conditions and my offer. Acceptance by another person should be on my terms and condition if it is not then it is not an acceptance.

Legal rules regarding consideration

- Consideration is required both for the formation and discharge of an agreement or contract - Consideration is taking up or forgoing an opportunity. Consideration is what you are ready to pay to get something that is of your liking. Consideration is very important without consideration there cannot be a contract. For example, if you're going for a contract with a person who is ready to sell his bike to you. You are interested in the bike, ready to pay Rs.50,000, that is your consideration you like you pay and you are ready for the contract. Another person's need is that he doesn't want the bike and wants the money. That is at the person's consideration. When the contract is formed the consideration is required when the contract is coming to an end, consideration is required. The consideration for the buyer is that he wants a bike, and wants to pay Rs.50,000, the seller doesn't want the bike, wants Rs.50,000. The people agreeing to it and paying the seller 50,000 contracts come to an end and the seller gives the bike to the buyer and the contract comes to an end. Discharge of an agreement means that the agreement is coming to an end. And it is a consideration that is required for the formation of a contract too.

- Consideration may be past, present, and future - Past means based on what you had entered into the contract. For example – you want a car which is a BMW and you're very interested but the price of the car was high. It was 35 to 40 lakhs of rupees Or more. And you promise yourself that I would be purchasing the car. So you start working and saving money one fine day, and at this moment you have 50 lakhs of rupees and in a very good position to purchase the car, you go to the showroom you see the car of your choice and you want to purchase it and you have the money, but the colour of the car you don't like it you want something else maybe you want to go for a silver, and the silver Colour was not present in the showroom, the showroom people say you have to wait, After one month or so it will be available and you said okay whenever this thing comes you just inform me and this is for the future when you're ready to take the car you got the money you got the car but the colour choice is not yours so you are ready to wait for the future for that car so this becomes a future consideration. You are ready to shell out money for the car and this becomes a future consideration.

- Consideration may be either positive or negative - If you are considering without any condition, then it is a positive one. It would be negative if certain conditions are attached to it.
- Consideration must be done at the desire of the promisor - For example, I want to sell the car for five lakhs of rupees I am the promisor and it is my offer and it is my consideration whatever terms and conditions are mentioned by me that I want half in cash half in cheque and I want to sell it for five lakhs of rupees this is my consideration since I am giving an offer, so this should be at the desire of the promiser
- Consideration may be furnished by the promisee or any other person - Anyone who wants to go to the contact and wants to purchase anything can form a part of the consideration.
- Consideration must be lawful - It should be legal. You cannot go for a contract or consideration with a terrorist or enemy or a person who is in the jail, as it would be an unlawful one.
- Consideration must be real and not illusionary - It cannot be such a contract that human beings cannot fulfill. For example you want to hire a mechanical engineer Who can build bridges, ropeways and you want to build a ropeway in the entire India, in the next two days. This is not real, this can only happen in the movies is cannot be a practical thing and it is not possible and it is not a consideration.
- Consideration need not be adequate - Actual price of things should be according to the person's financial status. For example I have a TV, LGTV 50 inches colour TV, I want to sell that TV for Rs.2000 and it is in very good condition you must be thinking that the price is not adequate how can you sell a TV for 50 inches, colour TV for 2000, in good conditions this cannot be a part of a contract but this can be a part of a contract, contract happens on whatever terms and condition both the parties are agreeing to

if I being an offeror I want to sell the TV for Rs.2000 that can be done doesn't matter when the other person is ready to pay for the same thing it can be a consideration.

- Consideration must not be the performance of existing duties - The consideration for some other agreement that has been done in the past cannot be a consideration for the present contract. If I had already promised a person I will be giving my cell phone to the person for Rs.10,000, and I had promised at one year back and presently I am ready to sell my engineering books, per book I am ready to sell for Rs.600, now these are the two things that had happened when I had promised in the past and now I'm going for something else, the cell phone I had promised in the past that cannot be consideration for the selling of engineering books. These are two different things, first one would be a past consideration for a past contract. Selling of the engineering books would be a present consideration, and a present contract.

- Consideration must be of some value in the eye of law - Consideration should be legal in the eyes of law. For example, if you're going into a contact with a minor, which is not at all legal in the eyes of law, it cannot be a consideration for the contract. Maybe the minor is having lots of property and you want to grab the property. But he is a minor, so it is not legal and it is not a part of a consideration or a contract.

CONTRACTUAL CAPACITY - *Who all should be competent enough to go into a contrac?*

- Every person is competent to contract who is of the age of the majority according to the law to which he is subject and who is of sound mind, and is not disqualified from contracting by any law to which he is subject – The capacity to form a contract. How should a person be who is competent enough to go into a contract. He should at least be 18 years old. You should be a sane person, you shouldn't be an idiot or a lunatic, not suffering from any kind of mental illness. No drunkard, they are not of sound minded and they cannot enter into a contract. If the law has already stated that these kinds of people cannot enter into a contract and you being a fool you offer a contract, it cannot be taken as a part of a contract.

For example, in the Law, it is stated, in Hindu law if you're going for a second marriage you need to divorce your 1st wife. And you don't want to divorce your first wife or husband and you go for a marriage with the second person that cannot be a contract. Because it has already been declared as null or void. If you are entering into contract with a minor again you are disqualified from the law and it cannot be a contract. If you're entering into a contract with a foreign enemy, like a person who is staying in Pakistan, These kinds of people. If you're entering into a contract with these kinds of people then it is not a legal one in India.

- Mental deficiency- The people who can think and cannot suffer from any kind of mental illness. Those people who have thinking capacity can give rational judgment are considered as sane. We can enter into a contract with these kinds of people. Beyond this, we cannot enter into a contract with those who are not in their senses, lunatic, mad, idiots, and drunkards.

(Sound mind he is capable of understanding it and forming a rational judgement as to its effect upon his interest)

Mental incompetence- Alzheimer disease, where the person forgets. You cannot enter into a contract. These people don't know what they are thinking. How can you enter into a contract with them?

Idiots- Who is IQ level is very less

Lunatics and insane persons- mad people.

Minor (<18)- less than 18 years of age.

Drunkenness- they are drunk throughout the day and they are not in the senses and how can you Enter into a contract.

- legal disability (alien enemy, insolvent, imprisonment)- insolvency means bankruptcy, if you don't have anything in your bank, these kinds of people cannot enter into a contract. Imprisonments serve jail punishment for certain kinds of criminal offence or civil offence and these kinds of people cannot enter into a contract.

Free consent

- *Agree upon the same thing in the same sense*. When you're getting into a contract you should willingly enter into a contract; no one can force you. If someone is forcing you, then it is not a contract.

Consent is not free when caused by:

- Coercion - When you're physically harming someone. For property, you want to sell your property, customers are coming for the property, and your friend wants to have a property but is not in a position to pay, he comes with a gun and just wants to take the property forcefully that becomes coercion and it cannot be free consent.
- Undue influence - Here, you are emotionally trying to influence someone. For example, seniors can influence juniors, the elder brother can influence you, your parents can influence you, etc. These kinds of influences mean it becomes undue influence, means you are not thinking. Someone is forcing you to think and this becomes an undue influence and not free consent.
- Fraud - Here, you are intentionally hiding certain facts. For example, you are selling a medicine chlorophyll, it is a malaria medicine. You being a chemist you know this medicine's expiry date is already over. Sometimes people are in such a hurry they don't check the expiry, they come and they just pick up the medicine and without checking. And the patient is serious. This is kind of a fraud. It is not free content because when you know something, you are hiding the facts. This doesn't come under free consent, And it cannot form a contract.
- Misrepresentation - Giving facts that are not true.
- Mistake - You are given out the facts unintentionally. For example – you have a property in your hometown, Your dad wants to sell that property and he has informed you that you are staying in the city. Why don't you see some people who would be ready to purchase the property. And there was no interaction between you and your dad. One fine day you got a buyer and took him to the village, and there you saw that your dad had already sold off the property to someone else and it is a mistake but it is unintentional one you didn't know the fact. Mistakes could be by law or facts. The one which I gave an example of as a mistake of fact. And the mistake of law is that you should be having good knowledge regarding Indian law if you're in a foreign country then regarding the foreign law. For example in the Hindu religion if you're getting married second time you should be divorcing your first wife or

first husband but didn't want to find out what is the law and you are getting married for the second time without divorcing your first wife or husband and this is a mistake of law this cannot be considered as a contract and it is a mistake and not free consent.

Object and public policy

Anything that is against the public policy cannot be taken as a contract.

- Not be forbidden by law - Anything forbidden by the law cannot be taken as a contract For example, Getting into a contract with a minor, a terrorist, etc.
- Should not defeat the provision of any law - Whatever the law has already decided, the contract cannot be against it. Anything going against the law will not be a part of the contract. For example, making a contract with mentally ill person.
- Not to be fraudulent - Whatever object is being put in front, it shouldn't be fraud. You shouldn't intentionally hide the fact. For example, if you have a horse and if you want to sell your horse, but he is suffering from the disease, and because of that the horse will be dying in two days. And you want to sell that house because you don't want that horse. And you don't want to suffer for that horse so you ask your friend that I need to send a horse and your friend said that go ahead sell your horse and I am ready to Buy it, Your friend is ready to pay one lakh of rupees you take the money and within two days the horse is dead and it is fraudulent because you yourself knew this is a fraud and you went ahead with the contract, this cannot be the object for the contract. The very base of the contract is defeated and it cannot be a contract.
- Should not injure a person/property - Anything that is harming a person or a property cannot be an object of the contract.
- Should not be opposed by public policy - It shouldn't be moral or opposed to the public or public policy. For example public policies that you shouldn't be harming any kind of children, children shouldn't be harmed during the contract, children shouldn't be sold off to other countries and it is against the public policy. But you enter into a contract with someone and you're ready to sell

or kidnap, sell children to another country this comes against public policy. Children under 14 years of age cannot work in any company or cannot be a house worker. But you get a child who is less than 14 years old and you make that person work for you. It is against the public policy and it cannot be a contract.

❖ VOID AND VOIDABLE CONTRACTS

VOID

- An agreement that is enforceable by law at the option of one or more of parties thereto, but not at the option of other or others, is a voidable contract - Voidable contract means that you can keep aside that contact for some time until the condition is suitable for you. For example you are booking a flat in a posh locality in Pune. In Hinjewadi where their IT sectors, and the flats are very good and it is a posh area And you want to book a flat there. You go ahead and book a flat, the price of the flat is one crore. 3 bedroom flat when you are ready to pay one crores of rupees. You Have already paid 50 lakhs of rupees and another 50 lakhs you are supposed to pay after one month where you get the possession of the flat. The day you are planning to take possession due to some natural calamity, The building collapses or is destroyed. What happened is you didn't get your flat and 50,00,00 rupees is already with the builder and you don't have a flat. What you can do is you can take the money back from the builder and the builder says wait for a few months with the same money I will be making a new flat for and will be giving it to you. Another six months or one year and then you'll get it is a voidable contract where you keep aside a contract until and unless the terms and conditions are favourable and then you go ahead either you close the contract or go ahead with it.
- A contract that ceases to be enforceable by law becomes a void contract - The contact doesn't exist for example entering into a contract with a minor, the women who are in parda Who are covered from head to toe you cannot enter into a contract. You cannot enter into a contract with a country's enemy, you do not enter into a contract with an insane person and these kinds of things are void or the contract doesn't exist in the eyes of law.

Types of contact - On the basis of validity

- Valid contract - An agreement which has all the essential elements of a contract is called a valid contract.
- Void contract - A void contract is a contract that ceases to be enforceable by law. It doesn't exist in the eyes of law.
- Voidable contract - An agreement that is enforceable by law at the option of one or more of the parties thereto, but not at the option of other or others, is voidable contract.
- Illegal contract - A contract is illegal if it is forbidden by law; or is of such nature that, if permitted, would defeat the provisions of law.
- Unenforceable contract: A contract that is good in substance but because of some technical defect cannot be enforced by law is called an enforceable contract. These contracts are either void or voidable. When you started with the contract because it was a valid one, but then a long time has passed, then the contract cannot be enforced.
  1. Express contract - Where the terms of the contract are expressly agreed upon in words (written or spoken) at the time of formation, the contract is said to be an express contract.

     Express contract is whatever you are thinking regarding the terms and conditions you should be expressing.
  2. Implied contract - An implied contract is one that is inferred from the acts or conduct of the parties or from the circumstances of the cases.

     Implied contract means that without saying you think it is your responsibility to do so. The same example I would like to extend, the 400 rupees pen drive I have, my friend comes up and takes it. He was supposed to give me 400 rupees, that is quite obvious. But without paying he tries to leave the house or tells me I am now leaving. So there it is not an implied contract for him and I am not supposed to tell him that I have already given the offer, the price has been stated so he should be paying the price. No one is going to tell you that if you are purchasing that you have to pay the price of the same. So this is an example of an implied contract.

3. Quasi contract - A quasi contract is created by law. It is a legal obligation that is imposed on a party that is required to perform it. A quasi contract is based on the principle that a person shall not be allowed to enrich himself at the expense of another.

   Quasi contract is actually created by law, where the law doesn't permit anyone to enrich themselves on the expense of another. For example suppose a salesperson I had come to your house and that person was selling washing powder and suppose he had a round 5kg of washing powder with him and we were not interested in the washing powder and we said we are not interested in the washing powder and the salesperson requested that can he get a glass of water and you said ok fine so you call that person home and give him a glass of water and he drinks the glass of water and then while he was leaving he forgot to pick up his 3kg of washing powder and he left the house and you were in need of the washing powder and you open 1kg pack and you used it for washing clothes. So then the salesperson remembers and comes next day and says that by mistake i have left 3 kg of washing powder can you give it back and you said that it ok fine I have used 1 pack you can take the other two and he said it is ok that you used it you can pay me for the pack and you said that you won't pay him for that pack also. So in this case I can take you to court. So Quasi contract is created by law and it prohibits anyone from enriching themselves at the expense of another.

There are some other types of contracts too that are executed and executory contracts.

1. Executed contract - An executed contract is one in which both the parties have performed their respective obligation.

   For example you are in need of a shirt and you go to the market and the cost of the shirt is 2000 rupees so you pick up the shirt and pay 2000 rupees at the cash counter and you take the shirt and come home. Show the contract comes to an end. So you wanted the shirt you paid the money and the shopkeeper has handed you the shirt so this is executed contract where the obligations have been fulfilled by both the parties.

2. Executory contract - An executory contract is one where one or both the parties to the contract still have to perform their obligations in future.

    For example you have come travelling by train and you have landed with heavy luggage and you call a coolie to pick up your luggage and to put it in the taxi waiting outside the station. Show the coolie said that you have to pay him 200 rupees and you said yes so the coolie picks up the luggage and put it in the taxi and you don't pay him saying that you don't have change I'll pay you later on so therefore it is an executory contract where one of the party has performed his obligation and the other is still due.

❖ TYPES OF CONTRACT ON THE BASIS OF PERFORMANCE

1. Unilateral contract - A unilateral contract is one in which only one party has to perform his obligation at the time of the formation of the contract and the other party has already fulfilled it at the time of the contract (same as the executory contract).
2. Bilateral contract - A bilateral contract is one in which the obligation on both the parties to the contract is outstanding at the time of the formation of the contract (same as executed contract).

According to Section 37, Para 1 of the Contract Act, "the parties to a contract must either perform their respective promises, unless such performance is dispensed with or excused under the provision of this act, or of any other law."

The offer to perform the contract is called tender. Offer to perform or tender maybe called attempted performance. A tender, to be legally valid, must fulfill the following conditions. So when you are fulfilling the conditions of the contract, then only it becomes a valid tender.

A tender, to be legally valid, must fulfill the following conditions:

It must be unconditional.
It must be made at a proper time and place.
The person to whom a tender is made must be given a reasonable opportunity of ascertaining that the person by whom it is made is able and willing.

PERFORMANCE MADE BY WHOM?

Personal performance - In cases involving personal skill, taste, or credit, the promisor must himself perform the contract.

Performance by a representative - In all other cases, the promisor or his representative may employ a competent person to perform it. For ex- if a contract is taking place between two people, that i have a flat and i want to give on rent to another person, for 30,000rs monthly. This is between me and a person called X. And his friend is also present there. While getting into a contract if that person is not available then a third person can come and fulfil the contract.

Performance by a third person - When a promisor accepts performance of the promisee from a third person, he cannot later enforce it against the promisor.

❖ *PERFORMANCE MADE BY WHOM?*

* Death by promisor
  - Contracts involving personal skills or violation come to an end when the promisor dies. His hires or legal representative are not bound to perform such contract.: For example there is a contract with the carpenter who is building furniture, is doing something for your house or company and suddenly the carpenter dies, or in such a state that he won't be able to work and his family is not bound to fulfil the performance and the performance comes to an end.
  - In cases not involving personal skill or violation, legal representative of a deceased promisor is bound to perform the contract. Liability of the legal representatives is limited to assets obtained from the deceased. if it is not a personal skill, and the carpenter was having the specific skill any other person cannot have the same skill. A faculty like me, Other faculty won't be having the same skills I am having, for personal skills if one person is not that another person can't fulfil it. But in case of not being a personal skill and any other thing for a contract. If there is a legal representative and promisor of who has already made a promise, that legal representative can fulfil the contract and it can be taken as a performance. If there are certain kind of liabilities after the death of the promisor, if the promise is having certain property that would be utilised by the legal representative to fulfil the debts

Persons entitled to demand performance.

- Promisee (who had already promised)
- Legal representatives
- Third-party
- Joint promises

Time for performance

- When no time is specified, reasonable time is implied. For example, I have purchased a refrigerator and given instructions to the salesperson by tomorrow afternoon I need the refrigerator at my residence. This is a specific time, and that would be considered as a time for performance. And if I say whenever it is possible then I'm not giving a reasonable time, it shouldn't be like my refrigerator is coming after one or two years it should be in a reasonable time like a week.
- When time is specified, it has to be followed strictly.
- On application for performance by promisee

Place for performance

This applies to

- Delivery of goods - Generally, the goods are delivered and picked up from the place of business if the buyer is requesting the seller to deliver at the residence then that becomes a delivery of the goods and the place for performance of the goods.
- Payment of money - The payment of money is also done generally at the business place.

Performance of reciprocal promises

If I am making a promise and the same time I'm making a second and opposite promise, they become reciprocal promises. For example, I am selling dresses and also cosmetics. I have promised customers that today I would be selling dresses for 50% discount and at the same time, who ever takes that dress, would be getting one deodorant free with dress. This is a reciprocal promise happening at the same time.

- Mutual and dependent - In the above example, you'll be getting a dress with a free deodorant, so it is mutual and dependent.
- Mutual and independent - In the same example, a promise of 50% discount on dress and 20% discount on any items on cosmetics would become an independent one.
- Mutual and concurrent: When the same promises are made twice. For example, in the same example, I can say the dress for 50% for today but 20% discount, if you're taking it tomorrow.

Order of performance who has to do when: fixed by contract: for example – when you're entering into a contract you can fix when the money should be given, when you should be fulfilling the contract, these can be fixed during the time of contact.

Contracts that need not be performed

- When a new contract is substituted- for example: you have a cell phone, you are ready to sell the cell phone for Rs.20,000, you say I am selling the cell phone for Rs.20,000, and you convey the same to your friends. Suddenly in the evening you think why should I be selling this for 20,000, it is in such a good condition and all other things. I should be selling it for Rs.30,000, Rs.20,000 is too less. This becomes a new thing. This you cannot substitute with your previous one. That 20,000 your friend will be purchasing That would be a contract for the previous one. Now you're thinking about 30,000 means you're cancelling the previous one and now you have to go out with the second contract.
- A person rescinds it (who has the option of 'voidable') - You can put aside the contract until and unless the situation is favorable. For example – you have been offered a position as an HR manager in IBM, the salary offered is 70,000 per month. And you are supposed to join in one weeks time, you are ready to join everything is ready, the documents are ready, and everything is done. The day when you join, the head of IBM comes to you and says sorry we cannot take you now you have to wait for another one month, because the person who was supposed to leave that position, hasn't left the position. He is still in that position so we cannot give you that position. So it depends on you whether you

want to leave that job, or you want to wait for one month to get that position. This is rescinding, The contract comes to an end there is no need to continue with the contract.

- Promisee neglects or refuses to afford the promisor circumstances for performance - The promisee doesn't want to fulfill the terms and conditions of the contract, means you are supposed to pay Rs.5000 for a book, it's a very good book and you are supposed to pay Rs.5000. But you had promised that I will be paying Rs.5000, but when the time came for you to pay Rs.5000, you only handed over Rs.1000 to me, then the contract comes to an end because I had given Rs.5000 as the price, when you agreed you didn't say anything the day you're supposed to pay, It is only Rs.1000, then the contact comes to an end.

- Impossibility or illegality - If it should be beyond the capacity of the human being, then only the contract can be made.

- If one person has the right to rescind a contract, he can keep aside the contact till the time is favorable.

Discharge of contract by new agreement.

- Substitution
  Of old contract by new contract
  Of a party to the contract by a new one
  The new thing is added to the contract then it becomes a, the contract comes to an end. For example you are selling your flat for 50 lakhs of rupees. The contract was you have to pay 25 lakhs in cash and 25 lakhs in cheque and you agreed to do so, and then you don't have cash of 25, lakhs you request me I cannot give you 25 lakhs in cash I can only give you 10 lakhs in cash, there The contract would be discharged because I had promised you to give the flat and you are promised me to pay 25 lakhs in cash and 25 lakhs in cheque But you're not able to give so you are the contract becomes null and void and new clauses are added, if I accept 10 lakhs of rupees cash means a new thing is added to the contract. You are the contract comes to a discharge stop

- Alteration (change in terms of the contract) - you are altering certain things, for example, you are selling your car in that the car there is a music system, and it is mentioned, for five lakhs of rupees, once the person comes to you you say fine with this car you take the music system also, there is a certain alteration and change in that, then contract comes to an end. Because I didn't mention whether the music system would be given free, I'm giving it free means the contract Is altered and the contract comes to an end or the discharge of the contract happens.

- Rescission (cancellation by mutual consent/non-performing/voidable)- for example – I have a bike I want to sell my bike for Rs.50,000, and this is a price I quote to the public for example my friend doesn't have 50,000 rupees and he wants to purchase the bike for Rs.40,000 I said yes this becomes rescission Means it is cancelled, the prices cancelled by mutual consent, I get Rs.40,000 and I sell my bike for the same price.

- Waiver (abandonment of a right that a person is entitled to) - for example – some students are not able to pay the fees of college, college fees one lakh of rupees in six months and they are not able to pay one lakh of rupees within six months since the student is a very good one they come and request the authority that I cannot pay one lakh of rupees can I pay Rs.50,000 and can you waive of my fees. So the same thing can happen: certain terms and conditions can be waived off depending on the situation.

- Remission (a promisee may give up part of his claim at his will) Whole/in part
Extend the time of performance
Accept any other satisfaction than performance
  - you can extend terms and conditions till a certain time, which becomes a remission.

- Merger (superior right and inferior right coincide and meet in the same person). example a person buys the land which he has taken for lease before)- Suppose you have been a tenant in a place for 10 years and now you have money to purchase the same flat, this becomes the superior one you are the tenant and now you become the owner. The previous contract comes to an end and it becomes a merger now you become the owner and a new contract would be made.

Discharge by operation of law

- Insolvency: If the party of the contact has become bankrupt, then the contact would come to an end.
- Merger: When you become much better than in your previous position, the contract comes to an end.
- Death: If death occurs to any of the party, then discharge happens.
- Lapse of time: If the contract is not accepted in the specified time, the contract ends.
- Unauthorized material alteration: If any changes have been made to the contract, then the contract comes to an end.

Discharge of contract by the impossibility

- Destruction of objects necessary for performance - for example – you wanted to purchase the flat and the flat itself got destroyed by certain natural calamity When the object is not there, and the discharge of the contract comes to an end.
- Change of law - for example, The person in the US can purchase the property in India that was the law, when that person comes to India and wants to purchase the property at that time that this law was made The person if he's a foreign person he cannot purchase the property in India and cannot be the owner then that becomes the change of law and the contract comes to an end.
- Personal incapacity - When it is not personally possible to continue with the contract. For example, you are sick, suffering from illness and that's why you are not able to fulfil the terms and conditions of the contract. You are insolvent. Criminally convicted for certain reasons then it becomes personal and capacity and you cannot go for contact.
- Non-existence or non-occurrence of an event necessary for performance - If a certain kind of event was supposed to take place for which this contact would have been valid. For example, if you wanted a bike Enfield bike, and you want the electric blue colour to that but that colour is not possible it would be available in the future after one or two months but suddenly you come to know that colour the company has discontinued this is the non-existence of the event and here discharge of contract comes to an

end. Because without the same colour you will not go ahead with the contract.

- The outbreak of war - Due to Covid 19, it's a kind of situation which is out of control so the discharge of contract can take place.

Breach

When promises are made and you're breaking the promise, it becomes a breach.

- If a party breaks their obligation as imposed by the contract, the contract is no longer binding on the other person
- Actual breach of contract - When the party breaks the promise. the bag example which I have given. I am breaking my promise. I have taken the money but still, I'm not ready to give the bag.
- At the time when the performance is due

If one of the parties is not fulfilling the promise. For example, I have a bag and I want to sell the bag for Rs.5000. It is a leather bag, and a person is ready to pay. I have got the payment but I'm not ready to give my bag. Then it is a breach and the contact would come to an end.

- One party fails or refused to perform his obligations
  - During the performance of the contract
- Express repudiation (by word or act refuses to continue to perform his obligation) - The same example no doubt I am getting the money but I might give the bagin the future, it is expressed reputation.
- Implied repudiation (makes by his act the complete performance of the contract impossible) - It is my mistake I promise and I am not fulfilling it by giving the leather bag to my friend for Rs.5000. And here it is an implied repudiation and a breach has been made, the contract comes to an end.
- Anticipatory breach of contract (done before the time of performance arrives): breach can happen in The future, you feel that you will be back in the promise.
  - by renunciation (Express repudiation)- you might feel that you may not keep the promise, I am feeling that I don't want to part with my bag because I feel this bag is much more costly and 5000 would be too less but since I have to give it but I'm not in a mind to give it so it becomes Express repudiation.

- By creating some impossibility (implied repudiation): I would say don't worry friend what I'll do it, I'll do some more design and I'll make this bag more decorative, and better and then I'll give it to you and it becomes an implied repudiation, in either case, I'm breaking the promise and I don't have any intention to give the bag that I am giving so many reasons.

Remedies in case of breach

- Suit for damages (dealt by the Indian Contract Act) - In the previous example, only my friend has given me the money so I have to give the money back.
- Dealt by Specific Relief Act, 1963
  - Bring an action for specific performance - My friend can go to any court and say this is the situation, and this kind of fraud has been made to me whatever you feel like you do. The court can go to any extent and they can relieve my friend.
  - Suit for injunction - Injunction means when a case continues for a long time, the court stops the case midway until and unless the condition is favorable. For example, I want to purchase a flat for two crores of rupees and the builder had already promised me. That I would be having a personal swimming pool in my flat but when the builder handed over my flat there was no swimming pool in the flat, and I didn't want to take the flat without swimming pool and I went to court I told the court regarding the same, the court ordered the builder until and unless the swimming pool is been made the flat cannot be handed over to the buyer. Until and unless the conditions are favourable the suit would be injuncted.
  - Claim for quantum meruit - It should be according to the actual price of the product. For example, I had purchased 3 kgs of mangoes and each KG was hundred rupees and I had paid Rs.300 for 3 KG of mango but when I got 3 kg of mangoes only one KG mango was good and other 2 KG were rotten. I am supposed to get only Rs.300 back. I cannot ask for Rs.500 because the actual price of mango is Rs.300 so it would be Rs.300.
  - Restitution
  - Suit for cancellation or rescission

- Suit for damages (loss or damage suffered by breach of contract): Damages in the case of monetary or physical quantity would be applicable. In the case of if you're purchasing a TV or refrigerator, it could be a second refrigerator or TV which you can get, if you go for money then you can get money also.
- Kinds
  - Ordinary or general damages: These damages arise on a breach. Both parties are aware of these damages at the time of entering into a contract. For example, difference in the contract price and the market price. Whatever you asked for and getting a different one, you can go for the money on the price back. For example, order 3 kgs of basmati rice But instead of three kgs you got brown rice, here it is an ordinary or general damage, the rice would be taken back on the Basmati rice would be given or if you don't want the rice you can go for the price.
  - Special damages breach of contract under some special circumstances: For example, you have been offered a job as a director of a company. But on the day of joining, the position was not vacant and you have already left your previous position, and this company saying that you are least have to wait for six months to get the new position. This is a breach of contract too and you can go to the court and you can ask your position back.
  - Exemplary damages show the courts strong disapproval for the conduct of the defendant and committing the wrong; example refusal to honour a cheque despite having funds): for ex-refrigerator, for that, you are supposed to pay 50,000 rupees. And you have given the cheque to the seller after they gave the cheque you had informed the seller that unless and until till I don't tell you to deposit the check you will not deposit it. You didn't give instruction for six months and the person couldn't deposit the cheque but you are already having money in your bank but still, you didn't pay for it again this is a breach of contract. And it will be treated as exemplary damage by the court and you have to take care of the same.
  - Nominal damages (breach involved is of a technical nature, some nominal damages (one rupee may be rewarded): technical nature like you had asked for certain quality and

you had got different quality, for example, you had asked for silk dress but you got a cotton dress, these are the nominal damages which you can get the money back for. The dress can be exchanged and you can get it back.

- Remote damage is not to be given for any remote and indirect losses or damages sustained because of the breach): if there is any kind of indirect loss, for example – you being a director of the company and heading a company owner of the company, University, you are taking admission for the students, the seat for MBA student was 200, other students were left to take admission since the seats are full you are not able to take the other children's but since you took the money And not able to give the seat to the remaining students. This is remote damage and here you need to give the money back this would be a breach of contract since you promised this student to give you a seat and you were not able to give the seat if you take in the money you can give it back but the seats can't be given. It is indirectly a loss of the student.

- Rules regarding the determination of amount of damages
  - Restoration of parties to a position where they would have been if the contract had been performed and not where they would have been if they never made the contract- for example, the example which I gave regarding the students, since I have promised the seat and you're not getting the admission in any other college it is because of that you only if the students are not being promised regarding the same they would have got an admission in some other college. Since they were entering into a contract that is why they were not applied to any other college, and they didn't get admission in any other college, and not even in your college. Is it your responsibility to give the seats to them Because they are suffering.

- Damages are recoverable under two cases
  - When they arise naturally in the usual course of things from such breach - When the damage is made intentionally, you can go for the damage. For example, I have purchased one kilogram Basmati rice, and the rice is spoiled, then it is the job of the seller to give new rice to you.

- Loss or damages that the parties knew, when they made the contract is likely to result from the breach of it: For example – you are entering into a contract with the company, and you will be there only for two months as a counsellor or a person who is giving certain kinds of advice or suggestions. During the two months, you would be getting 50,000 rupees, and after two months you won't be getting 50,000 rupees. When you entered into the contract you knew that it was an intentional one. This is a breach of contract and an intentional one, you knew it from before and if you're forgoing that thing the party would be suffering. This is a loss of damage that parties knew.

Suit for an injunction

- Preventive relief: If any kind of contract has been made and one of the parties not fulfilling the terms and condition of the contract a preventive relief is given. For example, you are joining as a faculty in a college, and the rule of the college is that you are not supposed to get paid for six months at a stretch. You cannot sustain yourself for six months without pay. In this case, a kind of preventive relief can be given where you can say that if the college is not paying for six months, at least they can pay salary for one month.
- This is an order of the court restraining the wrongdoer from doing or continuing the wrongful act complaining of: Usually granted to enforce negative stipulations in cases where damages are not adequate relief. The same example of faculty – they can't pay for six months, this thing was already conveyed that you can give little by little, but it was not carried on so the college was asked not to continue with the faculty because they are not getting paid. This is a suit for an injunction where the court prevents another person from being penalized for a job they are doing, for a contract which they mutually agreed on.

Suit for quantum meruit

- Quantum meruit literally means "much as is earned".
- Right to quantum meruit: The right to claim the compensation of the work already done

For example, If a carpenter is working for the whole day and he was supposed to be paid Rs. 500 per day. The carpenter has worked for 7 days. The employer paid for 5 days and for the pending two days he is not ready to pay. That is wrong. Carpenter has to be paid or the court can take action on the person who is at fault.

INDIAN CASE LAWS

1. Acceptance should be communicated: Felthouse v. Bindley

Can a person's silence be considered acceptance?

In this case, the petitioner, Mr. Paul Felthouse wanted to purchase a horse from his nephew, but the price he offered to pay for the horse was less than that his nephew was willing to sell it for. The horse, therefore, was still in his possession. The Uncle communicated his offer through a letter, saying, "If I hear no more about him, I consider the horse mine at £30.15s" The nephew could not respond to the letter because he was busy with an auction on his farm. Though he asked the auctioneer, Mr. Bindley, not to auction the horses, he accidentally did. Mr. Felthouse then sued the defendant for <u>conversion of his property</u>. The defendant argued that the horse was not actually Mr. Felthouse's property, as there existed no contract between him and his nephew at the time of the auction because Mr. Felthouse's offer was not accepted by his nephew and the nephew's silence cannot be considered to be an acceptance of the offer.

2. General Offer: Carlill v. Carbolic Smoke Balls Company

Can offers be open to the public in general? Can a general offer lead to a contract?

In this case, a company carried out advertisements about their product, carbolic smoke balls, that claimed that any person who took the smoke balls in the prescribed manner (i.e., three times daily for two weeks) will not catch influenza. In case someone does, the company promised to pay 100£ to them immediately. To show their sincerity regarding this offer, the company deposited a sum of 1000£ in a public bank. Now, the plaintiff, Carlill bought the smoke balls and used them as prescribed in the advertisement, but still ended up catching the flu. She filed a suit for the recovery of 100£ as promised in the advertisement. The company denied the payment saying there existed no contract between them and the plaintiff. It was held that a contract came into existence between the plaintiff and the company as soon as the plaintiff bought the smoke balls and used them as prescribed.

3. Offer and Invitation to Treat: Harvey v. Facey

Can a mere quotation of price be considered an offer?

In this case, the petitioner, Harvey communicated with the defendant, Facey, about a Hall Pen through telegram, saying ""Will you sell us Bumper Hall Pen? Telegraph lowest cash price-answer paid". The same day, Facey responded with the price of the Pen to be £900. To which, the appellant replied, "We agree to buy Bumper Hall Pen for the sum of nine hundred pounds asked by you. Please send us your title deed in order that we may get early possession." The defendant refused to sell at that price that they had initially quoted. It was finally held in this case that no contract came into existence between both the parties because their exchange of telegrams was merely an informational exchange where the appellant asked for the price of the Hall Pen and the defendant quoted the price. Therefore the appellant had no right to sue.

4. Offer and Counter Offers: Hyde v. Wrench

This is a leading case eliciting the concept of offers and counter-offers.

In this case, Wrench, the defendant offered to sell his farm to the petitioner, Hyde for £1000. The petitioner declined the offer. The defendant again reinstated his offer for selling the farm at £1000 to the petitioner's agent stating that it is the final offer from their side. The petitioner, through a letter, offered to buy the farm for £950. The defendant refused to sell the farm at that price. The petitioner, several days later, offered to buy the farm at the initial price of £1000. The defendant did not send any agreement to that and refused to sell the farm, because of which the petitioner sued for breach of contract. It was held that no contract came to arise between the parties as the price was not agreed upon. Rather, offers and counter-offers were exchanged.

5. Agreement, Not Contract: Balfour v. Balfour

Can a promise between married parties result in a legally binding agreement?

In this case, Mr. and Mrs. Balfour, who used to live together as a married couple in Sri Lanka, went for a vacation to England. During this time, Mrs. Balfour developed rheumatic arthritis. The doctor advised Mrs. Balfour to stay back in England as, according to him, Sri Lankan climate would worsen her health. Before Mr. Balfour returned to Sri Lanka, he promised to send £30 to her per month. During their stay away, the parties drifted apart and separated. It was held in this case that Mr. Balfour's promise to pay a monthly sum of £30 did not amount to a contract, as there was no intention to create a legal relationship on part of either of the parties.

6. Communication of Offer is Necessary: Lalman Shukla v. Gauri Dutt

In this case, the defendant's nephew went missing and the petitioner, who was a servant under the defendants was sent out in his search to Hardwar. After sending the petitioner, the defendant carried out an offer to the general public offering Rs. 501 to whomsoever finds the missing boy. The Plaintiff found the boy and helped return him back to his home. He had been paid the money he spent in going to search for the boy, i.e., his travel expenses. When he returned, he continued working for the defendants for about six months. After six months, he sued the defendants for paying him the prize money that was offered earlier. It was held that the petitioner was not entitled to the prize money, as he was only obliged by the duty he had as the defendant's servant to find the missing boy, and the reward was announced after he had already been sent.

7. Minor's Capacity to Contract: Mohori Bibee v. Damodar Ghose

Is a minor's agreement void *ab initio*?

In this case, the defendant, Darmodar Ghose, as a minor was the sole owner of his property. His mother was his legally appointed guardian. One Mr. Brahmo Dutt who was a moneylender, through his agent Kedar Nath, lent Damodar Ghose a sum of Rs 20,000 at 12% interest per year. The loan was taken by way of mortgaging the property. The same day this deal was made, Damodar Ghose's mother notified the appellant that Damodar was a minor, and anybody who would get into an agreement with him would do so at his own risk. Kedar Nath claimed that Damodar Ghose had lied about his age on the date of the execution of this deed, which turned out to be untrue. Therefore, Brahmo Dutt's appeal was dismissed and his request for the return of Rs 10,500 advanced towards him was also rejected. It was held that a minor's agreement is void *ab initio*.

8. Doctrine of Frustration: Krell v. Henry

In this case, the defendant agreed to rent a flat of the plaintiff to watch the coronation of King Edward VII from its balcony. The plaintiff had promised that the view from the flat's balcony will be satisfying since the procession will be perfectly visible from the room. The parties corresponded through letters and agreed on a price of £75 for two days. Nowhere in their written correspondence did the parties mention the coronation ceremony. The coronation did not take place on the days the flat was booked for, as the kind fell ill. The defendant refused to pay the whole sum of money that the parties had agreed upon, for this reason. It was held that it could be incurred from the circumstances surrounding the contract what the implied purpose behind the contract was. Due to the cancellation of the procession, the purpose of booking the flat was frustrated.

9. The remoteness of Damage: Hadley v. Baxendale

In this case, the plaintiffs were operators of a mill, that they had to shut down temporarily when the crankshafts of the mill broke. Plaintiffs then contacted the manufacturers of the engine to make a new engine on a similar pattern. A servant of the defendants was then sent to the carriers to transport the crankshaft to the engine manufacturers. The servant told the Defendants that the mill is shut down, so the crankshafts must be sent immediately. The defendants informed that whenever the old crankshaft is given to them, the new one will be delivered by 12 o'clock its next day. Due to the delay of the defendants, the delivery got delayed and the mill had to stay shut for several days. In this case, due to the involvement of a third party (the carriers), the delay and loss could not entirely be blamed upon the defendants. Whatever damages or loss rose, did not come to existence because of a direct breach of contract by the defendants.

The Sale of Goods Act, 1930

DEFINITION

SEC 4(1) of the Indian Sale of Goods Act, 1930, defines the contract of sale of goods in the following manner:

"A contract of sale of goods is a contract whereby the seller transfers or agrees to transfer the property in goods to the buyer for a price".

There are two parties in the Sales of Goods Act, one is the buyer and the other one is the seller.

The buyer is the person who purchases the goods, moveable properties, which can be transferred from one place to another. In that matter, goodwill can be taken as a movable property and can be considered a part of the Sale of Goods Act, 1930.

The seller is a person who is selling the goods and is the owner of the particular good. If you are not the owner of a particular good, then you don't have the right to sell the goods. Any person who is the owner of the goods can sell the goods for a price. Price is very important since it is a business. Without a price during the sale of goods, the act cannot take place.

There the price factor comes into play and the position of goods are being transferred from the seller to the buyer, that is, ownership of goods is transferred from the seller to the buyer.

❖ ESSENTIALS OF CONTRACT OF SALE

From the above definition, the following essentials of a contract of sale may be noted:

1. There must be at least two parties.
2. Transfer or agreement to transfer of the ownership of goods - The seller was the owner, but now the buyer is the owner while paying the price for the same.
3. The subject matter of the contract must necessarily be 'goods'. The sale of immovable property is not covered under this act. No other things will come under the Sale of Goods Act except for movable goods.
4. The consideration is the price.
5. A contract for sale can be in writing or by words.
6. All other essentials of a valid contract must be present. Essential elements are as follows: two or more parties, legal objectives, legal consideration, no minors, a sound mind of parties, willful agreement, and no criminal activity.

❖ "GOODS"

- Goods refer to every kind of movable property and include stock and shares, growing crops, grass, and things attached to or forming part of the land, which are agreed to be served before a sale or under the contract of sale.
- Actionable claims and money are not included in the definition of goods.
- Thus, goods include every kind of movable property other than an actionable claim of money. Example – goodwill, copyright, trademarks, patents, water, gas, and electricity.

Goods can be transferred, moved, or uplifted. From one place to another, the following objects can be a part of the Sale of Goods Act: Books, pen rice, wheat, bikes, cars, all plants, etc. However, money doesn't come under this act.

❖ *TYPES OF GOODS*

1. Existing goods - *Goods that are physically in existence and that are in seller's ownership and/or possession, at the time of entering the contract of sale account existing goods. Where the seller is the owner, he has a general property in them.* Physically present during the time of sale and it is in the possession on the ownership

of the seller. When the contract has been made, the goods are in the position with the seller and the seller is making the sale.

2. Future goods - *Goods to be manufactured, produced, or acquired by the seller after the making of the contract of sale are called future goods {section 2(6)}. These goods may be not yet in existence or be in existence but are not yet acquired by the seller. Example – A agrees to sell to B all the milk that his cow may yield during the coming year. This is a contract of the sale of future goods.* Goods that would be manufactured in future and required in future by the seller after making the contract. Once the contract of sale has been made, the goods can be procured in future.

3. Contingent goods - A type of future goods the acquisition of which by the seller depends upon a contingency, that is, the acquisition may or may not happen (section 6).
   Example – A agrees to sell to B a specific rare painting provided he can purchase it from its present owner. This is a contract for the sale of contingent goods.

It is a future good, but, at the same time, there is a risk factor contingency. It may or may not be available.

The term "contract of sale of goods" is a generic term and it includes:

– A sale and
– An agreement to sell.

Here, the seller transfers the ownership right to the buyer immediately after making the contract. It is the contract of sale, but the ownership rights are to pass on some future date upon the fulfilment of certain conditions. Then, it is called an agreement to sell.

A contract of sale means what is happening at the present, an agreement to sell means what will happen in future.

In a contract of sale, you go to a shop and you purchase a book. This is a contract act.

In the same example, if that book is not available in the shop but would be available within a week, and you agree to purchase the book in future, then it becomes an agreement of sale.

Differences between Sale and Agreement to Sale

SALE	AGREEMENT TO SALE
Ownership passes to the buyer - The seller was the owner and now the buyer becomes the owner.	Ownership remains with the seller - Seller is still the owner and the buyer hasn't got the position of the goods.
It is an executed contract - Terms and conditions have been fulfilled and the buyer has already got the position of the goods.	It is an executory contract – The seller is in the position of the goods, the buyer hasn't got the position, and the contract is yet to get over.
The risk of loss falls on the buyer - The buyer is in the position of good. If anything happens to the goods, it is the risk of the buyer.	The risk of loss falls on the seller - Because the seller has the property, the buyer is not in any risky position.
The seller cannot re-sale the goods - Since the goods are with the buyer, the seller cannot re- sell any of the goods that the buyer has taken.	The seller can sell goods to third parties – The seller can do this because the goods are in the position of the seller.
It can be in the case of existing and specific goods - Certain kinds of goods that you purchase don't exist. The goods that exist are specific. All the buyers don't go and purchase all kinds of goods; they buy only specific types of goods.	It can be in case of future and uncertain goods - The goods are not in the position of the seller, they are not available in the market for the future, and the future is uncertain one, and thus, the goods are not specific.
In case of breach of contract, seller can sue for the price of the goods - If the contract is not kept by the buyer with respect to giving or paying for the goods, for a limited time, it happens when the seller can ask for the price.	In case of breach of a contract, the seller can sue only for damages, not for the price - The position of the goods and the ownership of the goods have not been transferred yet.
The seller is only entitled to the rateable dividend of the price due if the buyer becomes insolvent: If the buyer is not in a position to pay, he has become insolvent and becomes bankrupt, then the property is taken by the official assignor of the liquidity. In this case, for any kind of price that was still pending with the buyer, an interest on that price can only be taken by the seller.	The seller may refuse to sell the goods to the buyer if no payment is done - If goods are already in the position of the seller and the buyer becomes insolvent, the seller can say he doesn't want to pay or give the goods to the buyer.

Which documents are considered as documents of title to goods?

The title means the ownership – if you are the owner, then only you are in the position to sell the goods, if you're not the owner you're not positioned to sell the goods. It is a document that can prove to you that you are the owner of the goods and the goods belong to you.

A document of title to goods may be described as any document used as proof of the possession or control of goods, authorizing or purporting to authorize, either by endorsement or by delivery, the possessor of the document to transfer or receive goods thereby represented.

The following are documents of title to goods-

- Bill of lading – It is an entry or a document where being a buyer, you have loaded your goods in the carrier, then the document is issued as a bill of lading.
- Dock warrant – If you are sending anything through the ship, the certificate that you get at the time of loading your things in the ship, it becomes a dock warrant. And it gives you the certificate that you are the owner of the things loaded on the property.
- Warehouse Keeper's certificate – When goods are kept in the storehouse, the storekeeper will give you the certificate stating the quantity, name, quality, price, etc. That certificate gives the right that you are the owner of the property.
- Warfinger's certificate – When you are transferring your goods from one place to another, the carrier which is carrying your furniture is a Warfinger and the certificate gives the entire description of the goods.
- Railway receipt – If you send the goods to the railway, description time, authority sign, place where it started, where it's going to end, it gives you a certificate stating that the goods belong to you.
- Warrant order for the delivery of goods etc. – If you have ordered something from an online shop, the mode of delivery is mentioned in the certificate. This also proves the title of the goods.

Meaning of Condition

A condition is a stipulation or the main feature based on which the goods have been purchased. It is given by the manufacturer.

This stipulation is essential to the main purpose of the contract and its breach gives the aggrieved party a right to terminate the contract. The contact can come to an end. It goes to the root of the contract. Its non-fulfillment upsets the very basis of contract.

WARRANTY

It is an added feature given by the traders, sellers, and wholesalers. It is not the main provision but it is also a kind of secondary thing, based on which the seller or the buyer can make a choice. If there is a breach of warranty, you can claim the damages but you cannot cancel the contract.

- It is a stipulation collateral to the main purpose of the contract.
- It is of secondary importance.
- If there is a breach of a warranty, the aggrieved party can only claim damage and it has no right to treat the contract as repudiated.

Differences between condition and warranty

CONDITION	WARRANTY.
Condition is a stipulation in a contract that is essential to the main purpose of the contract.	Warranty is a stipulation that is only a collateral or a subsidiary to the main purpose of the contract.
A breach of the condition gives the aggrieved party the right to sue for damages as well as the right to repudiate the contract. There is a breach of contract and then the party can ask the damages as well as cancel the contract.	A breach of warranty gives only the right to sue for damages, the contract cannot be repudiated. Only the damages can be asked for but the contract cannot be cancelled.
A breach of condition may be treated as a breach of the warranty in certain circumstances. It can be converted into a breach of warranty.	A breach of warranty cannot be treated as a breach of the condition. You can only ask for the damages but you cannot cancel the contract.

Express and implied conditions and warranties (types)

Feature conditions are there; those things should be mentioned in the package with the product that is called express condition.

Implied conditions – It means without expressing, we have to do it. For example, if you're hired a coolie to transfer your luggage from the train to the rickshaw stand, it is obvious that you need to pay him.

- Conditions and warranties may be either expressed or implied.
- They are said to be expressed when they are expressly provided by the parties.
- They are said to be implied when the law deems their existence in the contract even without the actual having been put in the contract (sections 14 to 17).

Implied conditions:

The implied condition means whoever is selling the goods, that person must be the owner. The things that are selected should be given to me.

- Condition as to title (Section 14)a (Rowland v. Duvall, (1923))
- Sale by depreciation (Section 15) (Bowes v. Shand, (1877))
- Condition as to quality or fitness (Section 16(1)) - Whatever I am purchasing, it should be of good quality, should be having an expiry date, and should be fit to a person.
- Condition as to merchantability [(Section 16(2) R.S. Thakur v. H.G.E. Corp; A.I.R.(1971)] - Whenever goods are hitting the market, they have to go through a lot of quality checks.
- Conditions implied by customs [Section 16(3)]- When you're getting anything exported or imported, it goes through a custom checking where the customs officer will check the product whether these products are according to the criteria if you're exporting anything or importing anything, it should be according to the custom quality. Then only it should be hitting the market and it is an implied condition.
- Sale by sample (Section 17)
- Condition as to wholesomeness - It is a liquid product, its quality should be preserved. It shouldn't be expired or contaminated. The seller must make sure that the product is safe.

Implied warranties

- Warranty of quiet possession [Section 14(6)] - Goods and services I'm paying for I have every right to enjoy them in my own home or enjoy them peacefully. For example, if you got a second-hand bike from a friend, and the next day someone else comes and says that the bike belongs to him, it is not quite possession. This thing is but implied that whatever price you're paying for goods or services and you should be having the right to enjoy it.

- Warranty against encumbrance [Section 14(C)] - If someone is coming and threatening you for certain goods and services, it is not acceptable. When you are getting something from the seller, the seller has to give you the warranty that this thing shouldn't be happening. If this thing happens, then the seller is punishable.
- Warranty to disclose dangerous nature of goods - When a seller is giving you any goods, it shouldn't be dangerous.
- Warranty as to quality or fitness by the usage of trade [Section 16(4)] - It should be of good quality and it should be fit enough for consumption and should have gone to the quality check.

These are the implied warranties that the seller should give and take care of.

❖ DOCTRINE OF CAVEAT EMPTOR

- Caveat emptor is a fundamental principle of the law of sale of goods.
- It means "cautious buyer", that is, "let the buyer beware".
- The buyer must be careful while purchasing goods of his requirement, and in the absence of the enquiry of the buyer, the seller is not bound to disclose every defect in the good of which he may be cognizant.
- Being the buyer, it is not the responsibility of anyone else to find out facts and figures regarding a particular good you are purchasing.
- No one is supposed to give you the details regarding the product. It is not the seller's responsibility to give you each detail regarding the product. You being the buyer should be aware of the pricing factors, features, and uses of the goods.

❖ EXCEPTIONS TO THE DOCTRINE OF CAVEAT EMPTOR

It is the seller's responsibility and the seller does this intentionally.

- In case of misrepresentation by the seller - The seller intentionally misrepresents certain facts. Being the buyer we cannot do anything. Being a buyer how are we supposed to know, This is the seller's fault.

- In the case of concealment of a latent defect - Certain defects in the product that the seller chose not to tell. This is intentional concealment by the seller. This is not your mistake but seller's.
- In case of sale of description - the description of goods selected and paid by you should be provided to you. If you are getting any other product, then it is not your fault, it is the seller's fault.
- In case of sale by sample - The sample of goods that you selected and paid for should be the particular goods that you get. If you get any other product, then it is not your fault, it is the seller's fault.
- In case of sale by sample and description - You should get the goods whose description was given and sample was paid for by you. If you don't get it, then it is not your fault, it is the seller's fault.
- Fitness for a particular purpose - Certain goods are intended for a particular purpose. The seller needs to make sure that the good goes through appropriate quality check. If the good doesn't go through the quality check, the caveat emptor doesn't hold True.
- Merchantable quality.

❖ *PASSING/TRANSFER OF THE PROPERTY*

- Transfer of the property in goods from the seller to the buyer is the main objective of the contract of sale.
- "Property in goods" means the ownership of the goods.
- A product may belong to A although it may not be in his possession and B may be in the possession of the product, although he is not its owner.
- It is important to know the precise moment at which the property of goods passes from the seller to the buyer for the following reasons.

The ownership is transferred from the seller to the buyer, the seller was the owner but now the buyer is the owner. And the buyer can do anything with the property.

In a contract of sale, ownership, and title, transfer of property takes place from the seller to the buyer.

CONTD-

- Significance – Time to transfer the ownership of goods decides various rights and liabilities of the seller and the buyer.
- Risk – Owner needs to bear the risk and not the person who merely has possession.
- Action against third-party – Owner can take action and not the person who merely has possession.

Since I was the owner previously, I have every right over the product. If anything goes wrong with the goods, then it was my liability and my responsibility. But, when the product is sold, this responsibility passes over to the new owner.

Risk is always with the owner. When the seller was the owner, then it was the seller's risk. Now the buyer has become the owner and the risk is with the buyer.

For example – risk factor and action against the third party. There is a birthday party going on, and I am getting a beautiful person with me with my friend, another one of my friend was coming from another side, and I'll ask my friend to keep my purse with her until and unless I come back by the time I met my friend, and I was coming back at the same time another person who was keeping I am in my bag somehow managed to grab my purse from my friend and ran away. The risk of the bag being lost is taken away by someone else. The risk is with me since I am the owner and I had given it to my friend, and the risk is not with my friend and my friend did not pay, anything so the risk was entirely mine.

Action against the third party – the person who has taken away The purse against that person. I am the owner of the person. I can take some action. Take that person to the police but my friend can't do that. Since I was the owner the risk is with me and any type of action against the third party that is only by the owner of the particular goods not with someone else.

❖ *UNPAID SELLER SECTION - 45*

A seller of goods is deemed to be an unpaid seller when:

- The whole of the price has not been paid or tendered.

- A bill of exchange or other negotiable instrument has been received as a conditional payment, and the condition on which it was received has not been fulfilled because of dishonor of the instrument or otherwise.

An unpaid seller is a person who hasn't got the entire money for the goods sold or part of the money has been paid. Being the buyer I have taken certain kinds of negotiable instruments. A negotiable instrument is a document through which we conduct business, through which we give a right to someone else. If I haven't paid the price to the seller, and the seller hasn't received part of the payment, then the seller is known as an unpaid seller.

- The term "seller" includes any person who is in the position of the seller. For instance, an agent of the seller to whom the bill of lading has been endorsed or an agent who has himself paid or is directly responsible for setting the price.
- The seller shall be called an unpaid seller even when only a small portion of the price remains to be unpaid.
- It is for the non-payment of the price and not for other expenses that a seller is termed as an unpaid seller.
- If full price has been tendered by the buyer and the seller refused to accept it, the seller cannot be called an unpaid seller.
- If the money is not paid then only the person is known as an unpaid seller. If the person was supposed to get anything other than the money, then the seller is not known as the unpaid seller because the buyer has already given the price of the book.
- Where the goods have been sold on credit, the seller cannot be called an unpaid seller. Unless:
  If during the credit period, the seller becomes insolvent, or on the expiry of the credit period, the price remains unpaid.

If I am getting my house and I go to the market and purchase certain kind of raw material for my house, good for the furniture work, send the Seller knows me, I get a credit period of one month, Pay my money unless and until the credit period is over the seller cannot be known as an unpaid seller because the time limit has already given to me. You are the seller cannot be an unpaid seller but if the credit period gets over and one month gets over soon and I was supposed to pay 2 lakhs and I still haven't paid then the seller would be called as an unpaid seller. And during the insolvency period, if the seller goes insolvent or bankrupt, the seller is not an unpaid seller.

❖ *RIGHTS OF AN UNPAID SELLER*

– Against goods: Where the property in goods is passed to the buyer; where the property in goods has not passed to the buyer: The ownership has already been transferred to the buyer, in another case whether ownership has not passed to the buyer means the goods are still in the possession of the seller The buyer still has to purchase it in the future, and the seller is still in the ownership of goods.

For example- where the property in goods has passed to the buyer- you have purchase of furniture, the money has been paid and the ownership is transferred from the seller to the buyer the deal has been done contract has been done when the buyer becomes the owner of the goods.

Example- where the property in Goods has not passed to the buyer- suppose you want to purchase the teak wood centre table, but the teak wood centre table which is designed is not available with the seller, it might be available within one month or so, the centre table was available but you need to transfer it to your house, then the property is still with the seller it's not with you.

– Where the property in goods has been passed to the buyer.

– Right of lien - The right of lien means the right to retain the possession of the goods until the full price is received. Circumstances under which the right of lien can be exercised are as follows: Where the goods have been sold without any stipulation to credit; where the goods have been sold on credit but the term of credit has expired; and where the buyer becomes insolvent. In such cases, the seller can stop the delivery, take the position of the goods, and inform the buyer that he is not going to send these goods to you until and unless the buyer pays him the entire price. This is the right of lien where the position of the goods can be retained till the full price is paid by the buyer to the seller.

Right of stoppage of goods in transit (Section 50–52):

- Right of stoppage in transit means the right of stopping the goods while they are in transit, to regain possession, and retain them till the full price is paid.
- Conditions under which right of stoppage in transit can be exercised are as follows:
  The seller must have parted with the possession of goods, that is, the goods must not be in possession of the seller. All these rights can only be enforced when the goods are still with the seller because the ownership is transferred from the seller to the buyer, but still the buyer is in the ownership of the goods then only these rights can take place

The seller has the right to stop the goods before they reach the buyer. For example, if the seller is transferring, say, furniture from Rajasthan to Uttar Pradesh through truck and he comes to know that the truck has already reached halfway and the buyer has become insolvent, then the seller has got every right to call back the truck from halfway and take the possession of the goods and wait till the price is given to the seller and then only the possession of the goods can be given to the buyer.

CONTD-

- The Goods must be in the course of transit.
- Buyer must have become insolvent.

When the buyer is not in a position to pay, then the seller can stop the goods in transit and take the position.

Right of resale

An unpaid seller can resell a good under the following circumstances:

- Where the goods are perishable - for example, being a Buyer you have ordered 5 quarters of salt and you have kept with the seller in the rainy season. You asked the seller to keep it with them for a week and then you'll be taking it. A week goes by then two weeks go by you're not contacted and seen by, The seller by informing you can re-sale the goods.

— Where the seller expressly reserves the right of resale if the buyer commits a default in making payment - When the contract has been made and the goods have been sold by the seller to the buyer, during that time, the seller says that if you're not paying a certain amount of money, within some predetermined time, then I can resell, and in that circumstances the seller can also resell the items.

— Where the unpaid seller who has exercised his right of lien or stoppage in transit gives notice to the buyer about his intention to resell and the buyer doesn't pay or tender within a reasonable time.

Where the property in goods has not passed to the buyer.

— Withholding delivery
— Stoppage in transit
— Resale

There the goods are in possession with the seller and the buyer has shown interest in the particular goods. For ex- i go to a shop and select a beautiful painting. Tand i ask the painter, i want this painting and the painter says i will give you the painting, just give me one week of time, the painting is with the painter, he is the owner, i have showed the interest that i will be purchasing, in this case, since the goods are still in position with the seller. And the buyer doesnt wants to take, then withholding delivery, within a weeks of time the painting will be reaching you but you haven't paid. Then the painting can withhold the painting and ask for the money. Stoppage in transit, if you are insolvent, the painter can stop the delivery. Resale- and the goods can be resold to the third party.

— Against the buyer personally
— Suit for price
— Suit for damages

If the buyer hasn't paid the money, a part of the money or whole of the money, then the seller can sue the buyer for price and can get the price.

If certain damages have been made to the goods or the buyer doesn't want to take the risk, then the buyer can be sued for damages.

Suit for breach of the contract

If you break a promise, there would be -

- Suit for price

Where under a contract of sale the property in the goods has passed to the buyer and buyer wrongfully neglects or refuses to pay for the goods according to the terms of the contract, the seller may sue him for the price of the goods.

- Where under a contract of sale, the price is payable on a day irrespective of delivery, and the buyer wrongfully neglects or refuses to pay such price, the seller may sue him for the price although the property in the goods has not passed and the goods have not been appropriated to the contract.
- **DAMAGES FOR NON- ACCEPTANCE:** Where the buyer wrongfully neglects or refuses to accept and pay for the goods, the seller may sue him for damages or non-acceptance. If being the buyer I'm not accepting certain goods, already I am interested in and conveyed my interest that I would be purchasing this particular good, and I don't accept it. For example, when I go to a dealer I select a TV, LG colour TV, asks the shopkeeper to deliver it to my house as he is known to me and I say that once it's delivered to me I will give you the cheque because at the moment I'm not getting the cheque. The seller says yes and the next day I don't want to accept the TV, I sent back the TV to the person who was getting it saying that I'm not going to accept it. The seller can take me to the court and sue me for the damages done for not accepting. I'm just done during the delivery from the shop to the residence, the truck on the vehicle which is getting the TV, the people who have come all the way, their time. For

this damages of non-accepting can be taken from the buyer if the buyer is not accepting the particular product.

- **DAMAGES FOR NON-DELIVERY:** Where the seller wrongfully neglects or refuses to deliver the goods to the buyer, the buyer may sue the seller for damages for non-delivery. If the buyer has already purchased a product and the seller was supposed to deliver them, the ownership has to transfer from the seller to the buyer, but the seller, after the transaction has been done, doesn't want to deliver to the buyer, then the buyer can sue the seller for non-delivery of the goods and the damages.

❖ *SALE BY AUCTION(section- 64)*

In the case of sale by auction, a notification will be given on a predetermined date. The process of auction is as follows:

1. At an auction, the sale is complete when the auctioneer announces its completion by the fall of the hammer.
2. A bidder is at liberty to withdraw his bid at any time before it is accepted by the auctioneer. The person who is bidding for the price, quoting the price, calling the price is at liberty to withdraw his bid at any time before it is accepted by the auction.
3. Advertisement to auction is not an offer but a mere invitation. When we are going for an auction, it doesn't mean it is an offer of goods, it is just an invitation to bid.
4. Auctioneer has the right to make any condition he likes. Whoever is going for an auction, it is not an offer, it is just an invitation. People who are invited have the right to attend, but the auctioneer has the right to make any condition.
5. Biddings can be withdrawn before acceptance - Before the auctioneer accepts the final price of the bidding, the bidder can withdraw from the auction, but if it is accepted, then the bidder cannot withdraw.
6. Pretended bidding by the seller to raise the price is voidable at the option of the buyer. If someone is pretending to bid to raise the price, then the bidding price can be set aside for some time.
7. No seller or any other person has advertised the good can bid at an auction.

Indian Case Laws

1. Chhunna Mal Ram Nath vs. Mool Chand Ram Bhagat

(1928) 30 BOMLR 837

Key Words: breach, recovery of damages, sale, delivery, dispensing with the performance

FACTS

Plaintiffs entered into contract for taking deliveries of the goods packed in wooden boxes from the defendants, which latter was to secure from London. Since British government prohibited the supply of such goods in wooden boxes, hence, defendants offered to supply the goods in bales to which plaintiffs refused and "*cancel[ed] the goods*" without claiming any compensation thereof in any of the correspondences. Plaintiffs later claimed damages for non-delivery.

ISSUE

Whether plaintiffs can claim any compensation.

HELD

Plaintiffs upon the ancillary breach of defendants claimed to have 'put an end to the contract' u/s 39; however, it is the plaintiffs themselves who by wrongfully refusing to take deliveries under the contract have given a chance to defendants to 'put an end to it'. Nevertheless, defendants did not exercise this option and by acquiescence continued it; but Plaintiffs by insisting on "*cancel[lation] of goods*" to be supplied by the defendants, had expressly dispensed with the performance by the latter such that no claim for damages could be brought against the any breach by latter.

Author: Vishrut Kansal

2. Kailash Sharma vs. The Patna Municipal Corporation and Ors.

Kailash Sharma vs. The Patna Municipal Corporation and Ors.

Citation: CWJC No. 9730 of 2006

Facts:

The Appellant-Company sold a certain number of fogging machines (used for killing mosquitoes) to the Respondent-Corporation for which the payment had to be made within one week of delivery. The Respondents did not pay within one week. The Respondent did not communicate with the appellants w.r.t the payment afterwards too. After 6 months of using the machine, the Respondents communicated with the appellants, but only to complain about the fogging machines' inefficiency. They said that the machines were defective. Next, the Respondents intended to return the machines. The Appellants have filed this suit to recover the payment of machines from the respondents. This Judgement is given after three year of the delivery of goods.

Issue: Whether the Respondents are liable to pay for the machines (liable to pay if repudiation of transaction not allowed).

Relevant Provision(s): Section 13(2), 32, 42 and 59 of Sale of Goods Act, 1930

Case Analysis:

According to section 42 of the Sale of Goods Act, the act of receiving the machine, after demonstration, using it and retaining it for a long time amounts to valid acceptance. In this case, the Respondents have accepted the machines.

The Court in this case discussed Section 32 of the Act (payment and delivery are concurrent conditions) and noted that the law provides that payment and delivery are concurrent but that is subject to an agreement otherwise. Here the agreement was for payment within one week of delivery. Furthermore, in the present case, three years are over.

Section 13 (2) of the <u>Indian Sale of Goods Act, 1930</u>, clearly states that where there is a warranty then at best the purchaser can raise a claim for damage but cannot repudiate the transaction itself as is being sought to be done by the Corporation. This section was read with Section 59 of the Act. Section 59 says that a buyer is not by reason of a breach of warranty (by the seller) entitled to reject the goods. He may sue for damages or for breach of warranty. Here too, the Respondents, after using the machines for a long time, cannot simply return the machines to the appellants without payment for the machines.

The court eventually held that the Respondent-Corporation is at fault in law for the non-payment. The facts are merely a pretext to withhold the payment.

Conclusion: Respondents were held to be liable to pay for the fogging machines as they could not legitimately return the machines after use/repudiate the transaction.

Author: Vishrut Kansal

3. Badri Prasad v. State of Madhya Pradesh & Anr.

<u>Badri Prasad v. State of Madhya Pradesh & Anr.</u>

1969 SCR (2) 380

(Ascertainment)

FACTS:

The appellant (A) entered into a contract in respect of certain forests and became entitled to cut teak trees with some specifications.[1] After a legislation[2] vesting the estate in the State, A was prohibited from cutting timber in exercise of his rights under the contract. On Feb, 1, the State said that A's claim to cut trees would be considered only if he gave up his claim to a sum of Rs. 17,000 which he had already paid under the contract and was willing to pay a further sum of Rs. 17,000 to the state. On February 5, 1955, A expressed his willingness to pay the additional sum but reserved his right to claim a refund of the first sum. The State rejected A's right to cut trees. A then filed a Suit claiming specific performance of the contract.

ISSUE: Whether the property was vested in the state by the Act or transferred to the Appellant?

CONTENTIONS (A)

1. The forest and trees did not vest in the State under the Act.
2. Even if they vested, the standing timber, having been sold to A, did not vest in the State.
3. In any event a new contract was completed on February 5, 1955, and the appellant was entitled to its specific performance.

HELD:

Trial Court: Favoured the Appellant, A

High Court (MP): Allowed the appeal of the State and dismissed the suit brought by A.

SUPREME COURT (SIKRI, J.) (favoured the State)

1. The forest and trees vested in the State under the Act.
2. Under the contract A had not become the owner of the trees as goods. The property in the timber could pass to A only when the trees are felled, but before they were felled, the trees had vested in the State.
3. Under the terms of the contract, there was no sale of the whole of the trees[3], and, it had to be ascertained which trees fell within the description of trees which the appellant was entitled to cut.[4] Till that was done they were not 'ascertained goods' within s. 19 of the Sale of Goods Act 1930.
4. Even if the letter of Feb 1 could be treated as an offer, there was no unconditional acceptance of the offer, because, there was a reservation by the appellant of his right to claim refund in his letter dated 5th Feb and hence there was no concluded contract.

4. Kalka Prasad Ram Charan v. Harish Chandra

Kalka Prasad Ram Charan v. Harish Chandra

AIR 1957 All 25

(Section 54(2) of Sale of Goods Act, Right of
an unpaid seller, Right to lien)

FACTS:

Harish (H) entered into a contract for sale of 67 thans of silk with
Kalka Prasad (K) (a partnership firm). 10 thans were delivered
immediately. Delivery of the remaining, were not accepted by K.
H sold off the remaining thans and then notified the K about the
sale. But due to a government control order the sale fetched a price
considerably less than what had been agreed between the two. H
brought a claim to recover the damages after deducting the price
from the sale.

HELD

Trial Court: There was a contract. Case awarded to H without
considering the question whether notice of the intended sale was
given to K.

HIGH COURT:

Contentions

H

1. Breach of contract, as delivery of the 57 thans not accepted and
   no payment made.
2. Two notices had been sent to K, one stating that if they did not
   accept the 57 thans they would have to pay damages and second
   stating that the 57 thans had already been sold.
3. S.54 (2) of SOGA not applicable as a seller's exercise of the right
   of lien begins when a demand for delivery is made from him by
   the buyer and is followed by a refusal by him. But since this did

not happen so it was not an exercise of lien, as per section 47[1] of SOGA.
4. Buyer (K) falsely denied the formation of contract, so cannot claim relief under section 54(2).

K

1. Completely denied the existence of any such contract.
2. Claimed they were agents for H for the sale of the silk.
3. Since, no notice of the sale had been given to K therefore he was not liable to pay any damages. (section 54 (2)[2] of SOGA)

Decision:

1. No notice was sent to K. H's own *munim* contradicted him in his deposition, claiming that only an oral statement was made, further H was unable to produce any secondary statement proving his statement.
2. If lien would arise only when demand for the said goods is made then the interpretation of section 47 would be very narrow. H had sold the thans in exercise of lien as per S.47 and that S.54 (2) would be applicable. The mere fact that K made a false claim about not entering into a contract is not sufficient to take the case out of the purview of section 54(2). Therefore seller cannot claim any damages from buyer.
3. As 67 thans were determined by both parties, the goods were ascertained and were in a deliverable state. Under Section 20[3], Sale of Goods Act the property in the goods passed to the buyer as soon as the contract was made, so the seller was merely a bailee.
4. H should have sued under S.55[4], claiming the full amount, but now the court cannot award him damages as that would give Harish a decree for an amount larger than what he had claimed. No damages can be claimed for the 57 thans. For the remaining 10 thans, K is liable to pay with interest.

[1] (1) Subject to the provisions of this Act, the unpaid seller of goods who is in possession of them is entitled to retain possession of them until payment or tender of the price in the following cases, namely:—(a) where the goods have been sold without any stipulation as to credit;(b) where the goods have

been sold on credit, but the term of credit has expired;(c) where the buyer becomes insolvent.

(2) The seller may exercise his right of lien notwithstanding that he is in possession of the goods as agent or bailee for the buyer.

[2] Where the goods are of a perishable nature, or where the unpaid seller who has exercised his right of lien or stoppage in transit gives notice to the buyer of his intention to re–sell, the unpaid seller may, if the buyer does not within a reasonable time pay or tender the price, re–sell the goods within a reasonable time and recover from the original buyer damages for any loss occasioned by his breach of contract, but the buyer shall not be entitled to any profit which may occur on the resale. If such notice is not given, the unpaid seller shall not be entitled to recover such damages and the buyer shall be entitled to the profit, if any, on the resale.

[3] Where there is an unconditional contract for the sale of specific goods in a deliverable state, the property in the goods passes to the buyer when the contract is made, and it is immaterial whether the time of payment of the price or the time of delivery of the goods, or both, is postponed.

[4] (1) Where under a contract of sale the property in the goods for has passed to the buyer and the buyer wrongfully neglects or refuses to pay for the goods according to the terms of the contract, the seller may sue him for the price of the goods.

(2) Where under a contract of sale the price is payable on a day certain irrespective of delivery and the buyer wrongfully neglects or refuses to pay such price, the seller may sue him for the price although the property in the goods has not passed and the goods have not been appropriated to the contract.

Beale v. Taylor

<u>Beale v. Taylor</u>

[1967] 3 All ER 253

(Sale by Description, Section 13 of Sale of Goods Act)

FACTS:

Taylor published an advertisement to sell a car describing it as "white, 1961, herald convertible...." Relying on that description

Beale came to see the car. Since he did not have a licence, he did not actually take a test drive, but just sat on the passenger side. After the test run he also saw a metallic disc on the rear of the car with the figure 1200 on it. He bought the car believing it to be the 1961 model. When he got the license he found the car unsatisfactory. On examination, the mechanic told him that the car was made up of two cars welded together, the front portion was one 948 model while the rear portion was the 1200 model. Further the car was found to be in unroadworthy and unsafe. Beale filed a suit claiming damages.

ISSUE: Whether the transaction was sale by description?

CONTENTIONS:

Plaintiff

B is entitled to damages (1) for breach of the condition as implied by sec. 13[1](Car should correspond with its description) (2) as money was paid on a consideration which had wholly failed (3) for breach of an implied condition of roadworthiness.

Defendant

It was not a sale by description but sale of a particular car as seen, tried and approved. The buyer had ample opportunity to inspect and test the car.

HELD

Trial Court: The sale was not a sale by description as B had seen, tried and approved the said car.

COURT OF APPEAL (SELLERS, J)

1. Both the parties are innocent because no one could see from an ordinary examination that it was made of two cars welded together.
2. There is a sale by description even though the buyer saw the car before purchasing it. A thing is sold by description as long as it is not sold merely as a specific thing but as something corresponding

to a particular description. The buyer relied in part on that particular description in buying the car.

3. Ideally the buyer should have returned the car to the seller, but since this is not the case, B is only entitled to the price difference (actual price-scrap value).
6. Digamber Pershad Kirti Prasad v. State of Uttar Pradesh and Ors.

Digamber Pershad Kirti Prasad v. State of Uttar Pradesh & Ors.

AIR 1996 All 1

(Section 2o and 26 of Sale of Goods Act)

FACTS:

Digambar Pershad, D got the contract of felling trees and collecting timber through **an agreement to sell**. D commenced the work of felling trees. All the trees were felled, sawn and timber was collected at a central point for transportations. D claimed that all precautions had been taken to avoid inflammatory material around the storage area, and watchmen were also appointed to keep vigil. Fire broke out and destroyed the timber. The state (S), however, demanded the amount due under the sale. D filed a writ petition against the State of UP.

ISSUE: Whether the title of the goods, actually pass to D at the time of signing of the contract?

CONTENTIONS:

Plaintiff (D)

1. Title to the goods had not passed to D as the stage of removing timber had not reached.
2. There was no completed sale but only an agreement to sell as the payment was yet to be made.
3. Before the sale was completed, the subject-matter of the contract was destroyed by fire and, therefore, the contract stood frustrated and hence D was not liable to pay.

Respondents (S)

1. The sale of the lot in question was completed the moment it was approved. D is liable to pay as the fire had taken place after the contract had been concluded.
2. The conditions in the contract clearly mentioned that the property and the risk in the goods both passed to D at the time of signing of the contract.

HELD (Petition DISMISSED)

1. **(w.r.t 1st issue)** Just because the payment had not been made in full and timber was not actually removed does not mean that transfer of property had not taken place. Transfer of property in the goods depends on the facts and circumstances and intention of the parties to the contract. The agreement was not subject to any future condition of the full payment, but the agreement became a concluded contract when the auction was accepted by the competent authority and the possession of the trees was transferred to D. Thus, Section 20[1] of SOGA would be applicable.
2. **(w.r.t 2nd contention of S)** S. 26[2] of SOGA is applicable. The condition (21) clearly provided that after 30 days from the date of acceptance of the contract or from the date of commencement of work, (whichever is earlier) the buyer will be fully responsible for the damage caused to the goods. Since this time had passed the risk was with the buyer.

LAW POINT(S)

To pass property in the goods actual delivery is not necessary, but if the goods are ascertained and in deliverable state, then the property will pass in the goods immediately upon the contract having been made, notwithstanding the time of payment of the price or the time of delivery of goods, or both, having been postponed.

[1] Where there is an unconditional contract for the sale of specific goods in a deliverable state, the property in the goods passes to the buyer when the contract is made, and it is immaterial whether

the time of payment of the price or the time of delivery of the goods, or both, is postponed.

[2] Unless otherwise agreed, the goods remain at the seller's risk until the property therein is transferred to the buyer, but when the property therein is transferred to the buyer, the goods are at the buyer's risk whether delivery has been made or not:

Chapter 3

The Indian Partnership Act, 1932

A partnership is a relation between persons who have agreed to share the profits of a business carried on by all or any of them acting for all. Partnership is coming together of people having the same ideologies, the same interest.

The difference between the Partnership Act and the Companies Act is in the case of the Companies Act, the entire liability is with the company. Most of the things are taken care of by the company. In the case of a partnership, two or more people share of profit equally or as decided as per the partnership deed where the partners decide at what ratio they will be dividing. The liability is also carried out equally by the partners in case the partnership firm is landing up in trouble. They agree to share both profit and liability. In case of a partnership, we are partners in profit and liability at the same time; each one of us would be sharing the responsibility as if we are representing another partner.

Partnership

1. The relationship between persons
2. Agreement
3. Common business
4. Sharing profit and loss
5. May be carried on by all anyone of the partners acting for all

The relationship between persons: There is a mutual agreement of sharing profit and liability and it is for a common business. Whatever we do has one purpose and profit and loss is being shared by other partners. It may be carried by all or any of them acting for everyone.

❖ FEATURES

What are the salient features of the Partnership Act?

1. An association of 2 or more persons: We cannot be a partner with ourselves. We need someone else, so it is an association of 2 or more people.
2. An agreement (oral or written, expressed or implied): You already know that an agreement can be an oral one or a written one; it doesn't need to always be a written one. An agreement that is oral or written expressed or implied means that the partners should express the terms and conditions, and it should be known by each one of them, and they all carry certain responsibilities.
3. Business: Without a business, there is no need for a partnership.
4. Profit/loss sharing: Profit and loss are shared almost equally by the partner's profit percentage. You can decide the ratio or you can go for sharing equal profit and liability.
5. Mutual agreement between partners: All the parties are agreeing to the same terms and conditions; no one is forcing them to agree.

❖ PARTNERSHIP DEED

There is an interesting fact that I want to share: In the case of a company, it is mandatory to go for a company's registration. Until and unless you are registering, you cannot start a company.

In case of a partnership, it doesn't mean that you cannot start a partnership. You can still start it without the need to register, but the only thing is that when you are registering yourself, you are becoming a legally recognized firm. Any kind of benefits that you should be getting from the court of the law will be definitely be coming to you if you're registered. Suppose you have a partnership firm and something goes wrong, like you have taken a loan or someone else has taken a loan from the partnership firm who is doing business with you or maybe the third party was supposed to deliver you 35 computers for your organisation but they only delivered you 10 computers and those computers are not in good condition.

What happens is that you said that the computers are bad according to the quality you better return the computers and give back the money, but that person, instead of taking back the computers, started fighting with you or telling you they are not going to take the computers back and not going to return the money. In these cases, what you do is you can take that person to court and the court would definitely listen to you and give you certain solution of the problem. But if you're not registered, then the partnership firm is no use for you. If you're not registered and something goes wrong, this firm cannot take any action, so registration is very important. If you're not registered, it doesn't mean that you cannot start. The registration can be done one day prior to when you are starting the partnership firm till your partnership firm comes to an end. There is no fixed date for registration, but in case of a company, before you start anything, you need to register.

A partnership is also a contract. It is an agreement between the partners, which is the basis of the contract. The partnership must have all the essential elements of a valid contract. It is in the interest of the partner that the agreement must be in writing.

A partnership is an agreement or a contract. It is a kind of document that would be giving you the right of starting the partnership firm and also give recognition to the partners. Any deed happens as a contact, so the partnership is also a contract. A contract is an agreement between the parties. When I was teaching you the sale of goods act the Indian contract act I talked with you at length regarding the valid contract but if you want I can again quickly tell you the elements of the valid contract- between two or more parties, between the major, is not minor, they should be mindful they should not be lunatic or idiot, they shouldn't be a drunkard, The partner should not be in some kind of criminal offence or jail if it is the case the contract cannot take place between the alien enemy of the country at the same time partnership act should be having legal consideration and objectives. These things should be there when we go for any kind of contract. If it is in writing then what happened the problem if anything goes wrong with the partnership deed or both the partners don't want to keep the terms and conditions one partner is going against the other partner then if it is in writing the terms and conditions, name of the partnership should be there, and if it is in writing then you can proced in the court and you can take the action against the other partner.

A partnership deed is a document that contains the agreement nature of the business, principal place of business, name of the firm, profit sharing ratio, valuation of goods, will on the death and retirement of partner management of the firm accounts, firm arbitration, etc. In case of a partnership deed like we did in the Companies Act, each detail regarding the company needs to be mentioned. Apart from the above mentioned details, it is also mentioned that if a partner dies, what will happen to his share; if the partner is retiring, what is the process of the retirement of the partner and who would be managing the account of the partnership firm; in case there is any kind of problem, then who will take care of that problem; etc. In the process of arbitration, if a company and a partnership firm is fighting, or if some fight is going on between the partners, then a third party is appointed by the court for either of the parties and that person is like a mediator listen to the problem and try to give a decision regarding the situation, and suggest how to overcome the problem. Arbitrator is appointed by the court and their decisions are binding on both parties. Arbitration only comes at the last stage where all the measures fail if the company or partnership firm is on the verge of winding. If there is a feud between the parties, then an arbitrator is appointed and both parties must accept their decision.

❖ TYPES OF PARTNERS

1. Active partners- A person who becomes a partner by an agreement is known as an actual partner. This partner is an activity engaged in the conduct of the business of the firm and is also known as an active partner. He is the agent of the other partners. He binds himself and he binds the other partners for all the acts which he does in the ordinary course of business of the firm. An active partner is a person who is there every day, taking care of the day-to-day activities of the partnership firm. In partnership firms, the partners are agreeing to certain terms and conditions, and they become the actual partners. They actively take part in the business and day-to-day activities of all the partnership firms. He also represents the other partners like a mediator. He represents the

entire partnership firm. Responsibilities of and activities done by the active partner are on behalf of others and also other partners would be responsible for any kind of activity related to the partnership firm done by any of the partners.

2. Sleeping partner: A partner who does not take an active part in the conduct of the business is known as a sleeping partner. He likes other partners to invest capital. He shares in the profits of the firm. He is equally liable for all the acts with other partners. This existence is kept secret from the outsiders dealing with the firm. He would be investing capital but his name would not be there. He will also be getting the profit and will be liable for the liability but there are two conditions: 1. His name won't be given up to the public. 2. He won't take part in the activities or will not be actively involved in day-to-day activity of the partnership firm.

3. Nominal partner: A partner who lends his name to the firm without having any real interest in it, does not invest in the business of the firm. He does not take part in the management of the firm. He doesn't share in the profits. Suppose I have a lot of money and I am interested in investing in something. And my friend has a partnership firm where there are two or three partners and they suggest that I invest some of my money in the partnership firm. At the same time, you will have your name and you don't need to take part in any kind of activities. If he's not investing, even then it's okay. Only the name will be there. If you want to have a name that you are a part of a big partnership firm. And because of the name, many people come forward and they don't take part and are not actively involved in any kind of activities of partnership firms. They don't invest much money but a little bit is okay. They don't take part in the management of the firm and do not share profit.

4. Partners in profits only: Sometimes, partners may agree that a partner shall get a share of the profits only. He shall not be liable to contribute towards the losses. Such a partner is known as a partner in profits only. When you're in a partnership deed, many partners don't want to share their liabilities. A good example will be the minor. Only the name would be there, but the minor will not be liable for any kind of liabilities, but being minor he'll only be involved in profit. Sometimes partners do agree for profit sharing, which is called partners in profit only.

5. Sub partners: When a partner agrees to share his profit with a third person, then the third person is known as a sub partner. Or a sub partner is in no way connected with the firm. He has no rights against the firm. He is not liable for the acts of the firm. Suppose I have a friend and my friend wants to share a certain amount of profit with me because he might have taken some loan from me and he was not able to give it back. So, through his profit, he can repay my loan. So, when a partner agrees to share his profit with the third person, then I, being the third person, become the sub partner and I being the sub partner is nowhere connected or related to the firm. I can be the third person from anywhere. I don't have any rights to the firm, its day-to-day activities, or any kind of other important things.

6. Partner by estoppels (holding out): Under certain circumstances, a person who is not a partner in a firm may be liable for its debts as if he were a partner. Such a partner is called partner by estoppels. For example, a retired IAS officer took post of honorary President of the business of a certain person who requested him for the same hold. He was liable for the debts of the company. A partner who is no longer a partner in the firm but he was a partner previously and has his name in that firm, any kind of debts in his name would be paid by the partner by estoppel. The insurance agents might not be associated with a particular company. Suppose a person already left ICICI Prudential. Since, he was supposed to get the money of the business he did from a customer, he might say that he still belongs to the ICICI Prudential. But he is no more there and he acts as if he is still a part of the company. In this case, if he is in getting any kind of loan or anything, then the company or the partnership firm can hold them responsible and he has to pay for all the debts he had incurred by taking the name of the company or the partnership firm.

7. Minor partner: According to Sec (ii) of the Indian Contract Act, an agreement with a minor is void. He is incapable of entering into a contract. But, in the contract of partnership, with the consent of all the partners, a minor may be admitted to the benefits of the partnership for the time being. Any agreement with a minor one is a legal one or it's a kind of a void one or a cancelled one, but if a minor wants, he can enter into a partnership firm as a partner and with the consent of the partner. For example,

I am a partner of a partnership firm XYZ and I have a brother who is a minor and I want my brother to join the partnership firm. But still, he is a minor and I can take permission from all the partners and my brother can become a partner there. But my brother won't be liable for any kind of losses or liability. My brother will only get the profit from the partnership firm and my brother, being the minor, can also act as an agent or be a part of the partnership firm and act like a partner.

❖ TYPES OF PARTNERSHIP

  i) BASIS OF DURATION - 1. Partnership at will
                                         2. Partnership for a fixed period
 ii) ON BASIS OF EXTENT OF BUSINESS - 1. Particular partnership
                                         2. General partnership

Based on duration

1. Partnership at will: It means that when we are entering into a Partnership Act, what happens is both the partners decide that they have a similar kind of business, so they come together and form a partnership firm that would be a partnership at will when both people have the same business and they have agreed to start a partnership firm. Any terms and conditions regarding the liability, how much profit sharing, regarding the winding up, registration, everything will be at the will of the partnership. They decide beforehand how much money would be investing and how much profit would be there. In case of liability who would be taken care of. Generally, both the parties have to take care of the liability.
2. Partnership for a fixed period: If you are starting with the partnership firm, say, me and my friend started with a partnership firm for a mobile shop and both of us decide that we would be continuing this shop for two years. When we go for the partnership deed, we will mention that this partnership is for two years. Once the two years come to an end, our partnership will be dissolving.

Based on the extent of the business

1. Particular partnership: The partnership firm would be for a particular type of business, we cannot go for different types of business. It is for a single type of business and for a particular

reason that becomes a particular partnership. Shop for clothing, business or chocolate-making business, etc. would be a particular partnership and for a particular period.

2. General partnership: General partnership means it is for a general condition and it follows all the rules and regulations of a partnership firm. And here, it is not mentioned that you know when they would be retiring, this will be for a fixed period. Registration of partnership firm is not mandatory, but yes, if you are registering, then what happens js you are getting all the benefits from the law. Again, like a partnership firm, you can get the backing of law if you are registered, but if you are not registering yourself, it doesn't mean that you cannot start the partnership firm.

❖ REGISTRATION OF PARTNERSHIP FIRM SECTION 58(1)

Registration of a partnership firm is not mandatory, but if you are registering you get all the benefits from the law. Anything anyone is doing wrong against the partnership firm, you can get backing of the law if you are registered, but if you're not registering yourself, it doesn't mean that you cannot start with the partnership firm.

1. Registration is not compulsory: Like I said, it is not compulsory to register. If you want to register, you can register. If you don't want to register, you can do that as well. But if you get yourself registered, you do it before or on the day of starting a business till the day the business comes to an end.

2. Details required in the application form: The details would be your name, the office, the place of the business, the date of partners joining a firm, name and address of partners, like the name and address of the partners, duration of the partnership firm like how many years or days you want to. For a partnership firm, all these things should be mentioned in the partnership deed.

3. Registrar confirms the registration and records the name in the register of the firm: When you are registering, you are giving all the details; you are filling up the forms of the partnership deed, and then, you are giving the details by providing all the documents. You then submit it to the registrar office and the registrar confirms the registration and record the name of your firm, and then, your partnership firm becomes registered and you can go ahead with your business.

❖ CHANGES ALLOWED AFTER REGISTRATION OF FIRM

1. Firm Name
2. Principal place of business
3. Opening or closing of branches: You can go for other branches too. They would be conducting the business, and at the same time, they can mention if they want to grow any business or close certain kind of business in the partnership deed.
4. Address of any partner
5. Constitution of form/dissolution: How and when will the dissolution take place.
6. Minor partner's decision after becoming major

❖ WHAT IF THE PARTNERSHIP IS NOT REGISTERED?

Which benefits would you not get if you are not registered?

1. Partners can't file suit against the firm or other partners. Section 69(1) - If there is a case going on regarding a certain kind of problem going on in the firm for example – ABC is your firm and XYZ is the second firm and suppose XYZ has taken money from you from the ABC firm, they had taken a loan from ABC firm and XYZ form was given a credit period from ABC firm for one month. A month they are supposed to pay ABC firm loan amount of Rs.5 lakh but one month passed but still, XYZ firm is not ready to give your money back. So, in this case, what will the ABC firm do if they are registered? They would have taken the case to the court with all the documents. And the court would have given the order to XYZ firm to pay the money to ABC firm. But since ABC firm is not registered, the only request they can make from XYZ firm is that give me back my money or in that case, partners cannot file suit against other partners or firm. For example, suppose there are three partners in ABC firm, and one of the partners have taken a certain amount of money from the account of the ABC firm, and have purchased a property under his name. You, being a partner, cannot take advantage of the company's funding and use it for the personal use. If you are using it for the personal use, you have to take permission from the other partners. If the other partners say yes, then only you can use it. But here Mr. X of ABC firm, hasn't taken any permission

from the partners YZ and has gone ahead and taken money from the partnership account and has purchased the property. In this case, if the partnership firm ABC was registered, then the partners can be taken to the court and he had to pay the money to the partnership, firm but since it is not registered, ABC cannot do anything regarding the situation. Students must understand the benefits of registering the partnership firm. If you are registering then no wrong can be done to the partnership firm. You have every support of the court and you can take the person who is doing wrong to you whether it is your partner or from the third-party or if it's another partnership firm.

2. Partners can't claim set-off. Section 69(3): Sometimes irrespective of the credit period given, people don't try to give money back from the person they have taken the loan. In this case, if the loan has been taken and the credit period has been given from the partnership firm and the partner or any other person is not giving back the money, without the registration, it becomes more difficult to penalise the person who has taken a loan.

3. Firm can't filed suit against partners. Section 69(2): If a partner is not ready to, who has taken some personal gain or has done business without any knowledge of the partners or has taken out money from the partnership firm lend out money from the partnership firm or has purchased certain kind of property or conducted and kind of business without the other partner's knowledge and this kind of things easily be liable since the partnership firm is not registered the partner cannot be held liable.

These are the things that make it necessary for the partnership firm to be registered.

❖ RIGHTS OF THE PARTNERS

RIGHT TO:

1. Take part in business: Whatever business you have if it is a cleaning business or a mobile business, TV shop business, bakery business, the partners or the how many partners are there, they should be taking part in the business. If they don't want to take part in the business, then they are not the active partners.

2. Partners to be consulted: In case of any kind of business-related issue, each partner should be consulted. This is the right of the partner no one can take away this right. If two partners think that they should be opening a second branch or they should be purchasing certain things from outside, this should be discussed with the third partner too.

3. Have access to books: Whatever monetary or financial things are recorded in the books or accounts. Anything and everything that is made a document of or whatever is written down, these things should be accessed and these books should be accessible to the partners. This is the right of every partner.

4. Share profits: This is again the right of the partner. When you start with the partnership firm and you have decided you would be dividing a profit 50-50 percent, then it is the right of every partner to get 50% of the profit; one person getting 50% and another getting 20% and another getting 30% is not what is mentioned in the partnership firm or deed when it is being registered.

5. Interest on capital (if agreed): Sometimes, if the partnership firm has landed in the problem we need the money and out of three or four partners one partner has put money and is ready to pay the money for the time being but if the partner is giving certain kind of money to the partnership firm so he is personally accountable to utilise a partnership firm account, this person who has given the loan or some amount of money to the partnership firm has got every right to get the interest on the particular capital whatever he has invested. It is the right of every partner to see to it the partner who has given a certain amount of money should be getting interested to depend on what you decide.

6. Interest on loan to a firm: If a partner has given a certain kind of loan to the firm, any kind of interest that is due to the partner has to be given to the partners.

7. Indemnity: Whatever the partner is doing, he should be held responsible for the same. The partner should be taking all the responsibility and should be accountable for any kind of actions he is taking in the partnership firm.

8. Use firm property: If the firm's property is being utilised for business and if one partner is utilising it, then the other partners also have the right to utilise it.

9. Be consulted on the admission of a new partner: Suppose there are two partners and another partner wants to join. Before joining in, all the partners have to be consulted regarding the newcomer.

10. Retire: When the partners want to retire, before retiring, one partner wants to retire the time has come for the partner to retire, they have to come together and consult and decide the Retirement procedure then that person can retire.

11. Carry on competing business after retirement: Suppose three of the partners started a baking business and, after one year, my third partner wants to leave this organisation or partnership firm and we say yes okay, so the third person leaves the partnership firm and wants to start another baking business similar to ours so for that also, before he leaves has to take permission from the partners and it should also be mentioned in the partnership deed that the partner who is retiring leaving the organisation can carry on competing the business. If he is competing with the business, the name cannot be the same. He can start the competing business after one or two months of leaving the previous organisation, he cannot start the similar business in the same name within next day of leaving the organisation. Further, the leaving or retiring partner needs to give a notification in the newspaper that he is not associated with this partnership firm. After the organisation has given permission and sanction from the court and after being registered, after being conveyed to the public henceforth this person is free from this partnership firm then only that person can start with a partnership firm of the same nature but without the same name.

12. Share subsequent profit: The profits which are coming should be equally shared.

13. Not to be expelled: It is very insulting for anyone, whether it is a partner or anyone else, that without giving them the reason why we are expelling them, we suddenly expel them. There should be certain terms and condition where the partners shouldn't be expelled. However, if the partner has done something wrong, then, depending upon the seriousness of the reasons and intense nature of the issue, they can ask the partner to leave. But, before that, a notification has to be given and the partner has to be conveyed. He has the right to know the reason, to give some

explanation as to why this act has done by him or her, and then only, the partner can be expelled..

14. Remuneration: If the partners want they can get remuneration or a salary, and since the profit is being divided between the partners, they can only go for profit instead of the salary of remuneration.

When a partner is in a partnership firm, he has all these rights if anything goes wrong with these rights and the partner is not fulfilling these rights or something is going against these rights then the partner can be penalised.

❖ DUTY.

1. Of good faith: This firm belongs to me and whatever things I would be doing should be for the benefit of the partnership firm. I cannot think about my gain should it be for partnership firm. I should be of good faith, I should be a good person and everyone should believe in me, I should be a sincere and hardworking person. A person who would be taking care of the partnership firm, we should be doing each and everything beneficial for the partnership firm.

2. Of greatest common advantage: Anything that would be done by the partner, whether it is an expansion of the business or purchasing of property, giving a loan, taking some kind of loan, investing money, it should be for a common advantage of the partnership firm; it shouldn't be for his personal use.

3. To render true accounts: Whatever give-and-take is taking place in the partnership firm, whatever money has been spent, or whatever money is coming should be recorded in the books of accounts. Anyone who demands should be provided with the account book and all the details should be written properly in specified details and it should be true.

4. To give full information: Every partner is liable to give full information regarding the business transactions or any kind of activity which has been done, on behalf of the partner, any kind of loan which might have been taken, any investment is done on behalf of the partnership firm, all this information should be given to each of the partners.

5. To indemnify or loss due to fraud: For each act, every partner is held responsible. If there is a fraud, from any partner then the partner should be held responsible. For example, a partner has left the organisation, he is no more a partner, but still, he is continuing the business and taking money. This is a fraud and the money that has been taken by the partner that should be accounted for and that person should be penalised.

6. To attend diligently: Every duty and responsibility, like meetings, business expansion plan, day-to-day activities of the partnership firm, handling the customers, all these things should be taken care of diligently.

7. To share losses: The partner has to share every loss that has been incurred by the partnership firm.

8. To account for personal profit: If any of the partners have done a business on behalf of the partnership firm, but has taken the money for themselves, it is a personal profit. So, they are accountable for this; they have to give a reason why they have gone for a personal profit.

9. To account for the profit of competing business: If there is a competing business and a profit has been made by the partnership firm, then the profit has to be shared by the partners.

10. To use the firm property for a firm only: It is the duty of the partners to use the firm's property only for the use of the firm, not for your personal use.

11. To act within authority: Whatever authority, liability, or responsibility has been given to the partnership firm in terms of business, expansion, customer making, profit, etc., everything has to be within the authority. Anything which is not mentioned in the partnership deed cannot be carried on by any of the partners.

12. Not to transfer his rights and interest: Whatever rights, duties, responsibilities, or profit a partner is making cannot be transferred to any other person or third party without the knowledge of the partners.

❖ LIABILITY OF FIRM AND PARTNERS TOWARDS THE THIRD PARTY

Third-party means a person who is doing business and is nowhere related to the partnership firm.

Section 26: Firms is liable for the activities of partners done within actual or implied authority – The entire partnership firm is liable for any kind of activity or liability that is incurred by any one of the partners. If one partner has been liable, then every partner is liable, and the firm is liable too.

Section 27: If the partner made any misappropriation of money, then the firm is liable if the act is within his authority – If the partner has made a mistake of not giving actual money when the actual money is taken. For example, the firm has taken the loan of Rs. 10,00,000 from a third party, and while giving back, they have only given me Rs. 7,00,000, all the partners are equally responsible for the remaining three lakh rupees.

Section 28(1): If firm accepted the liability implied (liability by holding out), then the form is liable for it – When you have taken the liability on behalf of the partnership firm, then you are liable. If that is the case, then the entire firm is liable. You cannot say that out of three partners, only one partner is liable for everything. Being a partner you are liable for each liability, even those of other partners.

Any kind of loan taken by any of the partners, business done by any of the partners, money which has to be repaid from any other partner, all the partners are liable and the entire partnership firm will be liable for the third parties from whom the loan has been taken.

❖ AUTHORITY OF PARTNERS

As per section 25, "Every partner is liable jointly with all the other partners or severally for all acts of the firm done while he is a partner". But the point to be noted here is that he is liable for only those acts that are within the authority of the other partners. Thus, we must know the concept of "Authority of partners".

Every partner is jointly responsible for every act they are doing on behalf of the partnership firm. If a partner lands up in a troublesome situation, then all the partners are responsible and they also land up in the trouble.

1. Expressed
   Specifically decided by all partners during the partnership deed

2. Implied

   Assumption by some indirect permission. For example, if you are a partner and you are getting another partner on board, so it is implied or assumed that you have taken permission from the other partners.

Simply put whatever authority decided during the partnership deed should be performed; no one can go beyond that authority.

3. Conditions to be satisfied: The act must be related to the firm, done in a usual way, done in the firm's name. It is implied that whatever things you are doing, it should be because you needed other firm needed it and the permission has been taken from all the partners and they know that is done and firms name.

4. Examples- The partner can: 1. Engaged a lawyer, 2. Purchase unusual good, 3. Appoint servants, 4. Make collection from debtors, 5. Sales of goods. 6. Settle the accounts etc.

5. If the act is outside the implied authority, then the other partners shall not be liable and that specific partner shall be personally liable. For example, out of five partners, if one partner has engaged a lawyer without even knowing, has sold any goods without other partners knowing, then obviously, the fifth person would be held responsible with no other partner being responsible.

   - to submit a firm's dispute to arbitration- if a partnership firm is going under a dispute, and the partner has gone ahead to the arbitrator and has submitted the firms dispute without consulting then this person should be held responsible.
   - Open a bank account in your name on behalf of the firm- This thing is done without taking permission of other partners then he is liable.
   - To compromise or relinquish the claim of the firm on outsiders – If anything is done with the outside or a third party then the fifth partner is held responsible.
   - To withdraw such a suit.
   - To accept any suit/liability against the firm.
   - To acquire/transfer immovable property for/of a firm –If he has made a certain kind of transfer of money, the person who has done this and has not consulted with the other partners will be held responsible.
   - To enter into partnership on behalf of the firm.

❖ POSITION OF A MINOR PARTNER IN FIRM

1. During the age of minority –
   - He can't be a partner but he can be admitted to the benefits of the firm. And he is introduced to the firm. He can only get the profit is not the liabilities, nothing is associated with him.
   - He can receive the profits and part of the property. Any profit can be entitled to the minor as decided in the partnership deed. If there is a property that everyone is getting, then the minor will also get a part of that.
   - He has the right to access books of accounts. The minor can have a look at books of account, financial records, and coming and going of the money.
   - He is not personally liable, only his share of profit and property are liable. If the partnership firm lands up in trouble, then minor is not liable. But the profit the partnership firm is making, it's given to the minor.
   - He can file a suit against the profit and property, but the firm can't file a suit against him. The minor ones and he's not getting his profit on the property. The minor can file a suit, but the partnership firm cannot file a suit against the minor or the property.

2. After attaining the age of majority- When a person is minor and has become a partner and is getting the profit, that contract changes when he becomes a major. The minor has to sign a contract again and go for a partnership deed according to the rules and regulations and can be considered as a partner. When he was a minor, it was a different case, a different contact. One contract cannot be used for both cases. When the minor becomes a major, he has to go for another contract and when he becomes a major, all the responsibilities and duties, position and benefit what are partners would be getting the same thing will also be given to the minor now has become the major. When he accepts everything he'll be getting all of these things, but when he rejects the partner will be the same because then he will be not liable for other liabilities, he can sue the partners for the share of profit and property. If he refuses to become a partner in the partnership firm where he was a minor, then the liabilities for him, like other partners, will be the same until and unless the

notice is given. Then, once he gets the notice and he is out of his responsibilities as a partner, then he is not liable for any kind of liabilities after he leaves the partnership firm. He can also sue the other partner for a share of profit and property if the other partner has not given him.

- Public notice by him/her within six months about the decision otherwise assumed to be a partner-
- *IF HE ACCEPTS:* a. Same position as that of others, b. Personally liable for the acts from when he was admitted to benefits. C. Share of profit and property are the same.
- *IF HE REJECTS:* a. Liability as per partner will be the same till the notice date, b. Not liable for further liabilities, c. He can sue the partner for his share of profit and property.

The dissolution of a partnership firm means that the relationship with the partner will come to an end. For example, if there is a partnership among A, B, and C come to an end. But the partnership between A and B comes into being.

The new firm with A and B is called a reconstituted firm.

Thus, retirement of a partner from a firm doesn't dissolve the firm. The firm continues with changed constitution. The partnership between continuing partners will be unaffected.

It depends upon what is the nature of your partnership firm. The day you decide that henceforth we are dissolving the partnership firm, the relationship comes to an end. For ex- ABC They were Partners for a mobile firm, after one year they dissolved It was for a fixed period. Out of the three partners A and B would like to continue the same with a different name, there A and B becomes new partnerAnd that becomes a reconstituted firm, if they want to they can continue the same name or they can go for a different name. It is not necessary that if one partner is retiring due to some reason that partnership would come to an end but yes if the partnership firm was between two people only and one person retires automatically the partnership would come to an end but if there are three or four partners and one partner retires it does not mean that the partnership firm will come to an end it can continue with other partners.

❖ RECONSTITUTION OF FIRM

1. Administration of partner - He can be admitted with the consent of all, not liable for any liability before his admission, liable for all responsibility after his admission.- when we are getting new people within the firm by taking the permission of other partners and any liability which was there before this partner joined. For example – today if I join our firm and before I joined the firm there was a liability of 50,00,00 of rupees in the partnership firm, but today I am joining and this amount was before I joined so this liability, I am not liable for this 50 lakhs rupees but after I joined within a month there is a liability of 50 lakhs rupees then that liability of after I joined becomes my liability also.

2. Retirement of partner - He can retire by the consent with all or by notice, liable for any liability before his retirement, and not liable for any liability after his retirement. When a person is retiring, a notice has to be given because the people who were doing business with the partnership firm should know who all are coming and going.

3. Expulsion of partner - He can't be expelled even by majority but only by a legal suit. Expulsion by majority is allowed if they can prove that expulsion is in the interest of firm and done in good faith. If a partner is not doing well or maybe has done some kind of criminal offence, or has gone against the value of the partnership firm, he can be expelled; you cannot expel a partner until and unless a legal case has been filed. And Going on with the partner. the majority you cannot take the decision but this has to be done legally but you can go for a majority decision in that case if we feel as partners this is for the interest of the partnership firm. For example if the partner has interaction or is dealing with a mafia, terrorist then it is not in the interest of the partnership firm so the majority decision can come and the partner can be expelled but before that also the partner should be given notice or a chance to put forward his case. Partner has to be present in front of other partners and given a chance to explain this kind of behaviour.

4. Insolvency of partner - By default, the insolvency of any partner results into dissolution of firm. An insolvent partner is not liable for any further liability.: The partners have become totally bankrupt can be reconstituted firm. If there is an insolvency by

default the firm comes to an end. Out of five partners of two partners have become insolvent then those two partners, and a partnership firm decides and they want to carry on with the partnership they can ask the partners to leave and he is in solvent partners are not responsible for any kind of liabilities.

5. Death of partner - By default, the death of any partner result in resolution of firm. However, other partners may decide otherwise in an agreement. The deceased partner is not liable for any further liability. If the partnership is between two partners only, and if one partner dies, then partnership firm automatically dissolves.

DISSOLUTION IS OF 2 TYPES:

1. Dissolution of firm – Activities of the firm shut down:
2. Dissolution of partnership – Some of the partners goes out by death, retirement, etc.

Dissolution without court intervention:

Where do you dissolve the Partnership Act without having court intervention?

1. By the consent of partners - This can be done by consent of the partners or free will of the partners.
2. By contract between partners - This can be done when two partners have already decided that after a fixed period of time, they will resolve a partnership firm without taking the help of the court.
3. Compulsory dissolution - This happens in case of insolvency of all partners and when business of firm becoming unlawful: two partners were there one partner became insolvent from concerned end if one partner is carrying out a certain kind of business with terrorists it is an unlawful business then the partnership will come to an end.
4. Dissolution due to contingency - Such contingencies include expiry of fixed term, completion of adventure, death of a partner, or insolvency of a partner.
5. Dissolution by notice - If a partner is retiring or being expelled, and if the case has been taken to the court, the court may order to dissolve the partnership.

Dissolution with court intervention

1. Insanity of partner - When there are more than one partner and one partner becomes mentally ill, the remaining partner may take this case to court

2. Permanent incapacity of partner - When a partner has gone into a state of coma, met with an accident, or paralysed, and cannot take care of business any further, then the remaining partners need to take the help of the court.

3. Misconduct of partner - A partner has insulted other partners or a third party in some way, or started purchasing property or taking money from the partnership firm for personal use, this kind of misconduct can be taken to the court.

4. Persistent breach of agreement - If there is a breach of agreement between partners, the court has to deal with it.

5. Transfer of interest - When partners are not transferring profits to each other, that is, one partner is taking the profit and other partners are not getting the profit, then in this situation, the court has to intervene.

6. Perpetual losses in business – When a partnership firm is not able to make a profit and is in continuous loss, this case can be taken to the court to find out the solution.

Effects of dissolution of the firm

1. After public notice, partners are not liable for further liabilities; Any private profit under firm's name must be accounted for by the firm - When a firm is going for a resolution, a public notice has to be given and any kind of liabilities have to be taken care of by the partners. Any kind of personal profit that has been incurred in the name of the firm, must also be recorded.

2. Partners can sell off all the firm assets to pay from liabilities and can share the surplus - The liabilities of five crore rupees and the partner agreed to give only Rs.2,00,00,000s of rupees another three crores of rupees have to be given to the third-party whom these partners have taken the liability, The partners and decided to sell off the properties and give those 3 crores of rupees to the third party.

3. Partner shall keep the authority for decision regarding dissolution of firm - When it is the dissolution of a firm, it is the rights and responsibilities of the partner to decide whether they want to dissolve or not.

4. Losses on realization shall be adjusted first from past profit, and then from the capital and if any balance remains, then it is shared by solvent partner - When the dissolution is taking in place, This all of the property to give out, the partners are not able to pay them the property would be sold, once a property sold off it is distributed in stages if there are any kind of losses which partners is going through that lost Needs to be adjusted from the property sold. From the capital whatever money we can get that can also be given off as liability and if any balance is left that would be given to the solvent partners. the partners are insolvent any kind of losses will be adjusted from the past profits, whatever profits that have been made in the past that can be adjusted to the losses that profits can be given as loss and then from the capital whatever is left would be distributed and will be shared to the solvent partner.

5. Payment can be made as the external debt of firm, partners loan, partners capital, surplus shared by all partners and PSR - Any payment left after dissolving whatever money is left whatever loan is there that would be given off, partners loan will also be given off if any partner has taken the loan behalf of the partnership firm and the loan is pending that will also be incurred if partner has invested any kind of Capital and if their surplus, it will also be shared by all partners PSR means partner shared ratio. When you're going for the partnership firm you first decide in which ratio you need to divide the profits. It can be 50-50%, 10%, 30% and in this particular ratio the profit will be distributed.

The dissolution can take place at will and it depends on what the partners have already decided or you can take the help of the court to dissolve your firm. When you are dissolving, it is the responsibility of the partners to give back any kind of liabilities that they have incurred.

Effect of dissolution of the firm

1. After public notice, partners are not liable for further liability. any private profit under firm name must be accounted for. When the partners are opting for dissolution, a resolution or a notice has to be given that the partnership firm is coming to an end.
2. Partners can sell all the firm assets to pay firm liabilities and can share the surplus. Any kind of surplus can be distributed.

3. Partner shall keep the authority for dissolution of the firm.
4. Losses on realization shall be adjusted first from past profit, and then from the capital and, if balanced, then it will be shared by solvent partners.

The Indian Case laws

1. AVIATION TRAVELS PVT. LTD. vs. BHAVESHA SURESH GORADIA

Citation: 2020 Latest Caselaw 213 SC
Judgement Date: *02 Mar 2020*

Before:- R. Banumathi and A.S. Bopanna, JJ.

Civil Appeal Nos. 1890-1891 of 2020(Arising out of SLP(C) Nos.5374-5375 of 2019). D/d. 2.3.2020.

Aviation Travels Pvt. Ltd. - Appellant

Versus

Bhavesha Suresh Goradia And Others - Respondents

For the Appellant:- R.F. Totla, Ashutosh Dubey, Pritesh Burad, Ms. Rajshri Dubey, Abhishek Chauhan, Rajendra A., Sushil Pandey, Advocates.

For the Respondent:- Shree Prakash Sinha, Ms. Marina Wheeler, Rakesh Mishra, Nawalendra Kumar, Ms. Mohua Sinha, Shekhar Kumar, Ms. Anisha Upadhyay, Advocates.

JUDGMENT

R. Banumathi, J. - Leave granted.

2. These appeals arise out of the impugned judgment dated 09.07.2018 passed by the High Court of Judicature at Bombay in Appeal (Lodging) No.224 of 2018 in Notice of Motion No.580

of 2018 in Suit No.2865 of 1994 in and by which, the High Court dismissed the Notice of Motion filed by the appellant and declined to set aside ex-parte judgment and decree dated 07.10.2003 passed against the appellant in Suit No.2865 of 1994 and the impugned order dated 26.10.2018 passed in Review Petition (Lodg.) No.20 of 2018 whereby the review petition filed by the appellant was dismissed.

3. Brief facts which led to the filing of these appeals are as under:- Respondent No.1 filed a suit being Suit No.2865 of 1994 before the High Court of Bombay against the appellant and respondents No.3 to 24 for permanent injunction and compensation of L 1 crore for trespass, nuisance and damages allegedly made by appellant-Defendant No.1. It is stated that respondents No.3 to 6 are present trustees of a private trust known as "Parikh Goradia Trust" and respondents No.7 to 24 are beneficiaries of the said private trust. The appellant carries on business as travel agent and also inter alia of running a restaurant called "Woodlands Garden Cafe" i.e. respondent No.2. It was stated by respondent No.1 that the trust-Parikh Goradia Trust came into existence under an Indenture of trust dated 01.04.1976. Clause 3 of the said Indenture provides that the trust shall come to an end on 30.09.1985 and the trust fund will be divided amongst beneficiaries of the trust. However, despite the trust having come to an end on the stipulated date, the trustees thereof have failed and neglected to distribute the property and fund of the trust amongst the beneficiaries.

4. By an agreement dated 06.10.1978 executed between the trust and the petitioner and a letter dated 06.08.1982, the trust agreed to sell to the appellant a part of the said property for a consideration of L 10,00,000/-. Defendant No.1A-respondent No.2-M/s. Woodlands Garden Cafe is a partnership firm registered under Indian Partnership Act, 1932 by virtue of a partnership deed executed on 01.04.1989. The appellant executed a leave and licence agreement dated 10.04.1989 with respect to the said premises in favour of respondent No.2-M/s. Woodlands Garden Cafe for a period of ten years to run the restaurant therein. Since the year 1989, respondent No.2-M/s. Woodland Garden Cafe is in occupation and possession of the said premises by doing restaurant business thereon. Case of the first respondent is that respondent No.2-M/s. Woodland

Garden Cafe was closed down for repairs and renovations in the year 1992 and in the course of these repairs, the appellant caused considerable damage to the property and carried out unauthorized and illegal construction.

5. Respondent No.1 filed Suit No.2865 of 1994 to direct the appellant (defendant No.1) to pay a sum of rupees one crore to the trust together with interest @ 24% per annum and for permanent injunction restraining the appellant from carrying on repairs and renovations in the premises and also to ensure that no damage or loss or injury is caused to the said property of the trust either in the course of the renovation or the repairs carried out by the appellant and other reliefs. Vide order dated 07.10.2003, the Court noted that no written statement has been filed and the Court held that the first respondent's claim in the suit is clearly unchallenged. Vide ex-parte decree dated 07.10.2003, the High Court decreed the suit and directed the appellant and respondent No.2 to pay respondent No.1 and the beneficiaries of the said trust a sum of L 77,02,500/- with interest thereon @ 6% per annum from the date of filing the suit till the date of payment or realization. By the said ex-parte decree dated 07.10.2003, the Court also granted relief in terms of Clause (b), (c) and (g) (i.e. permanent injunction, mandatory injunction and costs of the suit) of the prayer clause against the appellant and respondent No.2.

6. The matter remained as such for quite some time. The appellant took Notice of Motion No.580 of 2018 dated 02.02.2018 praying to set aside the ex-parte judgment and decree dated 07.10.2003 and that the appellant be permitted to file written statement and defend the suit. It was stated that the summons of the original suit and the proceeding thereof were never served upon the appellant at its registered address and/or any other address where the appellant was carrying on its business and also on the ground that Rule 90 of the Bombay High Court (Original Side) Rules (for short "Bombay High Court Rules") has not been followed.

7. Vide order dated 19.04.2018, learned Single Judge dismissed the Notice of Motion No.580 of 2018. The learned Single Judge noted that the ex-parte decree dated 07.10.2003 shows that an advocate was engaged on behalf of the appellant and respondent No.2 and the said advocate has filed vakalatnama and there is no

question of having to thereafter serve a party personally. The High Court held that along with the affidavit, a Power of Attorney dated 29.04.1993 was said to have been executed by the appellant in favour of one K. Shrinivas Rao and there is also a rubber stamp and circular common seal of the appellant in the Power of Attorney and the Power of Attorney is said to have been notarized in Mumbai and the seal of the Notary is also visible. Pointing out that the defendant No.1 through its Power of Attorney had engaged a lawyer and there was a validly executed vakalatnama by a constituted attorney K. Shrinivas Rao and also that writ of summons was in fact served on the appellant and respondent No.2 (original defendant No.1A) by bailiff attached to the office of Sherrif of Mumbai, the learned Single Judge dismissed the Notice of Motion No.580 of 2018.

8. Being aggrieved, appellant preferred Appeal (Lodging) No.224 of 2018 challenging the order declining to set aside the ex-parte decree. The said appeal was dismissed by the Division Bench vide impugned judgment dated 09.07.2018. The Division Bench of the High Court opined that the appellant had engaged M/s. Narayanan & Narayanan, Advocates who placed on record of the suit a vakalatnama duly signed by the constituted attorney of the appellant. The Division Bench also noted that the record indicates that the advocate for the appellant represented the appellant in the suit on several dates including appearing at interlocutory application stage and engaging a senior advocate to argue on behalf of the appellant. The Division Bench held that appellant's Notice of Motion as well as the appeal is misconceived. The appellant then filed Review Petition (Lodg.) No.20 of 2018 along with the Notice of Motion for condonation of delay of 27 days in filing the review petition. The said review petition also came to be dismissed vide impugned order dated 26.10.2018 on the ground that there was no error apparent on the face of the order or any other ground is made out to entertain the review petition.

9. We have heard the submissions of Mr. R.F. Totala, learned counsel for the appellant and Mr. Shree Prakash Sinha, learned counsel for respondents No.1, 9 and 10 and carefully perused the contentions and impugned judgment and other materials on record.

10. The High Court has noted that on behalf of the appellant, M/s. Narayanan & Narayanan, Advocates has entered appearance and filed a vakalatnama duly signed by the constituted attorney of the appellant. The Power of Attorney dated 29.04.1993 was executed by the Chairman and Managing Director, Mr. Kudralli Subanna Nagraj of the appellant company and the same was executed before the Notary on 29.04.1993 and the signature of the executant was also identified by the advocate. The High Court noted that the said Power of Attorney inter alia authorized the attorney to accept the summons, notice and other processes issued to the advocate from any Court, Government or authority concerning the suit premises. The High Court also pointed out that there are several clauses in the Power of Attorney which authorize the constituted attorney to do acts in regard to the litigation. The High Court has referred to the affidavit filed by K. Shrinivas Rao in reply dated 20.07.1994 to the Notice of Motion No.1847 of 1994 for interim relief wherein, it was stated that he is a constituted attorney of the appellant (defendant No.1). K. Shrinivas Rao also stated that he was Director of appellant company till the year 1989 and at the time of filing the affidavit in 1994, he was a partner in respondent No.2-firm.

11. Insofar vakalatnama dated 20.07.1994 filed by M/s. Narayanan & Narayanan, Advocates on behalf of the appellant and respondent No.2, contention of the appellant is that they never instructed the said M/s. Narayanan & Narayanan, Advocates to appear on behalf of the appellant in the original suit. Case of the appellant is that vakalatnama dated 20.07.1994 was signed by K. Shrinivas Rao claiming himself to be a constituted attorney of defendant No.1. The stand of appellant is that defendant No.1 never authorized the said K. Shrinivas Rao to sign vakalatnama on behalf of the appellant in the original suit. Insofar as the Power of Attorney dated 29.04.1993 is concerned, the appellant contends that it was a general Power of Attorney and the appellant company never passed any board resolution nor executed any such Power of Attorney authorizing K. Shrinivas Rao to sign vakalatnama on behalf of the appellant in the suit; the said K. Shrinivas Rao signed the vakalatnama for and on behalf of respondent No.2. Stand of the appellant is that the appellant never authorized K. Shrinivas Rao to appear on behalf of the appellant in the original suit No.2865 of 1994.

12. The High Court rejected the stand of the appellant and observed that page 18 of the Power of Attorney is a typed name of the Chairman and Managing Director and there is also a rubber stamp and circular common seal of the appellant and the Power of Attorney was executed by the Chairman and Managing Director of the appellant company Mr. Kudralli Subanna Nagraj. The High Court has also pointed out that the Power of Attorney dated 29.04.1993 has been notarized in Mumbai on 29.04.1993 and the seal of the Notary is also seen in the Power of Attorney.

13. On behalf of the appellant, it was contended before the High Court that even assuming that the vakalatnama was filed on behalf of the appellant through Power of Attorney, Rule 79 of the Bombay High Court Rules requires personal service of the writ of summons on a defendant even if appearance was entered on his behalf by an advocate. To the said contention, the High Court opined that Rule 79 of the Bombay High Court Rules speaks of a waiver of the requirement of serving the writ of summons personally, if the advocate undertakes in writing to accept service of that writ of summons and to file a vakalatnama. The High Court pointed out that Rule 79 contemplates a stage before the vakalatnama is in fact filed and once the vakalatnama is filed, there is no question of having to serve a party personally thereafter. The High Court pointed out that in Suit No.2865 of 1994, vakalatnama was filed by the Power of Attorney in the suit itself and there is no question of having to thereafter serve a party personally. After referring to the affidavit in reply at pages 62 and 63 of the paper book, the High Court observed that summons was in fact served on the advocates for the appellant and respondent No.2 by bailiff attached to the office of Sherrif of Mumbai and there is an affidavit of service dated 18.08.1999 made by the bailiff's clerk to that effect. Observing that the Court has personally checked the original affidavit of the bailiff and the file and pointing out that there is no affidavit in rejoinder, the learned Single Judge has dismissed the Notice of Motion No.580 of 2018.

14. According to the appellant, the High Court erred in holding that the Power of Attorney dated 29.04.1993 is genuine. It was urged that the alleged Power of Attorney is said to have been notarized at Mumbai before Advocate Raja who was representing respondent No.2 in the original suit whereas, the appellant

company is located in Bangalore. Learned counsel for respondent No.1 has submitted that the appellant herein surrendered and/ or sold all its rights and interest in the property in question to respondent No.2 on 30.04.1993 and the present appeal is a proxy litigation on behalf of respondent No.2. It is the contention of respondent No.1 that since K. Shrinivas Rao duly constituted the Power of Attorney of the appellant has filed his reply on 20.07.1994 and the said reply was filed through M/s. Narayanan & Narayanan, Advocates in which the appellant through the Power of Attorney has stated that the premises in question was acquired by the appellant with the contribution made by respondent No.2- M/s. Woodland Garden Cafe and therefore, respondent No.2 also should be heard before any order is passed in the suit. It was submitted that based on the reply affidavit filed by K. Shrinivas Rao, respondent No.1 filed application for amendment and the amendment application was allowed on 26.07.1994 and respondent No.2 was impleaded as defendant No.1A. It is therefore, submitted that filing of vakalatnama on behalf of the appellant by its duly constituted Power of Attorney K. Shrinivas Rao and subsequent impleading of respondent No.2 clearly shows that the appellant and respondent No.2 were duly served and participated in the proceedings and were aware of the decree dated 07.10.2003. It was contended that the appellant has not approached with the correct averments and in view of the incorrect stand taken by the appellant, the High Court rightly rejected the Notice of Motion refusing to set aside the ex-parte decree dated 07.10.2003.

15. Though various contentions have been raised as to whether appellant was served or not and entered appearance in the suit, we are not inclined to go into the merits of the contentions. In our view, an opportunity has to be given to the appellant for contesting the suit. It is because the suit was filed for recovery of damages of L 1 crore and respondent No.1 claimed interest @ 24% per annum. By the judgment dated 07.10.2003, the Court has directed the appellant and respondent No.2 to pay a sum of L 77,02,500/- and L 42,70,772.46, total amount payable under decree is L 1,20,03,282.96. The Court also directed the payment of subsequent interest @ 6% per annum on the said amount of L 77,02,500/- till date of reliasation.

16. As pointed out earlier, the suit claim was for damages. The damages to the property if any, can be ascertained only after the parties adduce the oral and documentary evidence. We have no reason to believe that the appellant would have benefitted by deliberately not contesting the suit as they would in any event be saddled with interest if their conduct was to drag and prolong the suit. Considering the nature of the claim and other facts and circumstances and in the interest of justice, we are of a view that an opportunity has to be given to the appellant to contest the suit subject to terms. The appellant has also in that regard shown its bona fide by depositing L 60,00,000/- in compliance of the order dated 18.02.2019. By the order dated 24.01.2020, we have also directed the appellant to deposit further sum of L 35,00,000/- for which the appellant sought for some more time for compliance. Considering the request, two months further time is granted to the appellant for deposit of the said amount.

17. Insofar as the amount of L 60,00,000/- deposited by the appellant, by our order dated 24.01.2020, we have permitted respondent No.1-plaintiff to withdraw the said amount. Since there are number of other beneficiaries of the trust viz. respondents No.7 to 24, the amount has to be disbursed to the trustees/beneficiaries as per their entitlement. It is open to respondent No.1 and other trustees/beneficiaries of the trust to file appropriate application before the High Court for disbursement of the amount (pending disposal of the suit) and the High Court shall consider and pass appropriate order as per the entitlement of the respective parties. The disbursement of the said amount will be subject to the outcome of said suit. Permission for withdrawal of the amount of L 60,00,000/- by respondent No.1 and other trustees/beneficiaries is without prejudice to the contention of both the parties in the suit.

18. In the result, the impugned judgment dated 09.07.2018 passed by the High Court of Judicature at Bombay in Appeal (Lodging) No.224 of 2018 in Notice of Motion No.580 of 2018 in Suit No.2865 of 1994 and the impugned order dated 26.10.2018 passed in Review Petition (Lodg.) No.20 of 2018 are set aside and these appeals are allowed. The Suit No.2865 of 1994 is ordered to be restored. The appellant and respondent No.2 shall file their written statement within four weeks from today and

learned Single Judge of the High Court shall afford sufficient opportunity to both the parties to adduce evidence and dispose the said suit in accordance with law.

19. Insofar as direction for deposit of L 35,00,000/-, two months further time is granted to the appellant for deposit of the said amount and on such deposit, the same shall be invested in a nationalized Bank for a period of six months with a provision of auto renewal. Deposit of L 35,00,000/- would be subject to the outcome of the suit. No costs.

2. **Partnership Act, 1932, Section 14** - Partnership property - Property used for partnership purposes is necessarily not the partnership property - Property belonging to a partner does not become partnership property by being used for the purpose of partnership - There must be some evidence of an intention to treat the property as a part of the capital of the business - Where a partner brings certain property into the common stock as part of his capital, it becomes partnership property - Act has also specifically included the goodwill among the partners of the firm subject to any contract between the partners, in all accounts for determining the shares. (M/s.D.R. Associates Vs General Manager, East Coast Railways & Ors.) 2005(1) Civil Court Cases 328 (Orissa)

3. **Partnership Act, 1932, Sections 16, 37 and 50** - Partnership firm - One of the partners died and the firm stood dissolved - New partnership firm constituted in which new partners introduced - Held, surviving partner is liable to render accounts till the date on which the firm stood dissolved. (Smt.Sarojini, LRs. of Deceased 1st defendant Vs Kumari Bhagyavathi & Ors.) 2005(3) Civil Court Cases 327 (Madras)

4. **Partnership Act, 1932, Sections 20, 22** - Firm and its partners - Liability - A partnership firm has no independent entity of its own and all the liabilities against the firm or all acts done by any one of its partners for and on behalf of the firm shall bind all the other partners as well - Section 20 is an exception to the implied authority - Partners by contract between themselves extend or restrict the implied authority of any partner - However, notwithstanding any such restriction, any act done by a partner on behalf of the firm, which falls within his implied authority, binds the firm, unless the person with whom he is dealing knows

of the restriction or does not know or believe that partner to be a partner - Onus to prove that such authority of partner is restricted is upon the person who claims such a restriction. (State Bank of India Vs M/s.Simko Engineering Works) 2005(1) Civil Court Cases 319 (P&H)

5. **Partnership Act, 1932, Section 24** - Partnership firm - Partner is an agent of the firm - Notice to agent tantamount to the principles and vice versa - Notice to a principal is notice to all his agents and notice to an agent of matters connected with the agency is notice to his principal. (Ashutosh Vs State of Rajasthan & Ors.) 2005(2) Apex Court Judgments 657 (S.C.) : 2005(3) Civil Court Cases 606 (S.C.)

6. LANDMARK JUDGEMENT-EFFECTS OF NON REGISTRATION OF PARTNERSHIP FIRM

There is a possible confusion on the case that whether the subsequent registration of the firm will cure the initial defect in the filing of the suit. It has arisen for consideration in D.D.A. v. Kochhar Construction Work and Anr. The court stated that the provision of the Act it was not possible to subscribe to the view that subsequent registration of the firm will cure the initial defect, because of the proceedings. They not have been instituted as the firm in whose name the proceedings were instituted was not a registered firm on the date of the institution of the proceedings.

IN THE SUPREME COURT OF INDIA

Civil Appeal No. 4092 of 1998
Decided On: 07.11.2006
Purushottam and Anr.
Vs.
Shivraj Fine Art Litho Works and Ors.
Hon'ble Judges/Coram:
B.P. Singh and Altamas Kabir, JJ.

1. In this appeal by special leave the plaintiffs are the appellants. Their suit against original defendant nos. 1 to 9 was decreed for the sum of Rs. 8,92,815.14 by the Third Joint Civil Judge (Senior Division), Nagpur in Civil Suit No. 52 of 1980. On appeal by

original defendants 1 to 3, the High Court in First Appeal No. 35 of 1988 by its impugned judgment and order of April 10, 1992 allowed the appeal and dismissed the suit holding that in view of the provisions of Section 69(2) of the Indian Partnership Act (hereinafter referred to as the 'Act'), the suit was not maintainable, the plaintiff being an unregistered firm.

2. The facts of the case are not in dispute and they will be briefly noticed. Plaintiff No. 1, Pursushottam, carried on business as whole- sale paper merchant in the name and style of "Dinesh Paper Mart" as the sole proprietor of the concern. During this period he supplied goods to the defendant firm namely - Shivraj Fine Arts Litho Works, a firm registered under the Partnership Act. Defendants 2 to 9 were the partners of the said firm. In the year 1974, Special Civil Suit No. 9 of 1974 was filed for dissolution of the defendant partnership firm and for rendering of accounts. During the pendency of the suit a receiver was appointed initially to take possession of the properties of the firm and to run the business of the firm. Later joint receivers were appointed, and it is not in dispute that at the relevant time defendant No. 2 and defendant No. 12 were in management of the aforesaid registered firm - respondent No. 1 herein as joint receivers.

3. The aforesaid Purushottam had business dealings with the respondent No. 1 - firm. Goods were supplied and payments made from time to time. It is not in dispute that the amounts due and payable to the plaintiff No. 1, Purushottam were fully paid up as on March 20, 1974, that is, before the date of appointment of Receiver. Even after appointment of the Receiver, successive Receivers purchased goods from Plaintiff No. 1, Purushottam, herein for the business of respondent No. 1 - firm. A khata was maintained by plaintiff No. 1-Purushottam in which payments made were duly entered, and at the end of the year the amount outstanding as on December 31, was carried forward to the next year. The defendant firm acknowledged their liability to pay the amount entered in the khata by making an endorsement in the khata. As at the end of the financial year 1979 a sum of Rs. 6,22,713.06 was the balance due from the defendant firm to plaintiff Purushottam. The plaintiff was also entitled to interest at the agreed rate of 18% per annum on the balance outstanding for more than seven days.

4. With effect from January 1, 1980 the proprietary - firm of Purushottam (Plaintiff No. 1) was taken over by a partnership of which plaintiff Purushottam was also a partner. The said partnership firm took over all the assets and liabilities of "Dinesh Paper Mart" and continued their business in the same name. Though the said partnership firm came into existence on January 1, 1980, an application for registration of the firm under the Act was made on January 14, 1980. While the said application was pending, the instant suit was filed on March 31, 1980. Later, on November 29, 1980, the Plaintiff No. 2 - firm was granted registration under the Act. It would thus appear that though the newly constituted partnership firm had applied for registration on January 14, 1980, on the date on which the suit was filed, that is on March 31, 1980, it was an unregistered firm and registration was granted later on November 29, 1980. This therefore, gave rise to the objection urged on behalf of the defendants relying on Section 69(2) of the Act that the suit by an unregistered firm was not maintainable to enforce a right arising from a contract.

5. The High Court took the view relying upon authorities that the suit was barred by Section 69(2) of the Act, and even if registration was subsequently granted, that would not cure the defect. Repelling the argument that in any event Plaintiff No. 1, the erstwhile proprietor may be entitled to enforce his claim, the Court held that once he had transferred his rights to the partnership which took over all the rights and liabilities of the proprietary concern, he lost his exclusive right to recover the amount since that had become an asset of the partnership firm over which he as a partner had no exclusive right. He, therefore, did not have any enforceable subsisting claim after the partnership came into existence, and, therefore, no relief could be granted to him in his personal capacity as erstwhile proprietor of the concern.

6. Shri V.A. Mohta, Sr. Advocate, appearing on behalf of the appellants before us advanced three main submissions. Firstly, he submitted that once registration is granted, even though after the filing of the suit, the suit should be held to be maintainable as from the date on which registration is granted subject to the law of limitation. Secondly, he submitted that Plaintiff No. 1, Purushottam in his personal capacity could sue the respondent firm for the amount in question, if the firm of which he was a

partner was for reason of non- registration unable to maintain a suit. Lastly, he submitted that Section 69(2) of the Act is not attracted to a case where the contract in question is not with the unregistered firm and for this he relied on the judgment of this Court in Haldiram Bhujiawala and Anr. v. Anand Kumar Deepak Kumar and Anr. MANU/SC/0144/2000 : [2000]1SCR1247.

7. In Shreeram Finance Corporation v. Yasin Khan and Ors. MANU/SC/0341/1989; it was held by this Court that a suit filed by the existing partners of the firm after reconstitution was not maintainable if the newly added partners were not shown as partners in the Register of Firms under the Act. In that case the suit was filed in the name of the current partners as on the date of the suit, whose names were not shown as partners in the Register of Firms maintained under the Act. It is no doubt true that in the aforesaid decision the bar was attracted not on account of non-registration of a partnership firm but on account of the fact that the persons suing had not been shown in the Register of Firms as partners of the firm. Counsel for the respondent submitted that Section 69(2) of the Act is mandatory and unless the conditions specified therein are fulfilled, a suit by a partnership Firm will be hit by the bar contained in that provision.

8. The question as to whether the subsequent registration of the firm would cure the initial defect in the filing of the suit arose for consideration in D.D.A. v. Kochhar Construction Work and Anr. MANU/SC/1279/1998 : (1998)8SCC559. This Court held that in view of the clear provision of the Act it was not possible to subscribe to the view that subsequent registration of the firm may cure the initial defect, because the proceedings were ab initio defective as they could not have been instituted since the firm in whose name the proceedings were instituted was not a registered firm on the date of the institution of the proceedings. This Court also noticed the difference of opinion amongst the High Courts and concluded thus: Counsel for the respondents, however, invited our attention to two decisions which take a view that subsequent registration of the firm can cure the initial defect provided the registration is before the period of limitation has run out. Our attention was drawn to M.S.A. Subramania Mudaliar v. East Asiatic Co. Ltd. and Atmuri Mahalakshmi v. Jagadeesh Traders. However, the High Court of Patna in Laduram Sagarmal v. Jamuna Prasad Chaudhuri and the High Court of Madras in T. Savariraj Pillai v. R.S.S. Vastrad & Co.

take a contrary view and hold that the suit is incompetent ab initio. We have considered these decisions, but in the light of the plain language of Section 69 of the Partnership Act read with Section 20 of the Arbitration Act and in view of the decision of this Court reported in Shreeram Finance Corpn. We are clearly of the opinion that proceedings under Section 20 of the Arbitration Act were ab initio defective since the firm was not registered and the subsequent registration of the firm cannot cure that defect.

The same view was also reiterated in U.P. State Sugar Corporation Ltd. v. Jain Construction Co. And Anr. MANU/SC/0681/2004 : AIR2004SC4335. These decisions squarely answer the first submission of Shri V.A. Mohta. The submission must therefore be rejected.

9. The second submission urged on behalf of the appellants is also squarely answered by a judgment of this Court reported in Addanki Narayanappa and Anr. v. Bhaskara Krishnappa (D) and Ors. MANU/SC/0281/1966 : [1966]3SCR400 This Court held:

It seems to us that looking to the scheme of the Indian Act no other view can reasonably be taken. The whole concept of partnership is to embark upon a joint venture and for that purpose to bring in as capital money or even property including immovable property. Once that is done whatever is brought in would cease to be the exclusive property of the person who brought it in. It would be the trading asset of the partnership in which all the partners would have interest in proportion to their share in the joint venture of the business of partnership. The person who brought it in would, therefore, not be able to claim or exercise any exclusive right over any property which he has brought in, much less over any other partnership property. He would not be able to exercise this right even to the extent of his share in the business of the partnership. As already stated, his right during the subsistence of the partnership is to get his share of profits from time to time as may be agreed upon among the partners and after the dissolution of the partnership or with his retirement from partnership of the value of his share in the net partnership assets as on the date of dissolution or retirement after a deduction of liabilities and prior charges.

The High Court has, therefore, rightly held that the partnership having come into existence of which Plaintiff No. 1 was a partner, and he having transferred to the said partnership all his assets and liabilities of his proprietary concern, he had no subsisting exclusive right to enforce the liability against the defendants since such rights as he had as the proprietor vested in the partnership. He could not therefore either file a suit or claim any relief in the suit filed by the partnership asserting his right as the erstwhile proprietor. The second submission also fails.

10. This brings us to a consideration of the third submission that the bar in Section 69(2) of the Act is not attracted to a suit in which the contract in question is not with the unregistered firm which is the plaintiff. Counsel placed considerable reliance on the judgment of this Court in Haldiram Bhujiawala and Anr. (supra), and submitted that the principles laid down therein applied to his case with full force. On the other hand, the respondents insist that the case is clearly distinguishable on facts, and in any case the observations relied upon by the appellants do not constitute the ratio, as it was wholly unnecessary to go into the question which did not fall for consideration after the first question was answered in favour of the appellants. It therefore becomes necessary for us to notice the relevant facts of the case, the questions that fell for consideration, and the principles laid down therein.

12. In the meantime on 10.10.1977 R.L. Aggarwal and his son applied in Calcutta for registration of the same trademark in their name claiming to be full owners of the trademark, without disclosing the dissolution deed of 16.11.1974. In these circumstances a suit was filed by the partnership firm with three of the sons of Moolchand as partners thereof being the first plaintiff. The second plaintiff in the suit was the fourth son of Moolchand. They claimed the relief of injunction restraining the defendants from using the said trademark, damages, and for destruction of the material etc. The defendants filed an application under Order 7, Rule 11, CPC for summary dismissal of the suit since Plaintiff No. 1 partnership firm was not a registered partnership firm on the date of the filing of the suit. The Trial Court dismissed the application and so did the appellate bench of the High Court of Delhi. The defendants appealed to this Court by Special Leave.

16. In Raptakos Brett & Co. Ltd. (Supra) this Court after noticing Section 69 of the Act observed:

A mere look at the aforesaid provision shows that the suit filed by an unregistered firm against a third party for enforcement of any right arising from a contract with such a third party would be barred at its very inception. To attract the aforesaid bar to the suit, the following conditions must be satisfied:

   (i) That the plaintiff-partnership firm on the date of the suit must not be registered under the provisions of the Partnership Act and consequently or even otherwise, the persons suing are not shown in the Register of Firms as partners of the firm, on the date of the suit.

   (ii) Such unregistered firm or the partners mentioned in the sub-section must be suing the defendant-third party.

   (iii) Such a suit must be for enforcement of a right arising from a contract of the firm with such a third party.
   Relying upon the aforesaid analysis this Court in Haldiram Bhujiawala and Anr. (supra) held that the contract contemplated by Section 69 of the Act is the contract entered into by the firm with the third party defendant. The contract by the unregistered firm referred to in Section 69(2) must not only be one entered into by the firm with a third party defendant, but must also be one entered into by the plaintiff firm in the course of the business dealings of the plaintiff firm with such third party defendant.

17. With respect, we find ourselves in complete agreement with the principles enunciated in Haldiram Bhujiawala and Anr. (supra). Having regard to the purpose Section 69(2) seeks to achieve and the interest sought to be protected, the bar must apply to a suit for enforcement of right arising from a contract entered into by the unregistered firm with a third party in the course of business dealings with such third party. If the right sought to be enforced does not arise from a contract to which the unregistered firm is a party, or is not entered into in connection with the business of the unregistered firm with a third party, the bar of Section 69(2) will not apply.

18. In the instant case the contract was entered into with the respondent firm by the erstwhile proprietor of the concern namely Purushottam. The partnership firm came into existence later. The amount claimed in the suit were due to the proprietor Purushottam who carried on his proprietary business in the name and style of "Dinesh Paper Mart". When he entered into partnership with others, he contributed to the partnership by way of his contribution to the capital, all the assets and liabilities of his erstwhile proprietary concern. Thus, though the partnership firm, which

was unregistered, became entitled to enforce the contractual obligation of the defendant firm which it owed to Purushottam, the contract was not one entered into by the unregistered firm with a third party, nor was it one entered into by the unregistered firm in the course of its business dealings with the defendants. So viewed, the bar of Section 69(2) cannot apply to the suit filed by the Plaintiff - appellants.

20. We, therefore, allow this appeal with costs and set aside the impugned judgment and decree of the High Court and restore that of the Third Joint Civil Judge (Senior Division) Nagpur, in Civil Suit No. 52 of 1980 dated 29.4.1987.

The Negotiable Instruments Act, 1881

- *The law relating to negotiable instruments as contained in the Negotiable Instruments Act, 1881, which applies and extends to the whole of India.*

DEFINITIONS

- The word "negotiable" means "transferable by delivery" and the word "instrument" means "a written document by which a right is created in favor of some person or persons".
- Thus, the term "negotiable instrument" literally means "a written document that creates a right in favor of somebody and is freely transferable".

  The word "negotiable" means that you are transferring your right to another person and the instrument or document through which you are transferring this right should be a written document and the entire entity is known as a negotiable instrument. The written document gives a right to another person to obtain a certain amount of money. This concept is usually related to money matters.

  It involves giving you a favor and a right to do business with someone, and, at the same time, get the money related to the business, and this right is transferable. If I am giving you a cheque, it means I am giving you the right from my end, that is, I am transferring the right to you to receive the money that is given to you. This is the meaning of a negotiable instrument.

- A negotiable instrument is a piece of paper that entitles a person to a certain sum of money and is transferable from one to another person by delivery or by endorsement and delivery.
- Example – a promissory note, a cheque, a bill of exchange, and other documents, such as railway or ST receipts, dividends, warrants, railway bound payable, etc.

It is a piece of paper that is entitled, giving a right to another person to receive a certain amount of money that is due to the person who is giving this instrument. Negotiable Instruments are of different types. Promissory note is a written document where a promise is made from one person to another that on a predetermined date, some predetermined amount of money would be given to another person to whom this promissory note is handed to. Cheque is also given to a person whose money is due. A bill of exchange is another instrument where you get the money against the bill. Warrants on documents like railway or ST receipt or dividends are negotiable instruments because, through these, you are giving a right to another person to redeem the due money.

❖ CHARACTERISTICS OF NEGOTIABLE INSTRUMENTS

- *Free transferability or easy negotiability* – A negotiable instrument is freely transferable: One person can freely transfer the right of a particular instrument to another person. Example: I have taken a cell phone from my friend and I am supposed to pay Rs. 20,000 for the cell phone. So, instead of cash what I do is I give her a cheque. This cheque as a document, which is a part of the negotiable instrument. In that cheque, I'll put the money as Rs. 20,000 sign the cheque, and give it to my friend. This cheque is mine because I have an account in a particular bank, and on this right, I am giving the cheque to another person to deposit it in the said bank or any other bank and get the money that I was supposed to pay to her. Essentially, it implies transfer of rights to another person to redeem the amount of money that is due to the other person.
- *Title of the holder is free from all defects* – A person who takes negotiable instrument bona-fide gets the instrument free from all defects in the title. The holder, in due course, is not affected by the defective title of the transferor or of any other party. A holder is

a person who has the right to a particular negotiable instrument. For example, suppose I have given a cheque of Rs.10,000 to one of my clients and I don't have that money in my bank. In that case, the person who is holding that cheque becomes the holder. I have given him the right, as I have transferred him that right from my cheque to my friend's cheque. When the cheque is given to my friend, it has got no defect because it's given from a person who has got an account. If anything goes wrong with the cheque, like it has bounced, my friend is not liable for the same. It would be I, as a transferor, who would be liable for any kind of defect. The cheque that I have given is free from any defects; at any point of time, my friend can deposit the cheque and can get the money. In a nutshell, the person who is giving the negotiable instrument would be liable for any kind of defect, not the holder.

❖ PRESUMPTIONS

Presumption means whatever you are thinking or deciding.

- Of consideration: Every negotiable instrument was made or drawn for consideration. You, as a holder or the person who is getting a right, are presuming that any kind of negotiable instrument is being drawn or has been given to the holder to take care of the money that the person is getting. It is a consideration in such a way that the holder of the instrument would be getting the money.
- As to date: Every negotiable instrument bearing a date was made or drawn on such date. On a cheque or a promissory note, the date is mentioned. In case of a cheque, the date is valid for three or six months, and in the case of promissory note, the date is valid for one month or any other mentioned date. On the date that is mentioned there, it is presumed that till that date, that instrument is accepted within a reasonable time. For example, if I am giving a promissory note, the holder should be given a reasonable time for acceptance.
- As to time of acceptance: Every excepted bill of exchange is accepted within a reasonable time before its maturity. Until and unless I deposit within the due date, the cheque is of no use. The condition is any kind of exchange that is accepted, should be accepted within a reasonable time, and before the expiry date of

the particular instrument. The bill of exchange should be encashed within one month, if the check is for three months it should be in cash within three months after that it becomes expired. Any kind of negotiable instrument should be accepted in a reasonable time.

- <u>As to the time of endorsements</u>: The endorsements appearing upon negotiable instruments were made in order in which they appear thereupon. Endorsement means the signature and the amount. Whatever is written in the promissory note, bank draft, or cheque, all are endorsements that are legally viable. Whatever terms and conditions were there, when this negotiable instrument was drawn that, when the other person is giving you the same terms and conditions, should be there.

- <u>As to stamps</u>: A promissory note, bill of exchange, or cheque is duly stamped. When you are getting a legal document, it needs to be stamped by the organization. A cheque should contain name of the person who is getting it, name and signature of the person who is given it, and the amount. In case of a promissory note, the stamp of the company should be put. When they are accepting they are giving you a stamp they would be stamping and giving you the receipt, your cheque or your promissory note or anything similar. Their stamp is necessary because this is a proof that negotiable instrument has been deposited on so-and-so date.

- <u>As to holder in due course</u>: Every holder of the negotiable instrument is a holder in due course. Every negotiable instrument comprises the person who is transferring a bill of exchange in his name to another person's name; the person who is holding the particular negotiable instrument becomes a holder; and the time frame for which the negotiable instrument has been given. For example, suppose I need to pay Rs. 20,000 to my friend, my friend becomes a holder of that particular cheque that I am giving in due course, which means from that time onwards till the maturity, my friend becomes a holder.

- <u>As to the time of transfer</u>: Every transfer of negotiable instrument is made before its maturity. The validity of a particular document needs to be considered and the instrument needs to be attached within the particular time frame. If it is done, then it can be said that the negotiable instrument has been made within the time of transfer.

❖ TYPES OF NEGOTIABLE INSTRUMENTS

Negotiable instruments are of the following two types:

- <u>Negotiable instruments recognised by status</u>: Examples - Bills of exchange, cheques, and promissory notes. If you're getting a cheque, there is a status to the cheque: 'Yes, I got a cheque and this is my negotiable instrument'. A promissory note has the status that a person has promised another person to pay a certain amount of money, within a specific time.
- <u>Negotiable instruments recognised by usage or custom of trade</u>: Examples - Banknotes, exchequer bills, share warrants, bearer debentures, dividend warrants, shares certificates. If it is related to a business or to a particular type of business, it is known as a negotiable instrument that the person uses. Banknotes coming from a bank, so-and-so date this person would be given amount of money, exchequer bills – other bills which are also given from a company and it is like a promissory note, share warrants- As a document or certificate that so-and-so person is having so-and-so share from the company by usage and this gives you a guarantee for that dividend. Bearer Debentures – The person to whom the shareholder is giving them money and become owner a particular part of the company debenture is issued when the company is in the need of money or loan, they can get a loan and a document which is for a future project and they can get a loan in lieu of this particular document. A dividend warrant means when you are paying the dividend against the share which the person has already purchased The shareholder is a kind of a document which says this person is entitled to this much dividend. Share certificate as approved a particular proof of purchasing a particular share from a company. The example I am a shareholder and I have purchased a hundred shares from reliance, then reliance will give me the share certificate where a date would be given, the name of the person which is me would be given, and then how many shares I have purchased suppose a hundred shares, share value share is hundred rupees and I would be stated that I have taken a hundred shares on the face value is hundred rupees and this is the amount of money this person has paid and the share belongs to this person.

❖ BILLS OF EXCHANGE

- A bill of exchange is an instrument containing an unconditional order, signed by the maker, directing a certain person to pay a certain sum of money only to a person, or to the order of a certain person or the bearer of the instrument.

- Example: Mr. X purchases goods from Mr. Y for Rs.1000/-. Mr. Y buys goods from Mr. S for Rs.1000/–. Then, Mr. Y may order Mr. X to pay Rs.1000/– to Mr. S, which will be nothing but a bill of exchange. X is purchasing 1 kg mangoes for rs. 100 and X are purchasing from Y for 1000rs at the same time Y is also purchasing mango for 1000rs from another shopkeeper Mr S for rs.1000, instead of Y paying money to Mr X Mr Y directs Mr S the shopkeeper what you do is you give 1000rs to Mr S, and I will give you 1000rs back.

It is a kind of order given by one person in writing and signed. If I am giving a bill of exchange to my friend, I have to write and sign it and then I have to direct it to another friend or colleague.

❖ PROMISSORY NOTE

A promissory note is an instrument in writing (not being a banknote or a currency – note) containing an unconditional undertaking, signed by the maker, to pay a certain amount of money only to or to the order of a certain person or the bearer of the instrument. It is a promise made by one person. Suppose, you are in a company and the company has ordered around hundred pieces of computer and, at that time, the company hasn't paid the entire sum of money, each computer costs Rs.10,000 or Rs.20,000. At the time of order, money wasn't rendered to the vendor, some portion of the money is left to be paid, that is, some of the money can be taken as credit from the vendor, and a promissory note would be given by the owner of the company to the vendor, including the name of the person who you are supposed to give the money and it will be signed by you, mentioning the date, money to be paid, and maturity date.

❖ SPECIMEN OF A PROMISSORY NOTE

Rs. 5000/-	PUNE November 25, 2008

Three months after the date, I promise to pay Mr. X of Mumbai to order a sum of Rupees Fifty thousand for the value received.

A
To Mr.
Address............
....
Mumbai.   Stamp
                                                                 Signature of Mr Y

This is a specimen of a promissory note that contains the amount, date, sum of money, which day or month the money will be returned, address of the person whom I am paying, and the signature with a stamp after they received the money. This has to be done by the maker, so my stamp and signature will be there.

Essential characteristics of a promissory note

- A promissory note is a negotiable instrument. Through this instrument, only I would be able to get a certain amount of money that is pending. If I am doing a business, it is the amount of money that is due to me. This is a negotiable instrument because through this only the business is conducted and, at the same time, I have right to get the money transferred from one person to another.
- It must be in writing. It cannot be in the oral form.
- It is a promise to pay money only. A promissory note or any kind of negotiable instrument is related only to money, not to any other entity.
- It must be definite. The promise to pay must be definite. The definite sum of money must be there. Today, I am giving a promissory note to my friend, stating that I will be paying them one lakh rupees. Without mentioning the date this cannot be a promissory note because a specific date has to be mentioned, along with amount of money.
- It must be unconditional, that is, undertaking to pay must be unconditional. I cannot negotiate. For example, my friend has

given me a computer for one lakh rupees. I promised one lakh rupees. I cannot write in the promissory note that I will be paying Rs. 50,000. This is unconditional that I have to pay one lakh rupees. I cannot negotiate that amount of money that I am supposed to repay.

- It must be signed by the maker of the promissory note and there must be a certain payee. Whoever is making the promissory note should be a particular person and the person who would be collecting that money in lieu of him should be a particular person to whom this promissory note is issued.
- The amount of money in the promissory note must be certain
- Other formalities like the number, the date, the place, etc. are generally found on the promissory note but they are not essential in law.
- The promissory note must be properly stamped according to the provisions of the Indian Stamp Act, 1899. Stamp is a legal thing. If the note is not stamped, then a person might say that I haven't given this promissory note, but if the stamp and the date are given, it becomes a legal format. If a person has given a promissory note, but has not given the stamp as promised, the holder can take him to the court. It also gives you a proof that it is a legal formality and approves that this particular promissory note is prepared by a person on the mentioned date.

◈ CHEQUE

"A cheque is a bill of exchange drawn on a specified banker and expressed to be payable otherwise than on-demand".

I should have a bank account and the cheque should belong to that particular account. If I have an account in HDFC bank and I don't have an account in the Bank of Baroda, and I want to give a cheque belonging to Bank of Baroda, it is not at all acceptable. It should belong to the particular bank in which you have an account. And it gives a right to the person whom the cheque has been issued to go to the bank and demand the money from the bank within a specific period.

The maker of a bill of exchange or cheque is called a "drawer", the person thereby directed to pay is called the "drawee".

If I am giving a cheque, it means I become a "drawer", and the person who is withdrawing money from that cheque would be a "drawee"

Essential characteristics of a cheque

- A cheque is a negotiable instrument.
- It is a bill of exchange. While giving the cheque and getting the money by depositing it into the bank, the money is being transferred from my bank to the other person, so it is a bill of exchange.
- It is always drawn on a specific banker.
- It is always payable on demand. Until and unless you go and deposit the cheque, the bank is not going to come on its own to pay you the money. It has to be on-demand.
- In certain cheques, we just cross it, it is done on the top left of the cheque. The cross-checking means that it will be for a particular bank and if someone takes it away, he or she cannot encash it even if they want to. A bearer cheque means that the money already deposited and this cheque is given.
- A cheque requires no acceptance in the ordinary course of business as it is intended for immediate payment. This is not required for any course of business because the cheque has to be deposited and money has to be withdrawn. It is like an immediate payment.
- In case of a cheque, a drawee is always a specified bank, a drawer is a person who draws a cheque and who has an account in a bank, and a payee is a person to whom the cheque is made payable. The cheque, he/she has to have an account in a particular bank because without two people the drawer and drawee, Having an account in any particular bank, a cheque cannot be given to one another. It cannot be encashed.

❖ NEGOTIATION

"It is a process of transferring the ownership, right, title, the interest of a person in a negotiable instrument to another person to give a good title to the transferee and make a transferee or holder of such instrument".

It is a transfer of ownership, a right transfer through a negotiable instrument from one person to another.

- Negotiation does not mean a simple transfer. The simple transfer may not necessarily involve the transfer of property in the negotiable instrument, but negotiation implies the transfer of property or ownership. It is not a simple transfer, it is a transfer of ownership from one person to another, the right of demanding certain amount of money, which is due, is done through negotiation and negotiating instrument.

- For example, suppose I am handing over a cheque of Rs. 2 lakh to my friend. Here, I am negotiating the instrument to my friend, but if I'm asking my friend to keep that cheque safe, then it is not negotiating to my friend because my friend only becomes a caretaker of the cheque. I have not given the right to my friend to encash the cheque. My friend cannot be a holder; he will only be a caretaker or a bailee.

❖ FEATURES OF NEGOTIATION

- There must be a transfer of a negotiable instrument to another person. Negotiation must be done. Right must be transferred from one person to another.

- As a result of such transfer, the transferee must become the holder of the instrument. When the transfer is being made and right has been transferred, the person to whom this instrument has been transferred, that person becomes the holder of the instrument and gains the right to demand a certain amount of money that is due to the holder.

❖ MODES OF NEGOTIATION

- <u>Negotiation by delivery</u> – The negotiable instrument is transferred by delivery, either actual or constructive. It is the physical act of delivering the instrument or handing over the delivery, actual possession of an instrument is not passed. If I am giving a promissory note to one of my colleagues that within a month I would be giving my colleague around 5000 rupees, I need to hand this over to my colleague. If I'm handing this promissory note to my colleagues, this becomes actual delivery or a physical delivery and instrument is in actual position.

- Negotiation by endorsement and delivery – The negotiable instrument payable to order is negotiable by the holder by endorsement and delivery thereof. Endorsement has to be there, the amount should be there, the signature should be there, the date should be there. Then it becomes negotiable by endorsement and delivery, and it becomes viable and legal.

❖ ENDORSEMENT

"The literal meaning of the term endorsement is writing on an instrument".

Endorser – The person who signs on the back or the face of the instrument or the slip is an endorser.

- On my cheque, I'm signing. Then, I become an endorser.

Endorsee – The person to whom the instrument is endorsed is called the Endorsee.

- The person for whom this thing has been done becomes an Endorsee.

❖ TYPES OF ENDORSEMENTS

- General or blank endorsement – Endorser signs his name neither on the back or the face of the instrument. On the promissory note or cheque, they sign on the front side or at the back. When you go to a bank they say that you need to sign at the back of the cheque, you write your account number and then sign. If something goes wrong, then from the backside too, you can see whose account it is when it has been deposited. The person has an account in the bank and he is giving his right, transferring his right from that promissory note to others. The signature that we are doing at the bottom of the back, it becomes a general endorsement.
- Full or special endorsement – It specifies the name of the person to whom or to whom the payment must be made. The name of the person has to be mentioned, to whom we owe a certain sum of

money. When you're signing it, if you see a cheque, on the top right ins the company to whom we are giving the promissory note.

- *Partial endorsement* – *Endorsement is made for the balance of payment.* If you're purchasing a flat or car, you don't need to pay the entire amount of money. You can pay in more than one cheque, which becomes a partial endorsement.

- *Conditional endorsement* – *The liability of the endorser is limited or negative.* The endorsement is totally unconditional, to whom I'm giving the money, promissory note, or cheque. Then, the holder cannot come under any condition, there is no need of putting any kind of condition. The name of the person who is drawing, date, amount, stamp, and signature should be mentioned.

❖ DISHONOR OF NEGOTIABLE INSTRUMENT

- Negotiable instruments, promissory notes, and cheques may be dishonored by non-payment. Sometimes you give a cheque and it gets bounced back by the bank, because you don't have enough balance, The promissory note can also be a dishonored cheque. When we had given the cheque, at that time we had a certain amount of money in the bank and after that we didn't. So, the cheque becomes dishonored because the day that person or holder goes and deposits it, it might happen that we don't have enough money in the bank.

Bills of exchange may be dishonored by non-payment or by non-acceptance as they require acceptance from drawees.

The Indian Case Laws

Smt. Asha Baldwa v. Ram Gopal

This is one of the landmark judgments in Section 138. The petitioner had filed a petition under Section 482, CrPC to quash the proceedings instituted against him for committing an offence under section 138. He was alleged to have handed over the dishonored cheque to the respondent. She consented to such giving of the cheque. Hence, she is responsible for the consequences of giving the cheque.

The contention of the petitioner was that in accordance with Section 141(2) of the Negotiable Instruments Act, 1881, the allegations can be made against the Company only or its Partners or Directors only when the offence was committed with the consent or connivance or, is attributable to, any neglect on the part of, any director, manager, secretary or partners.

The Court held that the aim is that the person who promises to pay abides by his promise. Section 139 provides that it shall be presumed that the holder of a cheque received the cheque of the nature referred to in <u>Section 138 of The Negotiable Instrument Act, 1881</u> for the discharge, in whole or in part, of any debt or other liability.

Canara Bank vs Canara Sales Corporation & Ors.

The Supreme Court looked into the matter of cheque being presented for encashment and containing forged signatures.

It held that in cases where a cheque is presented for encashment but has forged signatures on it, the bank is freed from is legal liability of making any sort of payment against such cheque. If the bank made any payments in favor of such cheques, it would be concluded that the bank has acted anti-law by debiting the customer with amounts of the cheque.

<u>Dalmia Cement Ltd. V. Galaxy Traders & Agencies Ltd.</u>

Criminal Appeal No.957 of 2000

In this case the Hon'ble Supreme Court of India referred to the object of section 138 of Negotiable Instrument Act. The court observed that when the act was enacted, section 138 was incorporated with a specified object of making a special provision by incorporating a strict liability so far as the cheque as negotiable instrument was concerned.

Kishan Rao v. Shankargouda

The Supreme Court has reiterated on the scope of revisional jurisdiction of a High Court.

The Court held that the High Court is not to interfere with any of the Magistrate's order unless it seems to be completely unreasonable or there is no consideration of relevant material. Also, the Magistrate's order cannot be set aside on the mere ground that no other view on the issue is possible.

Jayalakshmi Nataraj v. Jeena & Co. (1996)

In this case, the Court adjudicated upon a Managing Director's liability under Section 138 of the Negotiable Instrument Act of 1881. It held that even though the Managing Director does not administer the day to day activities of the company, he/she can still be held guilty irrespective of the fact that he/she was unaware of the affairs.

Modi Cements Limited v. Kuchil Kumar Nandi (1998) 3 SCC 249

A three Judge bench of the Supreme Court held that even if a notice is issued to stop the payment of money before the payee has deposited the cheque with his bank, the act of crime is committed. Once the cheque is issued by the drawer, it must be presumed that just because a notice is issued by the drawer to the drawee or to the Bank, it will not stop action under section 138 by the holder of the cheque in due course. Thus, defense under strict interpretation of "insufficiency of funds" stands weak to some extent.

M/s Meters and Instruments Private Limited & Anr. v. Kanchan Mehta

A bench of Supreme Court comprising of two Judges made some points clear regarding dishonor of cheque. Directions were also issued for speedy trial of such cases under Section 138 of the Act of 1881.

Modern technologies were opined to be adopted to enable speedy disposal of the Section 138 cases. The Court noted that:

"Use of modern technology needs to be considered not only for paperless Courts but also to reduce overcrowding of Courts. There appears to be need to consider categories of cases which can be partly or entirely concluded "online" without physical presence of the parties by simplifying procedures where seriously disputed questions are not required to be adjudicated. Traffic challans may perhaps be one such category.

Atleast some number of Section 138 cases can be decided online. If complaint with affidavits and documents can be filed online, process issued online and accused pays the specified amount online, it may obviate the need for personal appearance of the complainant or the accused. Only if the accused contests, need for appearance of parties may arise which may be through Counsel and wherever viable, video conferencing can be used. Personal appearances can be dispensed with on suitable self-operating conditions."

Geekay Exim (India) Ltd. v. State of Gujarat (1998)

The Gujarat High Court held that though the element of mens rea is not important under Section 138, such element must be presumed to exist at the instance of every case. This means that the question whether mens rea should be considered or not while adjudicating, varies from case to case depending on their circumstances.

Jayawati v. Yogesh Kumar Gosain (Delhi High Court)

Another landmark judgment was passed by the Delhi High Court. In this case, the Court drew a distinction between traditional criminal cases and offence under Section 138. The purpose of such distinction was to validate that it is very much within the laws to refer a case of Section 138 for mediation.

Premchand Vijay Kumar v. Yashpal Singh

In this case of Premchand it was held by the Apex Court that upon a notice under section 138 of Negotiable Instrument Act being issued, a subsequent presentation of a cheque and its dishonour would not create another 'cause of action' which could set the section 138 machinery in motion. Only 4 Bhaskaran concomitants were spelt out in this judgement instead of 5.

Chandrabolu Bhaskararao's case

In the case of Chandrabolu, it was held by the High Court of Andhra Pradesh that it is not mandatory for promissory note to be an attestable document even if the signatures of the attesters are taken and after its execution it does not amount the material alteration. So it does not get quashed. So therefore, whether there were attesters or not at the time of its execution is immaterial, more so when its execution is admitted.

Bhutoria trading co. v. Allahabad Bank

It was pointed out by the Hon'ble court that where there are no circumstances that afforded any reasonable ground for believing that the payee was not entitled to receive payment of the cheques, the bank is deemed to have payment in due course.

Bhaskaran v. Shankaran Vaidhyan Balan

In this case, the Two-Judge Bench of the Supreme Court had held that the offence under Section 138 of NI Act can be completed only with the concatenation of a number of acts. However, this ruling was overruled by Supreme Court's judgment *in Dashrath Roop Singh case.*

Dashrath Roopsingh Rathod v. State of Maharashtra

A strict approach was applied by the Apex Court in its new judgement which sought to discourage the payer for misusing or carelessly issuing cheques. Thus, due sympathy was shown or given to the drawer.

Infact in this case it was observed by the Supreme Court of India that courts have been enjoined to interpret the law to eradicate ambiguity, and to ensure that legal proceedings have not been used as a device for harassment even of apparent transgressor of law.

M.M.T.C. Ltd. and Anr. Vs Medchl Chemicals and Pharma (P) Ltd. and Anr. (AIR 2002 SC182)

The Apex Court held that even though the cheque stands dishonored, the drawer of the cheque is to be held guilty as a complaint under Section 138 is maintainable. The burden of proof lies on the accused to show that he had issued an instruction to stop the payment because of valid reasons. In other words, the presumption as to existence of legally enforceable debt is rebut table as per Section 139. It further held that even a payee or the holder in due course of the cheque can file a complaint under Section 142 of NI Act and it need not necessarily be by a Director or duly authorized officer as the defect can be cured later. Complaint cannot be quashed.

Chapter 5

PART 1: The Companies Act, 1956

❖ What is a company?

- A company is a voluntary association of persons formed for the purpose of doing business, having a distant name and limited liability
- They can be Incorporated under The Companies Act (it may be any type of company)

Limited liability refers to a limited sum of money when the company is in trouble.

Incorporation refers to the registration. It can be any type of company, public or private, but its incorporation is necessary because, without incorporation, the company cannot become a legal company. Registration and incorporation of the company are very important.

❖ *FEATURES OF A COMPANY*

- A company is considered as a separate legal entity from its members: It has a distinct identity. It is a citizen of India. Whatever rights an individual is enjoying, the same rights would be enjoyed by the company. It is separate from the members, that is, people who are working in the company
- Independent corporate entity: It is different from any other companies or members.

Other features

- Limited liability (either by share or guarantee): By share means how much shares a particular shareholder is purchasing. They are liable to pay up a definite amount of money depending on their share in the company, when the company is in trouble.
- Separate property: Whatever a company has in terms of business or assets, it is separate from the members. No one is supposed to utilise that property for personal use; it is only utilised by the company.
- The income of the members is different from the income of the company: Whatever the members are earning per month, it is completely different from the income of the company. The income of the company is is separate.
- Perpetual succession: When a company is started, that is, incorporated according to the Companies Act of 1956 or 2013, that company would be there till its proper end. When the company is formed it can stay intact for generations. The name would be there, whether it is having any members or not.
- As it is a legal entity or a juristic person or an artificial person, it can sue and be sued: Since it is a legal entity and has a legal recognition of any harm done to the company in terms of business or loan, or in terms of any other issue, the company has every right to sue. And if the company is doing anything wrong, the law also states that the company can also be sued by its name.
- The company enjoys rights and liabilities that are separate from the members of the company: A company can recruit people and can take loans. There are rights and liabilities of a company. These things are entirely separate from the people who are working in the company.

❖ LIFTING OF CORPORATE VEIL - *A right given to a company*

- As the company is a separate legal entity, it has been provided with a veil/right that is separate as compared to that of individuals who are managing the company: It is a right that is given to the company. The company can carry on its duties and responsibilities under this corporate veil and no one is supposed to disturb the company and take care of its rights and responsibilities.

- But if the court feels that such veil has been used for any wrongful purpose, the court can lift the corporate veil and make the individual liable for such acts that they should not have done in the name of the company: If the court feels that these rights are being misused by any person, then that person can be sued by the court. When the court thinks that this veil is used for a wrongful purpose, the court can leave the corporate veil and make the individual liable for such an act. If any person is found to be doing anything wrong under the name of the company name, then that person is liable and can be sued by the court.

❖ CIRCUMSTANCES TO LIFT THE CORPORATE VEIL

The corporate veil can be lifted either under:

- Statutory provision: As provided by the Companies Act, 1956.
- Judicial interpretation: These circumstances are decided through judicial interpretations, which are based on facts of each case as per the decisions of the court.

❖ CAUSES FOR THE LIFTING OF CORPORATE VEIL

- *Failure to refund application money*: After the issue of shares to the public, the company has to pay back the initial payment to the unsuccessful applicants, and if they fail to do so the corporate veil can be lifted. When a share is issued to the people, they have to pay a certain amount of money, and then only the share can be prescribed to them. For example, if 20 people have paid the face value of the shares. Out of the 20 people, five people haven't been allotted the shares. The company must return the face value of the shares. If the company is not a turning then the corporate veil will be lifted and the company will be sued.
- *Mis-description of the company name*: While signing a contract if the company's name is not properly described, then the corporate veil can be lifted. For example, suppose the name of the company is Maruti Udyog, and for some reason instead of Maruti Udyog, the name is written only as Maruti, then it becomes a different company altogether. The court has every right to lift the corporate veil.

- *Misrepresentation in the prospectus*: In case of misrepresentation, the promoters, directors, and every other person responsible in this matter can be held liable. If for a certain reason the prospectors is missing certain things, then the court has every right to lift the corporate veil. The promoters, the directors, and every person can be responsible and can come under the court.

- *Fraudulent conduct*: In case of companies that are carried on with the intent to defraud creditors, the court may lift the corporate veil. For example, the company has a business in automobile, but instead of taking care of automobile business, the company has started, without informing anyone about, some other business like textile, then the shareholders of the company are into automobiles but actually, it is carrying on a business for the textile industry. It is a fraud and this kind of conduct, if it comes to the notice of the court, can take away the corporate veil and the company will be sued.

- *Holding subsidiary companies*: Subsidiary has a distinct legal entity from the holding company other than a few circumstances. So, if otherwise shown, the court may, under the act, lift the corporate veil of the subsidiary company. The holding companies and the subsidiary companies are two different companies. The holding companies have 51 shares of the entire company. It has every right to appoint people like directors. It takes care of day-to-day activities and advises on a day-to-day basis. If these rules and regulations for the holding and subsidiary companies are not being mentioned properly, then the court can lift the corporate veil.

❖ JUDICIAL INTERPRETATIONS BY THE COURT

- *Protection of revenue*: Whenever a company uses its name for tax evasion: for example, XYZ company were supposed to pay a tax of five crores, but the company is not paying the five crores of rupees and given a certain reason that my business, is not going well, the company is a sick company, and I cannot pay that much amount of money, and in this case, if the court comes to know about this and then the court can lift the corporate veil.

- *Prevention of fraud or improper conduct*: If the incorporation has been used for a fraudulent purpose, like defrauding the creditors, defeating the purpose of law, etc., then the corporate veil would be lifted. The corporate veil is the right and safeguard of the company. Company is safe in many ways from being penalised by the court but for these reasons, some kind wrongful reasons, harmful, or they are not paying tax, revenue then the corporate veil can be lifted and they can be penalised.

❖ *OTHER CIRCUMSTANCES*

- *Where a company is used to avoid welfare legislation*: If a company is formed to avoid the benefits to the workers or not taking care of the welfare aspect of the employees, then the corporate veil is lifted.
- For *determining the technical competence of the company*: to look into the competency of the company other shareholders or promoters (New Horizons Ltd and another V.union of India 1994) - A company is having a shareholder or a promoter, certain kind of rules and regulation for the people who could be shareholder and promoter but for certain reasons, if promoter shareholders and directors are not qualifying the capabilities to become the shareholder of promoter or director then the company's corporate veil can be lifted.

❖ *TYPES OF COMPANIES*

- Limited company (limited by shares or guarantee): Buy shares means the shareholder is paying some predefined amount of money when he purchased the shares. By guarantee means during the incorporation of the company, the shareholders will say when the company is going for the winding-up process; when in liability, the shareholders, the stakeholders, or members would be only paying money that they guaranteed.
- Unlimited company: Here, the company has unlimited liability. Unless and until the company comes out of the trouble, the people can help the company.
- Government company: Major chunk of the company is under the government. The government holds 51% of the shares. The government takes care of each and everything like roles and regulations is followed by the government.

- Foreign company: Here, the companies are in foreign countries and have different branches.
- Private company: Members of that company take care of the company. They are not allowed to take shares on the shares that are not issued to the public.
- Public company: The company can give away their share and the people purchase the shares and become the shareholders of the company.

❖ LIMITED COMPANY

- Limited by shares – In such companies, the liability is only the amount that remains and paid on the shares Suppose you have taken 20 shares and you have paid money for 10 shares. The money that you haven't paid for the amount of share purchased would be given during the time of winding up.
- Limited by guarantee not having a share capital – In this type of companies, the memorandum of association limits the member's liability. During the formation of the company for incorporation, the amount that the shareholders are guaranteed would be paid by the shareholders.
- Limited by guarantee having a share capital – In such cases, the liability would be based on the MOA towards the guaranteed amount and the remaining would be from the unpaid sums of the shares held by the person concerned.

❖ UNLIMITED COMPANY

- There is no limit on the liability of the members. The liability in such cases would extend to the whole amount of the company's debt and liabilities. It is not guaranteed that this amount would be paid by the shareholders or the stakeholders because liability is equally shared by the shareholders. So, until and unless the company is coming out of the trouble, the shareholders would keep paying.
- Here, the members cannot be directly sued by the creditors. The company has taken certain loans from the creditors. In this situation, the creditors cannot sue the members saying you have to pay the money or I will go to the court. It is the responsibility of the company that whatever money the shareholders are paying is good enough, the creditors cannot sue the members but the company.

- When the company is wound up, the official liquidator will call upon the members to discharge the liability. During the winding-up process, the company is a company and it is not able to show any kind of profit or business transactions for quite some time for two years or more, company becomes A sick company and company is wound up when the company is winded up at that time the entire property of the company is given to the official liquidator, from the court and appointed by the court. The property of the company is going to court, the liquidator will summon the members, shareholders and will ask them to discharge the liability, so that the company can wound up freely.

❖ GOVERNMENT COMPANY

- When 51% of the paid-up share capital is held by the government, that is, the government is having a major share from the company.
- The share can be held by the Central government or the state government. It would have the power to appoint members, people, or the workers, and set the rules and regulations that the company has to follow.

❖ FOREIGN COMPANY

- A company that is incorporated outside India but has a place of business in India.

❖ PRIVATE COMPANY

- A company that has a minimum of two persons. They have to subscribe to the MOA and AOA. A private company cannot have only one person, it should have a minimum of 2 persons.. When you are starting a company, it has to be incorporated, all the rules and regulations should be there in MOA and AOA, and it will start with 2 people. Then, it would be a private company.
- It should be having a minimum paid-up capital of one lakh or more as prescribed by the AOA.
- You can start with a minimum of two and a maximum 50 members.
- The rights to transfer the share are restricted in private companies. Since it's a private company, you are not supposed to give away

the shares to the public. Whatever shares are given, it would be taken by the members who are in the company, not the outsiders.

- It prohibits any invitation to the public to subscribe. The public has no say in the private company, only the company will be taking care of all of this.
- It prohibits acceptance of deposit from any person other than its members, directors or their relatives. any kind of deposit, the company is in trouble or money is required only the members, the workers who are working in the company they would be working will be taking care of everything like liabilities, no other people from outside will be helping them, only the director members and their relatives are eligible to help and deposit the money.
- If two or more are holding one or more shares in a company jointly, they shall be treated as a single member: If you are having one or more shares, then it's a private property, they both would be considered as a single member because they cannot share it with the outside people.

❖ EXEMPTION AND PRIVILEGES OF A PRIVATE COMPANY

- It can have a minimum of two members.
- It can commence business immediately after obtaining a certificate of incorporation: After the company is registered, you get a certificate of incorporation from the registration of that locality, stating that on some date, this company has started on someone's name.
- It need not issue a prospectus or statement in lieu of a prospectus. Since it is not giving away shares to any kind of people outside, there is no need for a prospectus or statement. Lieu means before the prospectus has been issued means like a pre-prospectus is issued, whether the prospectus is issued saying that at this date the main prospectus will be issued.
- It can have a minimum of two directors: private companies have a minimum of two directors.

❖ PUBLIC COMPANY

- A public company means a company that has a minimum paid-up capital of Rs.5 lakh or higher (as may be prescribed). If ive lakh is less than whatever is prescribed by MOA and AOA, it would be allowed.

- Which is a private company and is not a subsidiary of a company, which is a private company: If you're having a public company, a public company should be having a minimum paid-up capital of Rs.5 lakhs or more and if a private company is being converted into a public company than the private company shouldn't be a subsidiary company of any company. Subsidiary means it shouldn't be under any other company which should be an individual company.
- It includes any company that is a public company with a paid-up capital of less than five lakh then it has to enhance its paid-up capital as per the statutory requirement: If it is having less than five lakh rupees paid-up capital then it has to arrange for that much money which is the statutory requirement of the public company and it is already mentioned in MOA and AOA The the public company.

❖ CONVERSION OF COMPANY

- The Company Act provides for conversion of public company into a private company and vice versa.
- A private company is converted into public company either by default or by choice in compliances with the statutory requirements. under statutory requirements are under the companies act 1956, legal requirement under the companies act 1956, if you have a private company you can convert it into a public company by a choice Like you decide to change your private company and public company. That can be done and for that, you need to have all the papers ready and it should be according to the companies act 1956.
- Once the action for conversion takes place, a petition can be filed with the Central government with the necessary documents for its decision on the matter of conversation: When you decide you need to give a petition or a request to the Central government, all the rules and regulations are decided by the government regarding the conversion.

❖ INCORPORATION OF A COMPANY

- The promoters are the persons who decide on the formation of the company: incorporation is very important because we can't start a company without that, The promoter is the person who is thinking about the company, setting up of the company he is a person who thinks what will be the product of the company, place where the company would be set up. The shareholders, the directors. the blueprint where we know, What we are exactly doing. So the promoter takes care of the place, legal requirements of the company, everything which is required to set up a company. The basic formation of the company is taken care of by the promoter.

- They may have to enter into pre-incorporation contracts, which can be validated after the incorporation of the company for obtaining a certificate of incorporation: before you start the company the promoter can go for the pre-incorporation whereby there is an acknowledgement from the register that you can start a company once the incorporation is done and it can be converted into a certificate of incorporation.

❖ PROMOTERS

- The promoters are the persons who decide on the formation of the company. They can be remunerated for their services, but they have to enter into a contract before the incorporation of the company through a pre-incorporation of the company. Many promoters are often owners of the company.
- They will usually act as nominees or as the first directors of the company.
- They enter into contracts after the incorporation and before the commencement of business.
- They need not necessarily participate in the formation of the company. They take an active part but it is not necessary for them to participate. They can give their ideas and they can rest. They don't need to be active during the incorporation, if they want they can, but if they don't want, then they may not be active in the formation of the company.
- Promoters, in most of the cases, decide as to what type of company to be formed.
- In India, promoters generally secure the management of the company that is formed and have a controlling interest in the company's management.

❖ *LEGAL POSITION OF THE PROMOTERS*

- They cannot make a profit at the expense of the company. In case they do so, they may be compelled to account for it.
- They cannot sell their property to the company at a profit unless all material facts are disclosed at the independent board of directors or the shareholders of the company. If the promoter has some kind of property and he or she wants to sell the property to the company at a profit, it cannot be done unless and until it is discussed with the board of directors.
- If the company find out that the promoter has sold a property for a certain kind of profit then, the company can repudiate, that is, cancel the contract of sale and also can get the profit back. This can be done by recovering the profit made by the promoter.

❖ *PROMOTERS HAVETHE FOLLOWING LIABILITIES UNDER THE COMPANIES ACT, 1956*

- They can be liable for non-compliance of the provision of the act. If the promoter is not adhering according to the Companies Act, then the promoter is liable to be punished for non-compliance.
- Severe penalty may be imposed.
- The court may suspend the promoter from taking part in the management of the company. They might be penalized or suspended from the management of the company.
- If there are any kind of untrue statements is in the prospectors of the company then also the promoter is liable for the penalty.
- The liabilities are...
  a. To set aside the allotment of shares
  b. Sued for damages
  c. Sued for compensation
  d. Criminal proceedings (Depending upon the extent upon what the facts and figures not mentioned in the prospectus)

❖ *REQUIREMENTS ARE AS FOLLOWS*

1. Application for the availability of name- During the incorporation of the company the name should be there, deciding upon the name should be Available. Today if I'm going for reliance I cannot go for reliance, I have to go for something else.

2. Preparation of MOA and AOA - memorandum of association and articles of association is very important so that should be prepared when you're going for the incorporation of the company
3. Selection and finalisation of MOA and AOA: it's printing, stamping and signing- whatever things you need to write an MOA what things have to be mentioned in AOA, it should be printed and stamped, signed by the higher authority.
4. Preparation of other necessary documents.
5. Filling of the required documents for registration to obtain a certificate of incorporation and certificate of commencement of business- when you're going for a certificate of incorporation there is a specific format, filling of the document mentioned from application to stamping and signing of MOA AOA these things should be attached to the form and it should be submitted, the registered place where the business is set up and then only you can get a certificate of incorporation, and the business can start.

❖ MEMORANDUM OF ASSOCIATION (MOA)

– *It contains the fundamental conditions upon which the company can be incorporated.*
– *It contains the objectives of the company's formation.*
– *Anything done beyond the objectives specified in the MOA you will be ultra vires. The transaction will be null and void.*

CONDITIONS OF THE MOA

• It should be printed.
• It is divided into paragraphs and numbers consecutively.
• It is signed by at least seven and two persons in case of the public and private companies, respectively.
• It should be signed in the presence of a witness, who will have to attest the signature.
• Members have to take shares and write the numbers of share taken with full address.

❖ MOA OF A LIMITED COMPANY

– The name of the company with limited as the last word- Whatever company it is, it should be a limited one. Given the shares to the shareholders.

- The name of the state whether the registered office of the company is to be situated - The place of your company should be situated.
- The objects of the company stating the "main objects" and other objects- Reason why the company started and what is the main reason behind starting the company, main objective and other objectives should be mentioned.
- The declaration about the liability of the members is limited by shares or guarantee) - The liability of the members is limited by shares or guarantee that should be mentioned. They should be utilised during the winding up of the company,
- The amount of the authorised share capital, dividend into shares a fixed amount- The authorised share Means how many shares each person has taken and how much it is divided, whether it is a fixed amount or into shares should be mentioned.

❖ COMPULSORY CLAUSES IN MOA

- The name clause: It decides the name of the company based on the capital involved.
- The registration office clause: Where has the company registered its head office and other branches of the office.
- The objective clause: The main objective, ancillary object, and the other objects of the company are specified.
- The liability clause: What is the liability of its members, whether it is limited by shares or guarantees or unlimited. There can be alteration in the liability clause in future.
- The capital clause: the amount of the nominal capital of the company, the number of shares in which it is to be divided, alteration of the capital.
- The association of subscription clause: Here, the subscribers to the MOA declare that they agree to take the number of the shares in the capital.

The shareholders mention how many shares they are taking and they have to sign in the presence of 2 witnesses, who attest the signatures.

❖ DOCTRINE OF ULTRA VIRES

- The power exercisable by the company needs to be confined to the objects specified in the MOA, like sharing of profits, acquiring business, etc. The rules and regulations need to be followed by the company. If not followed, then the actions will be null and void. The objectives mentioned in MOA should be followed and intimated to all the members.

- If the company acts beyond the power or the objectives of the company that is specified in the MOA, the acts are considered to be of ultra vires, and the action is considered to be ineffective, that is, null or void.

❖ *THE CONSEQUENCES OF THE ULTRA VIRES TRANSACTIONS*

a. Injunction - Injunction means "stay order". Certain cases go on for quiet some period. If the case is going for too long, then the court puts an injunction, a stay order, until and unless the situation is favorable. In the case of ultra vires, companies' rules and regulations are not followed.

b. Directors' personal liability - Director of a company cannot have personal liability. He can have personal liability on his personal firm. Not at the expense of the company. If the director has a liability at the expense of the company, then ultra vires would be there. Suppose the director has purchased the property and taken money from the company's account and purchased personal property. Then, it is a personal liability and until and unless the director answers the same, it would fall under ultra vires.

c. If a property has been purchased and it is an ultra vires act, the company can have a right over that property.

d. The doctrine is to be used exclusively for the companies' interest - The doctrine, if it is for the companies' interest, then only it would be ultra vires. Others cannot use this ultra vires to attack the company. But if anyone is taking any kind of advantage at the expense of the company, then the doctrine of ultra vires would be there and the company is proceeding to be stopped until and unless the situation is favorable.

❖ *ARTICLES OF ASSOCIATION*

- *It is the company's bye-laws or rules to govern the management of the company for its internal affairs and the conduct of the business* - Any rules and regulation that the company is working on regarding the appointment of people, or how they would be taking care of the business, what kind of investment the company would be making, how many directors they would be working, will they give shares to the public or not, all these rules and regulations need to be mentioned in the articles of association. It even contains information regarding the liability.

- *AOA defines the power of its officers and also establishes a contract between the company and the members - What are the powers of a director, manager, etc., all would be mentioned in the AOA.*
- *AOA is a subsidiary power to the MOA.*
- *Anything done beyond the AOA will be considered to be irregular and may be rectified by the shareholders - If* anything is not mentioned, shareholders can go through it, and if something is missing, they can change it and get it done.
- *The content of the AOA may differ from company to company as the act has not specified any specific provisions -* MOA and AOA are different for different companies.
- *Flexibility is allowed to the person who forms the company to adopt the AOA within the requirements of the Company Law -* Whoever is forming the AOA, they have all the power and the flexibility to adhere to whatever they have mentioned in AOA.
- *The AOA will have to be conversant with the MOA as they are contemporaneous documents to be read together.*
- *Any ambiguity and uncertainty in one of them may be removed by reference to the other -* The MOA and AOA should be similar. You can compare them and remove them.

❖ CONTENTS OF THE AOA

- Share capital
- Lien on shares - The company has a right to declare how many shares they are ready to give out to the public at any point in time. If today they have decided to give a hundred shares to the public, due to some reason they find 50 shares of more than enough, we don't want to give more than 50 shares so they can stop giving the share.
- Calls on share - You can issue a letter to the public.
- Transfer and transmission of shares - Shares can be transferred from one shareholder to another shareholder.

- Forfeiture of the shares - In the person is not paying the amount of money, the shareholder is not paying the amount of money, which he/she was supposed to pay. Within a limited time, I was supposed to take a hundred shares and pay per share one rupee, I was supposed to pay 100 shares hundred rupees and pay them on by month-end and I was not able to pay and my shares are forfeited and I am not getting those share, I would only be getting the shares are paid for.

- Surrender of the share - I don't want to keep the share then I can surrender the shares. For example, I have 50 shares worth 50,000 rupees but I don't want to keep that much amount of shares, and I can give 25 shares or can surrender 25,000 shares to the company.

- General meetings - General meetings are important to know the working of the company and the situation in the company. General meetings are arranged where shareholders, directors, and promoters come and attend a meeting and any kind of important decisions are taken.

- Alteration of the capital - If you have started with the capital of five lakh rupees but if you want you can increase the capital, and you can increase it to 7,00,00 rupees or 10 lakhs of rupees depending on the requirement.

- Directors - Qualification of directors, how many directors are there, and how many directors are ready to join, along with the letter that they have agreed to join, all these things should be mentioned.

- Dividends and reserves - Shares, profits, and reserves can be used when there is a requirement, and you can use the money when it is required against the reserved.

- Accounts and audit - Who would be taking care of the account, who is the auditor, which audit firm would be taking care of the auditing of the company, etc., should be mentioned.

- Borrowing powers- Who would be the borrower, who would be the person taking the loan, or who has a right to borrow a loan should be mentioned.

- Winding up - If the company is not doing well and the company is a company or not doing well in the business for the past 3 to 4 years at a stretch, and it is winding up. What are the rules and regulations for winding up in terms of liability, members, capital, and creditors should be mentioned.

- Appointment of the preliminary contracts - The contacts that would be done with the company during the business should be there according to the format and should be mentioned.

❖ *RAISING OF CAPITAL FROM PUBLIC*

- The companies can raise money by offering securities for sale to the public - There is a requirement for money by the company or capital for the company. The company can give out shares to the public, which is the best way how they raise capital for the extended business or business they want to do.
- They can invite the public to buy shares, which is known as a public issue - In terms of the prospectus, call letter or share certificate can be issued and the public issue is made to invite the shareholders.
- For this purpose, the company may issue a prospectus, which may include a notice, circular, advertisement or other documents, which are issued to invest public deposit - A notice is given in which it is mentioned that the company is ready to give out some shares. They also mention the face value of the shares. There would be an advertisement and it would be issued in the public interest.

❖ *PROSPECTUS*

- It is an invitation issued to the public to purchase or subscribe to shares or debentures of the company.
- Every prospect must be dated. The date of publication and the date of issue must be specified in the prospectus – There should be a publication date and a date of issue.
- The golden rule of the prospectors is that every detail has to be given in strict and scrupulous accuracy. The material facts given in the prospectors are presumed to be true, else the relevant parties are held liable.

❖ *VARIOUS FORMS IN WHICH THE PROSPECTUS CAN BE ISSUED*

- **Shelf prospectus:** Prospectus is normally issued by a financial institution or bank for one or more issues of the securities or class of securities mentioned in the prospectus.

- Deemed prospectus: It is issued by the issuing house apart from the banks.
- Information memorandum - It means a process, which is undertaken before the filing of a prospectus.
- Even an advertisement, that the shares are available is considered to be a prospectus.

❖ CONTENTS OF THE PROSPECTUS

- General information
- Capital structure
- Terms of the present issue based on which you would be getting the share
- Management and projects of the company, what is the product of the company, what kind of future project company has, the credibility of the company in the market, who are the shareholders and directors of the company, and its working structure
- Management and perception of risk factor
- It is compulsory to register the prospectus with the registrar.

❖ CIVIL LIABILITIES FOR MISSTATEMENTS IN CASE OF ANY UNTRUE STATEMENTS IN THE PROSPECTUS

If some facts are not mentioned or if you're hiding some facts or fraud has been made, it leads to liabilities.

- The liability will lie on the director of the company since their signature is present on the prospectus.

Whose names are mentioned in the prospectus at the time of issue:

- Directors of the company
- Promoters
- Every other person who is an expert and has authorized his name to be issued with the prospectus

❖ REMEDIES FOR MISSTATEMENTS IN THE PROSPECTUS

- Rescind the contract - It is done only when there is misrepresentation relating to the material facts. The recession has to be done within a reasonable time.

- Claim damages - Damages can be claimed from the directors, promoters, or another person who has authorized their name to be written during the issue of the prospectus.

❖ *SHARE CAPITAL*

- Share: Share is defined as "an interest having a money value and made up of diverse rights specified under the article of association"- where is the ownership given to the public, where the public purchases the share, or part of a company and becomes a shareholder of the company or owner of the company. Along with the ownership, you have to pay a certain amount of money.
- Share capital: Share capital means the capital raised by the company by issuing a share.
- A share is a share in the share capital of the company including the stock.
- Shares give a right to participate in the profit of the company, or a share in the assets when the company is going to be wound up.

❖ *OTHER FEATURES OF A SHARE*

- Share is not a negotiable instrument, but it is a movable property. It is a movable property because you can transfer the shares from one person to another, you can also give back your shares to the company.
- It is also considered to be a good under the Sales of Goods Act, 1930.
- The company has to issue the shares certificate - When purchasing a share, a share certificate is mandatory that the company issues.
- It is subject to stamp duty.
- The call on share is a demand made for payment of the price of the share allotted to the members by the board of directors following the articles of association.
- The call may be for a full amount or part of it.

❖ *SHARE CERTIFICATE AND SHARE WARRANT*

- *Share certificate* - A share certificate is a document issued by the company and is a prima facie evidence to show that the person named therein is the holder (title) of the specified number of shares stated therein. This document specifies that you are the owner and this is your share. Any profit or dividend by the company will be given to you and you are liable to get that.

- *The company has to issue within three months of the date of allotment. In case of default, the allottee may approach the central government.* If the share certificate is not given within three months of purchasing the shares, then you can approach the central government and action would be taken against the company.

- *Share warrant* - The share warrant as a bearer document issued by the company under its common seal. It is a document and a warrant and it would be given by the company as a proof that you have this particular share.

❖ TRANSFER AND TRANSMISSION OF SHARES

- AOA_provides for the procedure of transfer of shares. It is a voluntary action of the shareholders. You can transfer your shares to some other person.

- Shares can also be transferred through a blank transfer where you can only sign, name and state that you are ready to transfer the share.

- Transmission of share is by operation of law. Example by death, insolvency of the shareholders, etc. Transmission of shares means you are transferring your entire shares to another person. It can only be done by the court. Insolvency means when the person becomes bankrupt. In any kind of business or company, bankruptcy is like a curse. If you become bankrupt you don't have any right. The shares would be taken entirely from you. They can be given back to the company or you can transfer them to someone else.

❖ BUY-BACK OF SECURITIES

- The company may purchase its securities back and it is popularly known as buyback of shares - When the company wants, it can buy back its shares from the people depending on what they have decided.

- To do so, the company has to be authorized under the AOA

- The listed company also has to seek permission from SEBI if it is listed under SEBI.

❖ *DIVIDENDS*

- The sharing of profits in the going concern and the distribution of the assets after the winding-up can be canceled as a dividend_- When the company is making a profit then the company gives a part of it to shareholders who have purchased the shares of the company.
- The dividends can be declared and paid out of after the company declares.
- Other than the equity holders, even the preferential shareholders can get the dividend. Rather they are the first ones to get the dividends. Preferential shareholders are those who have got the right to get the dividend before anyone else.
- Dividends are to be only in cash if otherwise specified in the AOA - If it is in cheque or any other mode, it has to be specified in AOA.
- In exceptional cases, even the central government may permit the payment of interest to shareholders, even though there is no profit - In certain cases, if the central government is okay, the dividend can be given, irrespective of the fact that the company is not in profit. Still the dividend has to be given. It only happens in cases where the company is not able to give a dividend to the shareholders till 2 to 3 years. Then, the central government takes such decisions.

❖ *DIRECTORS*

- The legal status of the director
- The director occupies a position of a:
  As a trustee – In relation to the company
  As agents – When they act on behalf of the company
  As managing partners – As they are entrusted with the responsibility of the company

It is working for the company by the company, it is like a mediator, he is managing partner, he manages the company his day to day activities, his responsibilities are taken by the director.

In case there is a requirement as per the AOA for the Director is bound to buy qualification shares, if acts are done by the director before he or she is disqualified, the act is considered to be valid: previously it was mandatory, as a director, you should be having a qualification share which was equal to the value of Rs. 500. Nowadays, it is not mandatory if the company decided to appoint you as a director you should be going for qualified share. Certain kinds of things which the director has done before he or she becomes a director is not considered as a disqualified director.

❖ DISQUALIFICATION

As per the company law, the following persons are disqualified from being appointed as a director:

- Unsound mind - The director is insane, he doesn't know what to think or suffer from a certain kind of mental disease, is a mad person, is a lunatic is that idiot these kinds of people cannot be the director. Since the director has to be a very matured person who should be having excellent thinking power, if the person cannot think, then he cannot be the director and he's disqualified.
- Discharged insolvent - If a person is insolvent, they cannot have a position of a director profile.
- Convicted by the court - If a person is a criminal, he cannot be a director.
- Not paid for the call on shares - Being a director, the director's call was also made, but he or she hasn't paid, then he/she is a disqualified person for the post of a director.
- Already directors in the maximum number of the company as per the provisions of the act-If you are a director for two or three companies, you still want to be a director for this company then you're not qualified.
- Disqualified by the court for any other reason - Any other reason could be you don't belong to this country, are a terrorist, etc.

❖ APPOINTMENT OF DIRECTORS

- The appointment can sometimes be based on proportional representation, like minority shareholders - The directors are appointed by the shareholders. Based on the proportional representation, the representation varies from company to company.

- There can be alternate directors, additional directors, casual directors - If the director is not present at the time of the general meeting or other important occasions, then you can send another director in his place who could act as a casual director. Additional director means as already a director to directors and you want extra one and you want to the extra director then that becomes additional director.
- The third-party can appoint the directors - The Wenders, bank any other people with whom the company does the business if the third-party wants to appoint a director and be appointed.
- Other than the shareholders and the first director, the Central government may also appoint directors.

❖ DUTIES AND LIABILITIES OF THE DIRECTORS.

- Fiduciary duties - The director working for the company should only be working for the company and the interest of the company. He or she shouldn't be doing anything against the company.
- To act honestly and with good faith
- Not to use confidential information for the company for your purpose
- Duty of care and to act reasonably while acting for the company

Statutory duties:

- Not to contact the company, where he or she or his relative has an interest in the contract - The legal rights, the company is going into a Business contract with other companies, if the relative of the directors present in the company. suppose A is the company, wants to enter into the contract with B company and the B company, The director of the company A is related then the director shouldn't be allowing company A to enter into the contract with B.
- Where he/she has an interest, they need to inform the board or seek prior approval while entering into the contract, otherwise a contract is voidable - If the company insists that they want to get into a contract, then they have to inform the board and seek the approval. If you're interested in the permission, you can go ahead with the contract.

- Duty to attend and convene meetings
- Duty not to delegate

❖ *THE DIRECTORS' LIABILITIES*

- The liabilities of a director can be either civil or criminal.
- If provided in the MOA, no liability may be unlimited, for a limited company, otherwise, it may be altered - If it is already mentioned in the MOA that the liability of the director can be an unlimited one, it is a limited one depending on the liability the director can be there.
- Liability may be for breach of fiduciary duties - The director is not working in good faith and giving out certain details of the company to others.
- The directors are personally liable for the following:
  Ultra Vires acts - They are going against the rules and regulations of the company, whatever is there an MOA and AOA, The director hasn't followed that then it would be the ultra vires act.
  Malafide acts - Any kind of information that has been given out from the company
  Negligent acts - Because of the director's negligence the company has suffered
  Liability for the acts of third parties - for example, Tata Motors, the director of Tata Motors was supposed to get automobile parts from one company ABZ company and it was supposed to come on Monday but it didn't come, any time after one week because of this the production of the company couldn't take place and the production was stopped, this is the liability and fault of the director because of which this happened, and the director is liable for such kind of act.

❖ *CRIMINAL LIABILITIES*

- Any untrue statement in the prospectus - For example- prospectors the company is doing very well. Doing profit The company is not a profit-making company it is just on verge of making a profit and these are untrue statements for this criminally liable for the director is there.
- Inviting any deposits in contravention of the law - Any kind of deposit from the people against the loan is a criminal liability.

- False advertisement - False advertisement regarding share is a criminal liability.
- Failure to repay the application money – Suppose they were hundred share taken by the people and due to some reason 50 shares were not allotted to the shareholders, and the shareholders have already paid the money, but the money of these 50 shares has to been paid back to the shareholders because they were not allotted the share if the company fails to do so then it is criminal liability.
- Concealing the name of the creditors - From whom you have taken money or bank or any other financial institute has given you loan those creditors have to be given, if not then it is criminal liability.
- Failure to lay the balance sheet - The balance sheet is the most important aspect of the company. If the balance sheet is not shown by the director, it is a criminal liability.
- Failure to provide information to auditors, etc. - When the auditor comes for auditing, each detailed information regarding the business, loans, future investments, etc. have to be given by the director to the auditor. If they are not given, then it would be a criminal liability.

❖ COMPANY MEETINGS

- A meeting may be conveyed by the director, the requisitionists, or the NCLT (National Company Law Tribunal) - It is the duty of the director to conduct a meeting, it should be by the director or the shareholders interested can also hold a meeting. If the NCLT wants to have a company meeting, they can also do so.
- Notice to be given by the secretary after the time and place have been fixed by the directors - When you're going for a meeting, the notice has to be provided by the secretary of the company and also the place where the meeting is held.
- Even the shareholders can call a meeting as an extraordinary general meeting (EGM) - Shareholders can call at any moment. For example, during the COVID-19 pandemic, the shareholders think the company is not able to tackle this situation, for payment purpose or business purpose during this time and the shareholders want to have an EGM, they can call for the same.
- NCLT can call an Annual General Meeting (AGM).

❖ CLASSIFICATION OF MEETINGS

Shareholders meetings:

a. Statutory meeting (which happens only once in a lifetime of the company) - It is regarding the rules and regulation that have to be followed, called by the court.
b. AGM - convened the transaction some special or important decision to be taken- a meeting takes place when a crisis or sudden things have happened and you need to have a meeting and the shareholders can call for a meeting.
c. Class meetings - This is the meeting of the shareholders, which is convened by the class of shareholders based on the kind of share they hold.

Other meetings:

*   AGM - It can be conducted based on the provision given in the articles or by passing a resolution in one AGM. This meeting happens once in a financial year. It is based on the provision mentioned in the articles of association and these kinds of meetings are held.
*   Board meetings - This is conducted for the smooth running of the company and for collectively taking the decision. The meeting may be conducted to call on shares, issue debenture, borrow money, make loans, invest the funds etc-

❖ HOW TO CONDUCT MEETING?

*   Written notice to be given
*   Notice to be issued under the authority of the company
*   In case of failure to give a notice, the person concerned may be punished with a fine and the proceedings of the meeting will be rendered invalid.

❖ RESOLUTION

*   A motion, when passed, is called a resolution.
*   The resolution in the general body meetings can be an ordinary resolution.

- Special resolution (notice of 21 days to be given) - The notice of this resolution has to specify the purpose. The number of votes to be cast in the favor of resolution is to be three times the number of votes cast against.

❖ QUORUM AND PROXY

- The minimum members to be present must be according to the provision of the law
- Public company - Minimum five members; private company - Minimum two members
- The quorum must be those members who are eligible to vote with respect to the agenda of the meetings.
- If the quorum is not present within half an hour of the appointed time, either the meeting stands, dissolved, or maybe adjourned on the same day next week or any other as may be determined by the directors.
- A person incapable of attending a meeting and those who are eligible to vote may appoint a proxy in writing to attend the meeting of the member and vote on his or her behalf. The proxy can only vote and cannot participate in the discussion.

❖ MERGERS, ACQUISITIONS AND TAKEOVER OF THE COMPANY

- Merger connotes union of two or more commercial interest, cooperation, undertakings, body or any other entities.
- An acquisition means when one company is taking over another company, it is not doing well.

The changing of a legal entity after mergers and acquisitions:

- In a merger, one of the companies loses its corporate existence and the survivor company acquires the assets as well as the liability of the merger company. One loses its entity and the other one starts its operation and becomes the boss of the former company. And they can take part in the meetings, appointments, and can go for different kinds of rules and regulation and day-to-day activities of the company.

- In an acquisition, acquiring ownership in the property means the purchase of a controlling interest in the share capital of another existing company. It is an act of acquiring assets and management of the company.

Winding-up

- It is the process whereby the life of the company ended and its property is administered for the benefit of its creditors and members.
- During the process, a liquidator is appointed to take control of the company. The liquidator will be responsible for the assets, debts, and final distribution of the surplus of the members.
- It is the process of discharge of liabilities and returning the surplus to those who are entitled to it.
- But even a company that is making a profit can be wound up in a special feature of winding up, which is different from that the process of insolvency.

How can the company be wound up?

- Bypassing a special resolution
- If there is a default in holding the statutory meeting
- Failure to commence the business
- If there is a reduction in the membership of the minimum number of the members as per the statutory requirement
- If it is not able to pay its debts

Modes of winding up

- Compulsory winding up under the supervision of the court. The just and equitable grounds can be like loss of substratum, where there is a deadlock in the management, etc.
- Voluntary winding up (members voluntary winding up the creditor)
- Voluntarily winding up subject to the supervision of the court

❖ WINDING UP PROCEDURE.

- Petition of winding up has to be filed by the concerned person to the prescribed authority.

- Liquidator to be appointed to safeguard the property of the company.
- Then, the court will hear the matter and pass necessary orders. It can dismiss the petition or pass an order of wind up.

❖ *DISSOLUTION OF THE COMPANY*

- *When the company ceases to exist as a corporate entity for all practical purposes, it is said to have been dissolved*
- *Dissolution has to be declared by the court*
- *It will not be extinct and will be kept under suspension for two years*
- *The order has to be forwarded by the liquidator to the registrar of the company within 30 days of the date of order of dissolution.*

When the company is not doing well and it is suspended for two years, there would be a dissolution. Liquidator has to forward this to the register of the company and then the process of dissolution can take place within 30 days of the date of the order.

INDIAN CASE LAWS

Mobile View

Supreme Court of India
Raja Narayanlal Bansilal vs Maneck Phiroz Mistry And Another on 31 August, 1960
Equivalent citations: 1961 AIR 29, 1961 SCR (1) 417
Author: P Gajendragadkar
Bench: Sinha, Bhuvneshwar P.(Cj), Gajendragadkar, P.B., Wanchoo, K.N., Gupta, K.C. Das, Shah, J.C.

PETITIONER:
RAJA NARAYANLAL BANSILAL

Vs.

RESPONDENT:
MANECK PHIROZ MISTRY AND ANOTHER.

DATE OF JUDGMENT:
31/08/1960

BENCH:
GAJENDRAGADKAR, P.B.
BENCH:
GAJENDRAGADKAR, P.B.
SINHA, BHUVNESHWAR P.(CJ)
WANCHOO, K.N.
GUPTA, K.C. DAS
SHAH, J.C.

CITATION:

1961 AIR 29		1961 SCR (1) 417
CITATOR INFO:		
R	1964 SC1552	(10)
R	1967 SC 295	(10,72)
RF	1969 SC 707	(42)
RF	1970 SC 940	(13,14)
F	1973 SC1196	(19)
R	1978 SC1025	(34,35)
RF	1981 SC 379	(67)
D	1988 SC 113	(5)

ACT:

Company-Investigation into affairs of-Inspector appointed under old Act, if can exercise powers under new Act-Constitution-Testimonial compulsion-Whether Provisions for Production of documents and evidence offend guarantee-Equal protection of the law-If provisions for investigation and Production of evidence offend guarantee-Indian Companies Act, 1913 (VII of 1913), S. 138 Companies Act, 1956 (1 of 1956), SS. 235, 239, 240, 645 and 646, Constitution of India, Arts. 14 and 20(3).

HEADNOTE:

On November 15, 1954, the Registrar wrote to the company of which the appellant was the Managing Agent under s. 137, Indian Companies Act, 1913, that it had been represented to him that the business of the company was carried on in fraud and called upon it to furnish certain information. On April 15, 1955, the Registrar made a report to the Central Government under s. 137(5) to the effect that in his opinion the affairs of the company were carried on in fraud of contributories and they disclosed an unsatisfactory state of affairs and that a case had been made out for an investigation under s. 138. Thereupon, the Central Government, on November 1, 1955, appointed an Inspector to investigate the affairs of the company and to report thereon. The Inspector was authorised under s. 140 to examine any person on oath, and he wrote to the appellant that he would examine him on oath in relation to the business of the company. On April 1, 1956, the Indian Companies Act, 1913, was repealed by the Indian Companies Act, 1956, which conferred wider and more drastic powers of investigation. On July 26, 1956, the Central Government accorded approval under s. 239(2) of the new Act to the Inspector exercising his powers of investigating into and reporting on the affairs of the company. In May 1957 the Inspector served notices upon the appellant calling upon him to attend his office on the date and the time specified for the purpose of being examined on oath and to produce certain account books and papers relating to the company. The appellant challenged the investigation and contended: (i) that since the Inspector was appointed under the old Act he had no jurisdiction to exercise the powers referable to the provisions of the new Act, (ii) that s. 240 of the new Act which provided for the production of documents and, evidence at such investigations offended Art. 20(3) of the Constitution, and (iii) that S. 239 of the new Act which conferred powers on inspectors for investigation and S. 240 offended Art. 14 of the Constitution.

418

Held, that the Inspector appointed under S. 138(4) of the old Act must be deemed to have been appointed under s. 235 of the new Act and had authority and power to issue notices under S. 240 of the new Act. Section 645 of the new Act provided that the appointment of an Inspector under the old Act shall, on repeal of the old Act and on coming into force of the new Act, have effect as if it was made under the new Act. Section 646 which provided that nothing in the new Act shall affect the operation of S. T38 of the old Act as respects inspectors was not an exception or proviso to S. 645 and the two sections being saving sections had to be read as independent of and in addition to, and not as exceptions to, each other.

Held, further that S. 240 of Indian Companies Act, 1956, did not offend Art. 20(3) of the Constitution. For invoking the constitutional right against testimonial compulsion guaranteed under Art. 20(3) there must be at the relevant stage a formal accusation against the party pleading the guarantee relating to the commission of an offence which may result in a prosecution. The enquiry undertaken under S. 240 by the Inspector was in substance an enquiry into the affairs of the company; at this stage there was no accusation, formal or otherwise, against any specified individual. The mere fact that a prosecution may ultimately be launched against the alleged offenders would not retrospectively change the complexion or character of the proceedings held by the Inspector when he makes the investigation.

Maqbool Hussain v. The State of Bombay, [1953] S.C.R. 730, S. A. Venkataraman v. The Union of India, [1954] S.C.R. 1150, M. P. Sharma v. Satish Chandra, District Magistrate, Delhi, [1954] S.C.R. 1077, Thomas Dana v. State of Punjab, [1959] Supp. 1 S.C.R. 274 and Mohammed Dastagir v. The State of Madras, [1960] 3 S.C.R. 116, relied on.

Held, further that SS. 239 and 240 of the Indian Companies Act, 1956, did not violate Art. 14 of the Constitution. These sections denied the company and persons in charge of the management of such companies the ordinary protection afforded to witnesses under S. 132 of the Evidence Act and under S. 161(1) and (2) of the Criminal Procedure Code. As they were entrusted with the financial interests of a large number of citizens it was legitimate to treat such companies and their managers as a class by themselves and to provide for necessary safeguards and checks against abuse of power by the managers. The basis of the classification is founded on an intelligible differentia which has a rational relation to the object sought to be achieved.

Shri Ram Krishna Dalmia v. justice Tendolkar, [1959] S.C.R. 297, applied.

JUDGMENT:

CIVIL APPELLATE JURISDICTION: Civil Appeal No. 268 of 1959.

Appeal from the judgment and decree dated September 3, 1958, of the former Bombay High Court in Appeal No. 28/1958. A. V. Viswanatha Sastri, Ganpat Rai and I. N. Shroff, for the appellant.

M. C. Setalvad, Attorney-General for India, B. Sen and T. M. Sen, for the respondents.

1960. August 31. The Judgment of the Court was delivered by GAJENDRAGADKAR J.-The appellant Raja Narayanlal Bansilal of Bombay is the Managing Agent of a Limited Company named the Harinagar Sugar Mills Limited. By virtue of the power conferred on him by s. 137 of the Indian Companies Act, 1913 (VII of 1913), the Registrar wrote to the mills on November 15, 1954, that it had been represented to him under s. 137(6) that the business of the company was carried on in fraud, and so he called upon the company to furnish the information which he required as set out in a part of his letter (Ex. A). On April 15, 1955, the Registrar made a report (Ex. AA) to the Central Government under s. 137(5) of the said Act. This report showed that according to the Registrar the affairs of the company were carried on in fraud of contributories and they disclosed an unsatisfactory state of affairs. The report pointed out that the appellant was the Managing Agent of the company as well as its promoter, and that it was suspected that under a fictitious name of Bansilal Uchant Account the company was advancing money to the several firms owned by the appellant which were ostensibly purchased from the company's funds. The report further stated that between the years ending in September, 1942 and 1951 about Rs. 19,200 were paid for Harpur Farm and Rs.;. 39,300 for Bhavanipur Farm, and accounts disclosed that the Uchant Account was chiefly operated upon for purchasing such lands out of the funds of the company though the purchase in fact was for and on behalf of the appellant. The Registrar also added that he had reason to believe that the Managing Agent was utilising the property of the company in some cases for his personal gain, and concluded that, in his opinion, a case had been made out for an investigation under s. 138.

On receiving this report, on November 1, 1955, the 'Central Government passed an order under s. 138(4) of the said Act (Ex. B) appointing the first respondent Maneck P. Mistry, who is a Chartered Accountant, as an inspector to investigate the affairs of the company from the date of its incorporation. The said inspector was asked to point out all irregularities and contraventions of the provisions of the said Act or any other law, and make a full report as indicated in a communication which was separately sent to him. This separate communication (Ex. BB) prescribes the mode of enquiry which should be adopted by inspectors. It requires that while investigating the affairs of companies the inspectors should bear in mind that for a successful prosecution the evidence in support of a charge must be clear, tangible and cogent, and that their reports should specify with reference to the evidence collected during the investigations the points specified under paragraph 2(a) to (e). In the course of their investigation the inspectors are asked to make use of the powers available to them under s. 140 of the said Act including the right to examine a per- son on oath. The investigation should be conducted in private and the inspectors are not entitled to make public the information received by them during the course of the investigation.

Pursuant to the powers conferred on him by the said order respondent 1 wrote to the appellant intimating to him that he would examine him on oath in relation to the business of the company under s. 140(2) of the said Act (Ex. C). Meanwhile on April 1, 1956, the Companies Act of 1913 (VII of 1913) was repealed by the Companies Act of 1956 (1 of 1956). For the sake of convenience we would hereafter refer to the repealed Act as the old Act and the Act which came into force on April 1, 1956, as the new Act. On July 26, 1956, the Central Government purported to exercise its power under s. 239(2) of the new Act and accorded approval to respondent 1 exercising his powers of investigating into, and reporting on, the affairs of the appellant including his personal books of accounts as well as the affairs of the three concerns specified in the order. These three concerns are M/s. Narayanlal Bansilal, who are the Managing Agents of Harinagar Sugar Mills, the Shangrila Food Pro ducts Limited and, Harinagar Cane Farm. It appears that the appellant is the proprietor of the firm of Narayanlal Bansilal. After this order was passed respondent 1 served upon the appellant the four impugned notices (Ex. E collectively) on May 9, 1957, May 16, 1957, May 29, 1957 and June 29, 1957, respectively. These notices are substantially identical in terms' and so it would be sufficient for our purpose to set out the purport of one of them. The first notice called upon the appellant to attend the office of respondent 1 on the date and at the time specified for the purpose of being examined on oath in relation to the affairs of the company, and to produce before respondent 1 all the books of accounts and papers relating to the said company as mentioned in the notice. The appellant was further told that in default of compliance with the requisition aforesaid necessary legal steps would be taken without further reference to him. The notice contains a list of twelve items describing the several documents which the appellant was required to produce before respondent 1.

After these notices were served on the appellant he filed a, petition (No. 201 of 1957) in the Bombay High Court and prayed that the High Court should issue a writ of certiorari or any other appropriate direction, order or writ under Art. 226 of the Constitution calling upon respondent 1 to produce the records of the case relating to the notices in question and to set aside the said notices, the proposed examination of the appellant and the interim report made by him. It further prayed for a writ of prohibition or any other appropriate direction, order or writ restraining respondent 1 from making any investigation under the said notices and from exercising any powers of investigation under s. 239 and/or s. 240 of the new Act and/ or from investigating into the affairs of any persons or concerns specified in the petition. The petitioner claimed these writs mainly on two grounds. He first alleged that since respondent 1 had been appointed under the old Act he had no jurisdiction to exercise powers referable to the relevant provisions of the new Act. This ground assumed that the said relevant provisions of the new Act are valid, but it is urged that the powers referable to the said provisions are not available to respondent 1 since he was appointed under the old Act. The other ground on which the writs were claimed challenges the vires of ss. 239 and 240 of the new Act. This challenge assumed an alternative form. It is argued that s. 240 offends against the constitutional guarantee provided by Art. 20(3) of the Constitution and it is also urged that certain portions of ss. 239 and 240 offend against another constitutional guarantee provided by Art. 14 of the Constitution. It is thus on these three contentions that the petitioner claimed appropriate writs by his petition before the Bombay High Court. These pleas were resisted by the Union of India which had been joined to the proceedings as respondent 2. Mr. Justice K. T. Desai, who heard the petition, rejected the contentions raised by the petitioner, and held that no case had been made out for the issue of any writ. This decision was challenged by the appellant before the Court of Appeal in the Bombay High Court; the Court of Appeal agreed with the view taken by Desai, J., and dismissed the appeal. Thereupon the appellant applied for and obtained a certificate from the High Court, and it is with the said certificate that he has come to this Court by his present appeal. On his behalf Mr. Viswanatha Sastri has raised the same three points for our decision.

Let us first examine the question whether or not the first respondent has jurisdiction to exercise the powers under the relevant provisions of the new Act. It is common ground that if respondent 1's powers to bold the investigation in question are to be found in the relevant provisions of the old Act and not those of the new Act the impugned notices issued by him would be without authority and jurisdiction. In dealing with this question it is necessary to examine the broad features of the relevant sections of the two Acts.

We will begin with the old Act. Section 137 of the old Act deals with investigation by the Registrar. Section 137(1) provides that where the Registrar on' perusal of any document which a company is required to submit to him is of opinion that any information or explanation is necessary in order that such document may afford full particulars of the matter to which it purports to relate he may, by a written order, call on the company to furnish in writing the necessary information or explanation within the time to be specified in the order. Section 137(5) requires the Registrar to make a report in writing to the

Central Government if no information is supplied to him within the specified time, or if the information supplied to him appears to him to disclose an unsatisfactory state of affairs, or does not disclose a full and fair statement of the relevant matters. Thus s. 137(1) to (5) deal with the investigation which the Registrar is empowered to make on a persual of the document submitted to him by a company under the provisions of this Act. Section 137(6) deals with a case where if it is represented to the Registrar on materials placed before him by any contributory or creditor that the business of a company is carried on in fraud or in fraud of its creditors or in fraud of persons dealing with the company or for a fraudulent purpose, he may, after following the procedure prescribed in that behalf, call for information or explanation on matters to be specified in his order within such time as he may fix, and when such an order is passed the provisions of s. 137(2) to (5) would be applicable. This sub-section provides that if at the end of the investigation the Registrar is satisfied that the representation on which he took action was frivolous or vexatious he shall disclose the identity of the informant to the company. This provision is obviously intended as a safeguard against frivolous or vexatious representations in respect of the affairs of any company. The provisions of this section are substantially similar to the provisions of s. 234 of the new Act.

affairs of companies by inspectors, authorises the Central Government to appoint one or more competent inspectors to investigate the affairs of any company and report thereon in such manner as the said, Government may direct. The appointment of competent inspectors can be made by the Central Government in four classes of cases as specified in s. 138(1) to (4). It would be relevant to refer to two of these cases. Under s. 138(1) a competent inspector can be appointed in the case of a banking company having a share capital on the application of members holding not less than one-fifth of the shares issued, and under s. 138(4) in the case of any company on a report by the Registrar under s. 137(5). This section substantially corresponds to s. 235 of the new Act.

The other sections of the old Act to which reference must be made are ss. 140, 141 and 141A. Section 140(1) imposes upon all persons who are. or have been officers of the company an obligation to produce before the inspectors all books and documents in their custody or power relating to the company. Section 140(2) empowers the inspector to examine on oath any such person, meaning a person who is or has been an officer of the company in relation to the business of the company and to administer an oath to him. Section 140(3) provides that if a person refuses to produce a book or a document or to answer any question he shall be liable to a fine not exceeding Rs. 50 in respect of each offence. Section 141 provides that on the conclusion of an investigation the inspectors shall report their opinions to the Central Government, and shall forward a copy of their report to the registered office of the company; and it also provides that a copy of the said report can be delivered at their request to the applicants for the investigation. Then we have s. 141A which deals with the institution of prosecutions. Section 141A(1) provides that if from any report made under s. 138 it appears to the Central Government that any person has been guilty of any offence in relation to the company for which he is criminally liable the Central Government shall refer the matter to the Advocate-General or the Public Prosecutor. Section 141A(2) lays down that if the law officer who is consulted under (1) considers that there is a case in which prosecution ought to be instituted he shall cause proceedings to be instituted accordingly-, That in brief is the scheme of the relevant provisions of the old Act. We will now examine the scheme of the relevant provisions of the new Act. It has already been noticed that ss. 234 and 235 of the new Act are substantially similar to ss. 137 and 138 of the old Act. Section 239 of the new Act provides for the powers of the inspectors to carry on investigation into the affairs of related companies or of managing agent or associate. The sweep of the enquiry authorised by this section is very much wider than that under the corresponding section of the old Act. Sub-section (1) of this section authorises an inspector to investigate the affairs of a company and also the affairs of any other body corporate or person specified in cls. (a) to (d) if he thinks it necessary so to do. These clauses include several cases of body corporate which may have any connection direct or indirect, immediate or remote, with the affair of the company whose affairs are under investigation. It is unnecessary for our purpose in the present appeal to enumerate the said cases serially or exhaustively. It is conceded that the three other persons who have been called upon by respondent 1 to produce documents and give evidence fall within the purview of s. 239. As a result of the provisions of s. 239(1) the inspector has to report not only on the affairs of the company under investigation but also on the affairs of other bodies or persons who have been compelled to give evidence and produce documents during the course of the enquiry. The only safeguard provided against a possible abuse of these extensive powers is that in the case of any body corporate or person referred to in cls.

(b)(ii), (b)(iii), (c) or (d) of subs. (1) the inspector shall not exercise his relevant power without first having obtained the prior approval of the Central Government thereto.

Section 240 of the new Act imposes an obligation on the corporate bodies and persons in respect of which or whom investigation is authorised by s. 239 to produce all books and papers and to give all assistance in connection with the said investigation; that is the result of s. 240(1). Section 240(2) empowers the inspector to examine on oath any of the persons referred to in sub-s. (1) in relation to the relevant matters as specified. Section 240(3) deals with a case where a person refuses to comply with the obligation imposed on him by s. 240(1) or (2); and it provides that in such a case the inspector may certify the refusal under his hand to the court, and the court may thereupon enquire into the case, hear witnesses who may be produced against or on behalf of the alleged offender, consider any statement which may be offered in defence, and punish the offender as if he had been guilty of contempt of the court. Section 240(4) deals with a case where the inspector thinks it necessary for the purpose of his investigation that a person whom he has no power to examine on oath should be examined, and it provides that in such a case he may apply to the court, and the court may, if it thinks fit, order that person to attend and be examined on oath before it on any matter relevant to the investigation. This sub-section provides for the procedure to be followed in examining such a witness. Section 240(5) lays down that notes of any examination under sub-s. (2) or (4) shall be taken down in writing, and shall be read over to or by, and signed by, the person examined, and may thereafter be used as evidence against him. Having thus made elaborate provisions for the production of documents and evidence in the course of the investigation by the inspector, s. 241 deals with the inspectors' report and provides that inspectors may, and if so directed by the Central Government shall, make interim reports to that Government, and on the conclusion of the investigation shall make a final report to it. Section 241(2) provides for the supply of the copy of the said report to the several parties concerned as specified in cls. (a) to (e).

That takes us to s. 242 which deals with prosecution. Section 242(1) provides inter alia that if from any report made under a. 241 it appears to the Central Government that any person has in relation to the company been guilty of any offence for which he is criminally liable, the Central Government may, after taking such legal advice as it thinks fit, prosecute such person for the offence, and it imposes on all officers, and agents of the company, except those prosecuted, to give the Central Government all assistance in connection with the prosecution which they are reasonably able to give. That broadly stated is the position with regard to the relevant provisions of the new Act.

Mr. Sastri has drawn our pointed attention to the fact that the scope and nature of the enquiry authorised by the new Act are very much wider than under the old Act, and he has characterised the relevant, powers conferred on the investigating inspectors as draconian. He, therefore, contends that unless it is established that these powers are available to the inspector appointed under the relevant provisions of the old Act the impugned notices must be set aside; and his argument is that these powers are not available to the inspector appointed under the old Act. The decision of this question will depend mainly on the con- struction of ss. 645 and 646 of the new Act.

Section 644 provides for the repeal of the enactments mentioned in Schedule XII; the old Act is one of the enactments thus repealed. Ordinarily the effect of the repeal of the old Act would have been governed by the provisions of s. 6 of the General Clauses Act (10 of 1897), but in the case of the new Act the application of the said section is subject to the provisions of ss. 645 to 657 of the Act; that is the effect of s. 658 which provides that the mention of particulars in ss. 645 to 657 or in any other provisions of this Act shall not prejudice the general application of s. 6 of the General Clauses Act, 1897, with respect to the effect of repeals. In other words, though s. 6 of the General Clauses Act will generally apply, its application will be subject to the provisions contained in as. 645 to 657; this position is not disputed. It is now necessary to consider s. 645. It reads thus:

"Nothing in this Act shall affect any order, rule, regulation, appointment, conveyance mortgage, deed, document or agreement made, fee directed, resolution passed, direction given, proceeding taken, instrument executed or issued, or thing done, under or in pursuance of any previous companies law; but any such order, rule, regulation, appointment, conveyance, mortgage, deed, document, agreement, fee, resolution, direction, proceeding. instrument or thing shall, if in force at the commencement of this Act, continue to be in force, and so far as it could have been made, directed, passed, given, taken, executed, issued or done under or in pursuance of this Act, shall have effect as if made, directed, passed, given, taken, executed, issued or done under or in pursuance of this Act." The effect of this section is clear. If an inspector has. been appointed under the relevant section of the old Act, on repeal of the old Act and on coming into force of the new Act, his appointment shall have effect as if it was made under or in pursuance of the new Act. Indeed it is common ground that if s. 645 had stood alone and had not been followed by s. 646 there would have been no difficulty in holding that the inspector appointed under the old Act could exercise his powers and authority under the relevant provisions of the new Act, and the impugned notices would then be perfectly valid. Incidentally we may refer to the provisions of a. 652 in this connection. Under this section any person appointed to any office under or by virtue of any previous company law shall be deemed to have been appointed to that office under this Act.

It is, however, urged that the authority of the inspector which is in dispute is governed by s. 646.

This section provides:

"Nothing in this Act shall affect the operation of section 138 of the Indian Companies Act, 1913 (VII of 1913), as respects inspectors, or as respects the continuation of an inspection begun by inspectors, appointed before the commencement of this Act; and the provisions of this Act shall apply to or in relation to a report of inspectors appointed under the said section 138 as they apply to or in relation to a report of inspectors appointed under section 235 or 237 of this Act."

The argument is that the expression "nothing in this Act" includes s. 645 and so s. 646 should be read as an exception or proviso to

s. 645; and if that is so, all matters covered by s. 138 of the old Act must continue to be governed by the said Act and not by any of the provisions of the new Act. We are unable to accept this argument. In appreciating the effect of the provisions of s. 646 it is necessary to bear in mind that it occurs in that part of the new Act which deals with repeals and savings. Sections 645 to 648 are the saving sections, and ordinarily and in the absence of any indication to the contrary these saving clauses should be read as independent of, and in addition to, and not as providing exceptions to, one another. It is significant that whereas s. 646 provides for the continuance of the operation of s. 138 it does not make a corresponding provision for the continuance of the operation of a. 140 of the old Act which deals with the powers of the inspector to call for books and to examine parties. Besides, it may perhaps not be accurate to suggest that having regard to the provisions of s. 645, s. 646 is wholly redundant. It would be possible to take the view that cases falling under s. 138(1) of the old Act are intended to be covered by s. 646 as they would not be covered by s. 645. In regard to the case of a banking company covered by s. 138(1) s. 646 will come into operation and that may be one of the reasons for which s. 646 was enacted. It may be that the case of the banking company may also be covered by s. 35 of the Banking Companies Act 10 of 1949, but since a. 138(1) applied to the said case until the old Act was repealed the Legislature may-have, as a matter of caution, thought it necessary to provide for the continuance of the operation of s. 138 by enacting s. 646. However that may be, we feel no difficulty in holding that s: 646 should not be construed as a proviso to s.645 but as an additional saving provision. The words used in s. 645 are so clear, and the policy and object of enacting the said provision are in our opinion so emphatically expressed, that it would be unreasonable to hold that s. 646 was intended to provide for such a radical exception to s. 645. Where the Legislature enacts a saving section as a matter of abundant caution the argument that the enactment of the said section was not wholly necessary cannot be treated as decisive or even effective. Therefore, in our opinion, the High Court was right in coming to the conclusion that the inspector appointed under s. 138(4) of the old Act must by legal fiction, which is authorised by s. 645, be deemed to have been appointed under s. 235 of the new Act, and if that is so, respondent 1 had authority and power to issue the impugned notices under s. 240 of the new Act. The challenge to the validity of the impugned notices on the ground that respondent 1 had no authority to issue the said notices must, therefore, fail.

That takes us to the question as to whether the relevant provisions of s. 240, which empower respondent 1 to issue the relevant notices by which the appellant was called upon to give evidence and to produce documents, offend against the fundamental constitutional right guaranteed by Art. 20(3). It has been strenuously urged before us that the main object of the present investigation is to discover whether the appellant has committed any offenses, and so by compelling him to give evidence and produce documents he is denied the constitutional protection against self incrimination.

Article 20(3) provides that "no person accused of any offence shall be compelled to be a witness against himself". It may be assumed that the appellant is being compelled to be witness against himself in the present proceedings; but even so the question which arises for our decision is whether the appellant can be said to be a person who is accused of any offence as required by Art. 20(3). Mr. Sastri has contended that the words "person accused of any offence" should not receive a narrow or literal construction; they should be liberally interpreted because. the clause, in which they occur enshrines a fundamental constitutional right and the scope and reach of the said right should not be unduly narrowed down. In support of this general argument Mr. Sastri has naturally relied on the historical background of the doctrine of protection against self-incrimination; and he has strongly pressed into service the decisions of the Supreme Court of the United States of America dealing with the Fifth Amendment to the Constitution of the United States. The said Amendment inter alia provides that "no person shall be compelled in any criminal case to be a witness against himself". It would be noticed that in terms the Amendment refer to a criminal case, and yet it has received a very broad and liberal interpretation at the hands of the Supreme Court of the United States of America. It has been held that the said constitutional protection is not confined only to criminal cases but it extends even to civil proceedings (Vide: McCarthy v. Arndstein(1)). As observed by Mr. Justice Blatchford in Charles Counselman v. Frank

Hitchcock (2) "it is impossible that the meaning of the constitutional provision can only be that a person shall not be compelled to be a witness against himself in a criminal prosecution against himself. It would doubtless cover such cases but it is not limited to them. The object was to insure that a person should not be compelled, when acting as a witness in any investigation, to give testimony which might tend to show that he himself had committed a crime. The privilege is limited to criminal matters, but it is as broad as the mischief against which it seeks to guard".

In support of his plea that a liberal interpretation should be put on an article which enshrines a fundamental constitutional right Mr. Sastri has also invited our attention to the observation made by Mr. Justice Bradley in Edward A. Boyd and George H. Boyd v. United States (3). Says Bradley, J., "illegitimate and unconstitutional practices get their first footing in that way, namely by silent approaches and slight deviations from legal modes of procedure. This can only be obviated by adhering to the rule that constitutional provisions for the security of person and (1) (1924) 69 L. Ed. 158. (2) (1892) 35 L. Ed. 1110. (3) (1886) 29 L. Ed. 746,752.

property should be liberally construed". The learned judge has also added that any compulsory discovery by extorting the party's oath, or compelling the production of his private books and papers, to convict him of crime or to forfeit his property, is contrary to the principles of a free government, and is abhorrent to the instincts of an American. It may suit the purposes of despotic power; but it cannot abide the pure atmosphere of political liberty and personal freedom". In regard to this eloquent statement of the law it may, however, be permissible to state that under the English Law the doctrine of protection against self- incrimination has never been applied in the departments of Company Law' and Insolvency Law. There is no doubt that under s. 15 of the English Bankruptcy Act when a public examination of a debtor is held he is compelled to answer all questions as the court may put, or allow to be put to him, and that the answers given have to be signed by him and can be used against him in evidence (Vide: In Re: Atherton (1)); similar is the position under s. 270 of the English Companies Act. However, the general argument for the appellant is that in construing Art. 20(3) we may take some assistance from the broad and liberal construction which has been placed on the apparently narrow and limited words used in the Fifth Amendment to the Constitution of the United States of America..

Thus presented the argument is no doubt attractive, and its validity and effectiveness would have had to be fully and carefully examined if the question raised in the present appeal had been a matter of first impression; but the construction of Art. 20 in general and Art. 20(2) and (3) in particular has been the subject matter of some decisions of this Court, and naturally it is in the light of the previous decisions that we have to deal with the merits of the appellants case in the present appeal. In Maqbool Hussain v. The State of Bombay (2) this Court had occasion to consider the scope and effect of the constitutional guarantee provided by Art. 20(2). A person against whom proceedings (1) (1912) 2 K.B. 251.

(2) [1953] S.C.R. 730.

had been taken by the Sea Customs Authorities under s. 167 of the Sea Customs Act and an order for confiscation of goods had been passed was subsequently prosecuted before the Presidency Magistrate for-an offence under s. 23 of the Foreign Exchange Regulations Act in respect of the same act. It was urged on, his behalf that the proceedings taken against him before the Sea Customs Authorities was a prosecution and the order of confiscation passed in the said proceedings wag a punishment, and. so it was argued that the constitutional guarantee afforded by Art. 20(2) made his subsequent prosecution under s. 23 of the Foreign Exchange Regulation Act invalid. This plea was rejected. In dealing with the merits of the plea this Court had to consider the meaning of the words "prosecuted and punished" used in Art. 20(2). Article 20(2) provides that no person shall be prosecuted and punished for the same offence more than once, and the question raised was whether the proceedings before the Sea Customs Authorities constituted prosecution, and whether the order of confiscation was punishment under Art. 20(2). In construing Art. 20(2) this Court considered Art. 20 as a whole and examined the interrelation of the relevant terms used in the three clauses of the said article. "The very wording of Art. 20", observed Bhagwati, J., "and the words used therein" convicted", "commission of the act charged as an offence", "be subjected to a penalty", "commission of the offence", "prosecuted and punished", "accused of any offence "would indicate that the proceedings therein contemplated are of the nature of criminal proceedings before a court of law or a judicial tribunal. and the prosecution in this context would mean an initiation or starting of proceedings of a criminal nature before a court of law or a judicial tribunal in accordance with the procedure prescribed in the statute which creates the offence and regulated the procedure". Having thus construed Art. 20(2) in the light of the relevant words used in the different clauses of the said article, this Court naturally proceeded to enquire whether the Sea Customs Authorities acted as a judicial tribunal in holding proceedings against the person. The scheme of the relevant pro. visions of the Act was then examined, and it was held that the said authorities are not a judicial tribunal with the result that the "I adjudging increased rate of duty or penalty and confiscation" under the provisions of the said act did not constitute a judgment or order of a court or judicial tribunal necessary for the purpose of supporting the plea of double jeopardy. In the result the conclusion of this Court was that when the Customs Authorities confiscated the gold in question the proceedings taken did not amount to a prosecution of the party nor did the order of confiscation constitute a punishment as contemplated by Art. 20(2). This decision has been affirmed by this Court in the case of S. A. Venkataraman v. The Union of India (1). In that case an enquiry bad been made against the appellant Venkataraman under the Public Servants (Inquiries) Act, 1850 (Act XXXVII of 1850). On receiving the report of the enquiry commissioner opportunity was given to the appellant under Art. 311(2) to show cause, and, ultimately after consultation with the Union Public Service Commission the appellant was dismissed by an order passed by the President. The order of dismissal was passed on September 17, 1953. Soon thereafter on February 23, 1954, the police submitted a charge-sheet against him charging him with having committed offenses under ss. 161/165 of the Indian Penal Code 'and s. 5(2) of the Prevention of Corruption Act. The validity of the subsequent prosecution was challenged by the appellant on the ground that it contravened the constitutional guarantee enshrined in Art. 20(2). The appellant's plea was, however, rejected on the ground that the proceedings taken against him before the commissioner under the Inquiries Act did not amount to a prosecution. The relevant provisions of the said act were examined, and it was held that in an inquiry under the said Act there is neither any question of investigating an offence in the sense of an act or omission punishable by any law for the time being in force nor is there (1) [1964] S.C.R. 1150.

any question of imposing punishment prescribed by the law which makes that act or omission an offence. Mukherjea, J., as he then was, who delivered the judgment of the Court, has referred to the earlier decision in the case of Maqbool Hussain (1), and has observed that "the effect of the said decision was that the proceedings in connection with the prosecution and punishment of a person must be in the nature of a criminal proceeding before a court of law or a judicial tribunal, and not before a tribunal which entertains a departmental or an administrative enquiry even though set up by a statute but which is not required by law to try a matter judicially and on legal evidence". Thus these two decisions can be said to have considered incidentally the general scope of Art. 20 though both of them were concerned directly with the construction and application of Art. 20(2) alone.

Article 20(3) was considered by the Full Court in M. P. Sharma v. Satish Chandra, District Magistrate, Delhi (2). The question about the scope and effect of Art. 20(3) was raised in that case by a petition filed under Art. 32 of the Constitution. It appears that the Registrar of the Joint Stock Companies, Delhi State, lodged information with the Inspector-General, Delhi Special Police Establishment, against the petitioners alleging that they had committed several offenses punishable under the Indian Penal Code. The lodging of this information was preceded by an investigation into the affairs of the petitioners' company which had been ordered by the Central Government under a. 138 of the old Act, and the report received at the end of the said investigation indicated that a well-planned and organised attempt had been made by the petitioners to misappropriate and embezzle the funds of the company by adopting several ingenious methods. On receipt of the said First Information Report the District Magistrate ordered investigation into the offenses and issued warrants for simultaneous searches at as many as thirty four places. By their petitions the

petitioners contended that the search warrants (1) [1953] S.C.R. 730.
(2) [1954] S.C.R. 1077.

were illegal and they prayed that the same may be quashed as being
in violation of Art, 20(3). The plea thus raised by the petitioners was
ultimately rejected on the ground that the impugned. searches did not
violate the' said constitutional guarantee. Jagannadha das, J., who
spoke for the Court, observed that "since article 20(3) provides for
a constitutional guarantee against testimonial compulsion its words
should be liberally construed, and that there was no reason to confine
the content of the said guarantee to its barely literal import". He,
therefore, held that the phrase "to be a witness" means nothing more
than to furnish evidence, and such evidence can be furnished through
the lips or by production of a thing or of a document or in other
modes. He also pointed out that the phrase was "to be a witness"
and not "to appear as a witness" and so the protection afforded was
not merely in respect of testimonial compulsion in the court room
but may well extend to compel testimony previously obtained from
him. The conclusion of the Court on this part of the construction was
thus stated. The constitutional guarantee "is available to a person
against whom a formal accusation relating to the commission of
an offence has been leveled which in the normal course may result
in prosecution; whether it is available to other persons in other
situations does not call for a decision in this case". Since the First
Information Report bad been recorded against the petitioners in that
case it followed that the first test that a formal accusation relating to
the commission of an offence must have been leveled was satisfied.
The question which was then considered was whether there was any
basis in the Indian Law for the assumption that a search or seizure of
a thing or document is in itself to be, treated as compelled production
of the same; and it was held that there would be no justification
for treating the said search or seizure as compelled production; that
is why the challenge to the validity of the search warrants issued
against the petitioners was repelled. The effect of this decision thus
appears to be that one of the. essential conditions for invoking the
constitutional guarantee enshrined in Art. 20(3) is that a formal
accusation relating to the commission of an offence, which would
normally lead to his prosecution,, must have been leveled against the

party who is being compelled to give evidence against himself; and this conclusion, in our opinion is fully consistent with the two other decisions of this Court to which we have already referred. There are two other subsequent decisions of this' Court to which reference may be made. In Thomas Dana v. State of Punjab (1), according to the majority decision "prosecution" in Art. 20(2) means a proceeding either by way of indictment or information in a criminal court in order to put an offender upon his trial. It would be noticed that this conclusion is wholly consistent with the view taken by this Court in the case of Maqbool Hussain (2) and S. A. Venkataraman (3). In Mohammed Dastaqir v. The State of Madras (4) this Court had to consider Art. 20(3). The appellant in that case had gone to the bungalow of the Deputy Superintendent of Police to offer him a bribe which was covered in a closed envelope with a request that he might drop the action registered against him. The police officer threw the envelope at the appellant who took it up. While the appellant was still in the bungalow he was asked by the police officer to produce the envelope and he took out from his pocket some currency notes and placed them on the table without the envelope. The notes were then seized by the police officer and a rubber stamp of his office was placed on them. On these facts it was urged that in relying upon the evidence of compelled production of notes the prosecution had, violated the provisions of Art. 20(3). In support of this contention the general observations made by this Court in the case of M. P., Sharma(5), were strongly pressed into service. This Court, however, rejected the appellant's arguments and held that the prosecution did not suffer from any infirmity. On the facts it was found that though the offence had in fact been already committed (1) [1959] Supp. 1 S.C.R. 274.

(2) [1953] S.C.R. 730.

(3) [1954] S.C.R. 1150.

(4) A.I.R. 1960 S.C. 756.

(5) [1954] S.C.R. 1077.

by the appellant, he had in fact not been accused of it at the stage when the currency notes were produced by him; it was also held that it could not be said that he was compelled to produce the said currency notes, because he might easily have refused to produce them,, and so there was no occasion for him to invoke the constitutional protection against self-incrimination.

What then is the result of these decisions ? They show that in determining the complexion and reach of its respective sub-clauses the general scheme of Art. 20 as a whole must be considered, and the effect of the inter-action of the relevant words used 'in them must be properly appreciated. Thus considered the constitutional right guaranteed by Art. 20(2) against double jeopardy can be successfully invoked only where the- prior proceedings on which reliance is plac- ed must be of a criminal nature instituted or continued before a court of law or a judicial tribunal in accordance with the procedure prescribed in the statute which creates the offence and regulates the procedure. It would be noticed that the character of the said proceedings as well as the character of the forum before which the proceedings are initiated or conducted are treated as decisive in the matter. Similarly, for invoking the constitutional right against testimonial compulsion guaranteed under Art. 20 (3) it must appear that a formal accusation has been made against the party pleading the guarantee and that it relates to the commission of an offence which in the normal course may result in prosecution. Here again the nature of the accusation and its probable sequel or consequence are regarded as important.

Thus we go back to the question which we have already posed: was the appellant accused of any offence at the time when the impugned notices were served on him ? In answering this question in the light of the tests to which we have just referred it will be necessary to determine the scope and nature of the enquiry which the inspector undertakes under s. 240; for, unless it is shown that an accusation of a crime can be made in such an enquiry, the appellant's plea under Art. 20(3) cannot succeed. Section 240 shows that the enquiry which the inspector undertakes is in substance an enquiry into the affairs of the company concerned. Certain documents are required to be furnished by a company to the Registrar under the provisions of the new Act. If, on examining the said documents, the Registrar thinks it necessary to call for information or explanation he is empowered to take the necessary action under s. 234(1). Similarly, under s. 234(7) if it is represented to the Registrar on materials placed before him by any contributory or creditor or any other person interested that the business of the company is carried on in the manner specified in the said sub-section the Registrar proceeds to make the enquiry. Thus the scope of the enquiry con- templated by s. 234 is clear; wherever the Registrar has reason to believe that the affairs of the company are not properly carried on he is empowered to make an enquiry into the said affairs. Similarly under s. 235 inspectors are appointed to investigate' the affairs of any company and report thereon. The investigation carried on by the inspectors is no more than the work of a fact-finding commission. It is true that as a result of the investigation made by the inspectors it may be discovered that the affairs of the company disclose not only irregularities and malpractice but also commission of offenses, and in such a case the report would specify the relevant. particulars prescribed by the circular in that behalf If, after receiving the report, the Central Government is satisfied hat any person is guilty of an offence for which he is criminally liable, it may, after taking legal advice, institute criminal proceedings against the offending person under s. 242(1); but the fact that a prosecution may ultimately be launched against the alleged offender will not retrospectively change the complexion or character of the proceedings held by the inspector when he makes the investigation. Have irregularities been committed in managing the affairs of the company; if yes, what is the nature of the irregularities ? Do they amount to the- commission of an offence punishable under the criminal law ? If they do who is liable for the said offence? These and such other questions fall within the purview of the ins- pector's investigation. The scheme of the relevant sections is that the investigation begins broadly with a view to examine the management of the affairs of the company to find out whether any irregularities have been committed or not. In such a case there is no accusation, either formal or otherwise, against any specified individual; there may be a general allegation that the affairs are irregularly, improperly or illegally managed; but who would be responsible for the affairs which are reported to be irregularly managed is a matter which would be determined at the end of the enquiry. At the commencement of the enquiry and indeed throughout its proceedings there is no accused person, no accuser and no accusation against anyone that he has committed an offence. In our opinion a general enquiry and investigation into the affairs of the company thus contemplated cannot be regarded as an investigation which starts with an accusation contemplated in Art. 20(3) of the Constitution. In this connection it is necessary to remember that the relevant sections of the Act appear in Part VI which generally deals with management and administration of the companies.

It is well-known, that the provisions of the Act are modeled on the corresponding provisions of the English Companies Act. It would, therefore, be useful to refer to the observations made by the House of Lords in describing the character of the enquiry held under the corresponding provisions of the English Act in the case of Hearts of Oak Assurance Co. v. Attorney General (1). In that case Lord Thankerton said "it appears to me to be clear that the object of the examination is merely to recover information as to the company's affairs and that it is in no sense a judicial proceeding for the purpose of trial of an offence; it is enough to point out that there are no parties before the inspector, that he alone conducts the enquiry, and that the power to examine on oath is confined to the officers, members, agents and servants of the company". We ought, however, to add that the last (1) 1932 A.C. 392.

observation is no longer true about the inspector's powers under s. 240 of the new Act. In the same case Lord Macmillan observed that "the object of the enquiry manifestly is that the Commissioner may either by himself directly or through the medium of a delegate obtain the information necessary to enable him, to decide what action, if any, he should take. The cardinal words of the section are those which empower the Commissioner or his inspector to examine into and report on the affairs of the society". Thus it is clear that the examination of, or investigation into, the affairs of the company cannot be regarded as a proceeding started against any individual after framing an accusation against him. Besides it is quite likely that in some cases investigation may disclose that there are no irregularities, or if there are they do not amount to the commission of any offence; in such cases there would obviously be no occasion for the Central Government to institute criminal proceedings under s. 242(1). Therefore, in our opinion, the High Court was right in holding that when the inspector issued the impugned notices against the appellant the appellant cannot be said to have been accused of any offence; and so the first essential condition for the application of Art. 20(3) is absent. We ought to add that in the present case the same conclusion would follow even if the clause "accused of any offence" is interpreted more liberally than was done in the case of M. P. Sharma (1), because even if the expression 'accused of any offence" is interpreted in a very broad and liberal way it is clear that at the relevant stage the appellant has not been, and in law cannot be, accused of any offence. Thus the tests about the character of the proceedings and the forum where the proceedings are initiated or intended to be taken are also not satisfied; but, as we have already indicated, such a broad and liberal interpretation of the relevant expression does not appear to be consistent with the tenor and effect of the previous decisions of this Court.

It is true that in his report the Registrar has made (1) [1954] S.C.R. 1077.

certain allegations on which Mr. Sastri has relied. He contends that the statements in the report do amount to allegations of commission of offenses by the appellant. What the Registrar has stated in his report in this particular case cannot be relevant or material in deciding the vires of the impugned section. The vires of the section can be determined only by examining 'the relevant scheme of the Act, and we have already Been that such an examination does not assist the appellants contention that Art. 20(3) is contravened. Besides, what the Registrar has stated in his report can hardly amount to an accusation against the appellant; it is a report submitted by him to the Central Government, and it is only intended to enable the Central Government to decide whether it should appoint an inspector. It is not as if the investigation before the inspector begins on the basis that the Registrar is the complainant who has made an accusation against the appellant, or that the function of the investigation is to find out whether the said accusation is proved or not. As we have already seen an enquiry under s. 240 may require a large number of persons to give evidence or produce documents but it cannot be said that any accusation is made against any of the said persons. In fact three persons have been served with similar notices in the present enquiry which shows that the inspector desires to obtain relevant evidence from them as from the appellant. How can it be said that an accusation has been made against the said three persons, and that incidentally helps to bring out the real character and scope of the enquiry. Therefore we do not think that the state- ments made in the Registrar's report, on which Mr. Sastri relies can really assist us in deciding the question of the vires of s. 240. It is also significant that the appellant has not challenged the validity of the impugned notices on any ground relatable to, or based on, the said report. The challenge is founded on. the broad and general ground that S. 240 offends against Art. 20(3).

We may incidentally add that it was in support of his argument based on the Registrar's report that Mr. Sastri sought to rely on the decision of the Calcutta High Court in Collector of Customs v. Calcutta Motor and Cycle Co. (1). In that case certain notices had been issued under s. 171A of the Sea Customs Act to certain persons to appear before the customs officials and to produce certain documents. The High Court took the view that "it appeared from the accusations made in the search warrants at the instance" of the customs authorities and those made in one of the notices by the customs authorities themselves, that the accusations of criminal offenses could not be excluded"; and so it was held that the requirements of Art. 20(3) were satisfied and the protection under the said article was available to the persons concerned. In our opinion this decision does not assist the appellant. It proceeded on the finding that accusations of criminal offenses could be held in substance to have been made against the persons concerned, and it dealt with the other points of law on that assumption. That being so, we think it unnecessary to discuss or consider the said decision. Our conclusion, therefore, is that s. 240 does not offend against Art. 20(3) of the Constitution.

That still leaves the challenge to the vires of the said section under Art. 14 of the Constitution, though we ought to add that Mr. Sastri did not seriously press his case under Art. 14, and we think rightly. The argument under Art. 14 proceeds on familiar lines. It is urged that the ordinary protection afforded to witnesses under s. 132 of the Indian Evidence Act as well as the protection afforded to accused persons under s. 161(1) and (2) of the Criminal Procedure Code, have been denied to the appellant in the investigation which respondent 1 is carrying on in regard to the affairs of his company, and that violates equality before the law. The scope and effect of Art. 14 have been considered by this Court frequently.: It has been repeatedly held that what Art. 14, prohibits is class legislation; it does not, however,, forbid reasonable classification for the purpose of legislation. If the classification on which legislation is based is founded on an intelligible differentia which distinguishes persons or things that are grouped together from others left out of the group, and if the differentia has a rational relation to the object sought to be achieved, then the classification does not offend Art. 14 (Vide: Shri Ram Krishna Dalmia v. Justice Tendolkar (1)). Now in the light of this test how can it be said that the classification made by ss. 239 and 240 offends Art. 14 of the Constitution ? A company is a creature of the statute. There can be no doubt that one of the objects of the Companies Act is to throw open to all citizens the privilege of carrying on business with limited liability. Inevitably the business of the company has to be carried on through human agency, and that sometimes gives rise to irregularities and malpractice in the management of the affairs of the company. If persons in charge of the management of companies abuse their position and make personal profit at the cost of the creditors, contributories and others interested in the company, that raises a problem which is very much different from the problem of ordinary misappropriation or breach of trust. The interest of the company is the interest of several persons who constitute the company, and thus persons in management of the affairs of such companies can be classed by themselves as distinct from other individual citizens. A citizen can and may protect his own interest, but where the financial interest of a large number of citizens is left in charge of persons who manage the affairs of the companies it would be legitimate to treat such companies and their managers as a class by themselves and to provide for necessary safeguards and checks against a possible abuse of power vesting in the managers. If the relevant provisions of the Act dealing with enquiries and investigations of the affairs of the companies are considered from this point of view there would be no difficulty in holding that Art. 14 is not violated either by s. 239 or s. 240 of the new Act.

The result is the appeal fails and is dismissed with costs.

Appeal dismissed.

(1) [1959] S.C.R. 297.

PART 2: The Companies Act, 2013

❖ What is a company?

- The word 'company' is derived from Latin words 'Com', which means 'with' or 'together', and 'panies', which means 'bread'.
- The company can be defined as an artificial, invisible, intangible person created under the law with a discrete and legal entity, perpetual succession, and a common seal.

An artificial person, or an individual, which is not a body or a soul, and is intangible, means that you cannot feel it; you can only see it.

The most striking characteristics of a company are:

1. Corporate personality: It has a personality or a legal entity that I have already explained.
2. Common seal: It has a specific mark, identified and recognized.
3. Limited liability: Shareholders or the stakeholders have committed to the company during the formation of the company that they are ready to pay some pre-decided amount when the company lands up in an adverse situation. For instance, suppose a company is having a debt with another company or another person and the total debt is Rs. 50 lakhs and the shareholders already promised that they would be paying one lakh, they will pay.
4. Perpetual succession: Once the company name is already registered, the company should continue irrespective of the fact whether the company is having a board of directors, members, or employees, so that the name should continue.
5. Separate property
6. Transferability of shares: Any shareholder can transfer his part of a share to any other shareholders. Then, that person would be the owner.
7. Capacity to sue and be sued: If a person is doing anything wrong with the company, then that company can take action against the person. The company can sue the person if he/she does anything wrong with the company.

❖ History of Companies Act in India

- The Indian Company Law began with the Companies Act, 1850, modeled on the British Companies Act 1844

- The Indian Companies Act of 1913 was based on the British Companies Act of 1908
- The Indian Companies Act, 1956
- The Indian Companies Act, 2013

Started in 1850, it was based on the views and ideologies of the British Companies Act 1844.

When it was again started in 1913, it included the British ideology of 1908.

The actual Companies Act started in 1956 and was later amended in 2013. It was amended because certain clauses in Companies Act of 1956 were not good enough to tackle certain problems that arose when a company went multinational.

Highlights of the Companies Act of 2013.

1. Passed in Lok Sabha: December 18, 2012
2. Passed in Rajya Sabha: August 8, 2013
3. Total number of Sections: 470
4. Total number of Chapters: 29
5. Total number of Schedules: 7
6. Effective from September 12, 2013
7. JJ Irani committee overlooked its formulation

To pass a law or act both the Lok Sabha and Rajya Sabha needs to agree. Rajya Sabha is the higher authority. First, the law/act goes to Lok Sabha and then it comes to Rajya Sabha. Once it is sanctioned by both, then it comes into effect. The Companies Act of 2013 was sanctioned on August 8, 2013. The committee that did this was the JJ Irani Committee, which is very well-known to sanction these kinds of acts.

Companies Act 1956 vs. Companies Act 2013

Structural Comparison

Companies Act of 1956	Companies Act of 2013
13 parts	29 chapters
658 sections	470 sections
15 schedules	7 schedules

❖ OBJECTIVES OF THE ACT OF 2013

- To promote the development of the economy - The major part of the companies act is to develop the economy's impact. Since most of the companies had become multinational, government thought there should be a kind of object, an idea, where the development of economy takes place and the country and the economy goes towards the financial aspect and growth of the country.

- To encourage transparency and accountability - Whenever a person or a shareholder is investing money in a company, that person has got every right to know regarding the policies, features, and products of the company. Then, only the person would be good enough to invest in the company. In transparency, whatever policies, rules, and regulations the people from the higher authority are discussing, taking up, they have to tell the people in the lower authority too, so that the higher and the lower people can understand the actual happening in the company, and the people become much better understanding, do better and accountable. There are different departments in the organisation, such as the finance, the IT sector, the HR department, and the marketing department. Apart from that, we have auditors and stakeholders, and everything should be accountable. I should be accountable or responsible for my actions. When there are accountability and transparency, people are more interested to invest in the company.

- To promote higher standards of corporate governance - The responsibility of the company is taken care of by maintaining good standards with respect to its product, quality, and policies, and the corporate needs to govern all these things, whether it is as per the rules and regulation of the company or of the government.

- To recognise new concepts and procedures to support business while protecting the interest of all stakeholders - When we are thinking about profit, we do forget that other people may be affected. For example, we are thinking a person's capacity in manufacturing is around 5 to 6 items in a day, but since we want profit we just make that person work and make, instead of 5 to 6, 20 items per day and it becomes very difficult for that person to do that, and that person suffers. Whatever policies a company is thinking of, it should be keeping in mind that other people would be affected by some policies. If the company is not giving any kind of dividend to the shareholders, the shareholders would be affected. Before taking this kind of decision a company should be thinking twice regarding its decision, as without the stakeholders, the company is at a loss.

- To set up an institutional structure in the form of various authorities, bodies, and panels (NCLT and NCLAT) - The companies act decided that they should be having different structures for different bodies and for different work. For example, for auditors, there should be a different room to take care of the audit. For directors, there should be a different board to take care of everything. If a manager is there, then there should be different legal panel. So, overall different departments to take care of different kinds of work.
- To enforce stricter action against fraud and gross non-compliance with company law provisions - Any kind of fraud happening anywhere the company can ensure strict action so that no one is doing any kind of fraud with the company.

❖ THE COMPANIES ACT 2013 (AMENDED)

ONE PERSON COMPANY

- *One person company is a hybrid of sole – proprietor and company form business and has been provided with concessional/relaxed requirements under the act.*
- *One person company - one director; one shareholder*

Proprietor ship which was there as a proprietorship firm but now it is given the name of one person company. A single person can be the owner of the company. He or she becomes a director of the company and one shareholder can be there. Previously, there was no company name. Now, they have given the name of the company to the proprietorship.

ASSOCIATE COMPANY

- *Associate company in relation to another company means a company in which that other company has a significant influence, but which is not a subsidiary and joint-venture company.*
- *Significant influence means control of at least 20 percent of the total share capital, of a business decision under an agreement.*

Subsidiary and joint venture company is different from an associate company. Associate company means that two companies become associates of each other and one of the companies has got a significant influence on the other company in terms of 20% of total share capital, and can also take part in their business decisions under an agreement.

DORMANT COMPANY SECTION - 455

– Where a company is formed and registered under the new law for the future project to hold an asset of intellectual property.
– An inactive company is one that has not been carrying on any business operation, or has not made any significant accounting transaction, or has not filed financial statements and annual returns for the last two financial years.

For example, if I have an FNCC company, and I am planning to go for an automobile company in the future then my automobile company would be a dormant company.

Inactive company means a company that is in the business but is not able to do any kind of significant transaction and has not filed financial statements for the last two financial years. It is not able to do well. It is more or less like a sick company, which has had no transactions for the last two years and it is not able to do good business, or not able to do well.

WOMEN DIRECTOR

– Every listed company shall appoint at least one woman director.
– Every other public company having paid-up share capital of Rs. 100 crores or more and a turnover of Rs. 300 crore or more as on the last date of latest audited financial statements shall also appoint at least one woman director.

Every listed company shall appoint at least one woman director, which was not listed in the Companies Act of 1956. This is an important clause that has been given in the Companies Act of 2013. In case a public company has a paid-up share capital of Rs.100 crores or more and the turnover should be Rs. 300 crores or more, then only they can have a woman director, which is mandatory.

ROTATION OF AUDITORS

- *Mandatory rotation of auditors for the listed and other specific class of companies*
- *Individual auditor to be rotated after a term of five consecutive years*
- *Audit firm to be rotated after two terms of five consecutive years*

An auditor is a person who would be giving you the actual picture of the company. Previously, one signal auditor could go on auditing different companies for many years. But, nowadays, it has been made mandatory by the Companies Act of 2013 that the auditor should be rotated. An auditor can audit a company for five years. After that, the auditor should be going to some other company and should leave this company. The audit firm can go on audit for a particular company after two terms of five consecutive years means that it can be there for two terms.

SUMMARY

Appointment or reappointment of an auditor:

1. Individual as an auditor – More than five consecutive years.
2. Audit firm – More than 10 consecutive years.

VIGIL (WHISTLEBLOWER) MECHANISM

- Vigil (whistleblower) mechanism provides a channel to the employees and directors to report to the management concerned about unethical behavior, actual or suspected fraud or violation of the code of conduct or policy.

If some people are getting harassed by the company, director, or employee, in terms of unethical behaviour, actual or suspected fraud, then they have every right to speak up and also report the same to the management, so that the management can take strict action against these kinds of people.

SECRETARIAL AUDIT

- *The secretarial audit is a process to check compliances made by the company and corporate law and other laws, rules, regulation, procedure etc. It is a mechanism to monitor compliance within the requirements of stated laws and processes.*

A secretarial audit is the check-in process to see if the company is following proper rules and regulations of the corporate law whichever is there in the Companies Act of 2013 and 1956, whether they are following the same or not. If not, then strict actions are taken. It is a kind of checkpoint to see whether these people are following the rules and the regulations or not.

FAST TRACK MERGER

- *The act simplified the procedure of merger and amalgamation of a certain class of companies, such as holding and subsidiary and small companies.*

The merger means when two companies come together, they both are different companies before the merger and the merger results in an amalgamation of two companies. Provision is between certain companies... like small companies – holdings, subsidiaries, and small companies. Do you know what the meaning of a holding is? A Holding means a company who is having the maximum share in another company. It means companies come together and one company takes over the other company, and if it is having a stake, a share of 51%, that company becomes the holding company, and the other one becomes a subsidiary company. The holding company has a lot of say regarding the recruitment decision-related policies. The subsidiary company has to listen to every decision made by the holding company. The small company also comes in this preview in fast track merger.

KEY MANAGERIAL PERSON (KMP)

Companies Act 1956	Companies Act 2013
No provision except in AS-18 related party disclosures.	Includes:
	CEO OR MD OR MANAGER
	COMPANY Secretary.
	WTD;
	CFO; and
	Such other officer as may be prescribed

(SECTION 51)

CEO	-	Chief executive officer
MD	-	Managerial director
WTD	-	Whole-time director

Companies Act 2013 has given importance to all the key managerial people – these are the people who would be seeing if the company can work or not.

BOARD COMMITTEE

Following committees of the board are mandatory for listed and prescribed class of companies:

- Audit committee
- Stakeholders relationship committee
- Nomination and remuneration committee
- Corporate social responsibility committee
- Social and responsibilities committee

Nowadays, companies have to go for such corporate social responsibilities because it is for the society, where, every year, they have to give 10% of their income for the society and many companies are going for that. Many companies are investing 10% of their total income in another turnover every year so that it is beneficial for the society as well as for the people in the society. It has now become a mandatory thing that every company has to go for it.

THE COMPANIES (AMENDMENT ACT) 2015

- Minimum capital requirement – Private or public company can be incorporated without the need of minimum paid-up share capital. Previously, if it is a private or public company, it had to be incorporated with a minimum paid-up share capital depending upon the strength of the company. But now, you can be a private or a public company depending without the need for minimum share capital.
- Common seal – The requirement of having a common seal has been made optional, which was previously mandatory.
- Declaration of dividend - No company shall declare dividend unless carried over past losses and depreciation in the previous year or years are set off against the profit of the company for the current year.

INDIAN CASE LAWS

1. **Soloman v. Soloman & Co. Ltd. (1895 - 99) Facts** - Soloman sold his business to a company named Soloman & Company Ltd., which he formed. Soloman took 20,000 shares. The price paid by the company to Soloman was 30,000, but instead of paying him in cash, the company gave him 20,000 fully paid shares of Re. 1 each and Rs. 10,000 in debentures. The company wound up and the assets of the company amounted to Rs. 6,000 only. Debts amounted to 10,000 due to Soloman and secured by debentures and a further Rs. 7,000 due to unsecured creditors. The unsecured creditors claimed that as Soloman & Co. Ltd., was really the same person as Soloman, he could not owe money to himself and that they should be paid their 7,000 first. Judgment - 1. A Company is a "legal person" or "legal entity" separate from and capable of surviving beyond the lives of its members. 2. The company is not, by law, the agent of the subscribers or trustee for them. 3. Soloman was entitled to 6,000, as the company was an entirely separate person from Soloman. 4. The unsecured creditors got nothing.

2. **Lee v. Lee's Farming Co. Ltd. (1960) Facts** - Lee incorporated a company of which he became the managing director. In that capacity, he appointed himself as a pilot of the company. While on the business of the company, he was lost in a flying accident. His widow claimed compensation for personal injuries to her husband while in the course of his employment. It was argued that no compensation was due because Lee and lee's Air Farming Ltd. were the same person. Judgment - 1. Lee was separate person from the company he formed and compensation was payable. 2. His widow recovered compensation under the Workmen's Compensation Act. 3. A member of a company can contract with a company of which he is a shareholder. 4. The directors are not precluded from being an employee of the company for the purpose of workmen's compensation legislation.

3. **Macaura v. Northern Assurance Co. Ltd. (1925) Facts** - Macaura was the holder of nearly all the shares except one of a timber company. He was also a substantial creditor of the company. He insured the company's timber in his own name. The timber was destroyed by fire and Macaura claimed the loss from the insurance

company. Judgment - 1. The Insurance Company was not held liable to him. 2. A shareholder cannot insure the company's property in his own name even if he is the owner of all or most of the company's shares.

4. **Gol ford Motor Co. v. Home (1933) Facts** - Home was appointed as a managing director of the plaintiff company on the condition that "he shall not at any time while he shall hold the office of a managing director or afterwards, solicit or entice away the customers of the company." His employment was determined under an agreement. Shortly afterwards, he opened a business in the name of a company that solicited the plaintiffs customers. Judgment - It was held that the company was a mere cloak or show for the purpose of enabling the defendant to commit a breach of his covenant against solicitation. The court will refuse to uphold the separate existence of the company where it is formed for a fraudulent purpose or to avoid legal obligations.

4. **Daimler Co. Ltd. v. Continental Tyre & Rubber Co. Ltd. (1916) Facts** - In a company incorporated in England for the purpose of selling tyres manufactured in Germany by a German Company, all the shares except one was held by the German subjects residing in Germany. The remaining one was held by a British. Thus, the real control of the English Company was in German hands. Question arose whether the company had become an enemy company due to war and should be barred from maintaining any action. Judgment - 1. A Company incorporated in the United Kingdom is a legal entity, a creation of law with the status and capacity which the law confers. 2. It is not a natural person with mind or conscience. It can neither be loyal nor disloyal. It can be neither friend nor enemy. But, it can assume enemy character when persons in defacto control of its affairs are residents in any enemy country, or whenever resident, are acting under the control of enemies. 3. It held that company was an enemy company for the purpose of trading, and therefore, it was barred from maintaining the action.

Workmen employed in associated rubber industries Facts - A subsidiary company was formed wholly by the holding company with no assets of its own except those transferred to it by the holding company, with no business or income of its own except receiving dividend from shares transferred to it by the holding company. Judgment Court held that the company was formed as a devise to reduce the profits of the holding company, and thereby, reduce the bonus to workmen.

F. G. Films Ltd. Case Facts - An American company produced a film in India, which was actually in the name of British company, wherein 90% of the share capital was held by the chairman of the American company that financed the production of the film. Judgment - The contention of the sensor board of films refusing to register the film on the ground that British company has acted merely as an agent of British company was correct. COI is conclusive evidence that all the requirements have been complied with.

Moosa Goola Arif v. Ibrahim Goola Arif Facts - Company registered on the basis of MOA & AOA signed by two persons and a guardian on behalf of five minor members. Guardian signed separately for each of five members. The ROC, however, registered the company and issued under his hand a certificate of incorporation. Petition Plaintiff contended that COI should be declared as void. Judgment - The court held the certificate to be conclusive for all purposes.

Jubilee Cotton Mills Ltd. Facts - The ROC issued a COI on Jan 8th but dated it Jan 6th, which was the date on which he received application. On Jan 6th, the company made an allotment of shares to Lewis. Judgment Court held that the certificate was conclusive evidence of incorporation on Jan 6th and that the allotment was not void on the ground that it was made before the company was incorporated. Decided case on objects clause of MOA.

Crowns Bank Case Facts - A company's objects clause enabled it to act as a bank and further to invest in securities and to underwrite issue of securities. The company abandoned its banking business and confined itself to investment activities. Judgment Court held that the company was not entitled to do this.

The Consumer Protection Act, 1986

❖ WHO IS A CONSUMER?

- A consumer refers to any individual or household that uses goods and services generated within the economy - For example, suppose you are boarding Air India flight to Bangalore. So, you are paying for the ticket before you are boarding the flight, so you become the consumer because you are the one who would be getting to know the service. You are the one who is using the service, so then you become the consumer.

- Consumer is defined as someone who acquires goods or services for direct use or ownership rather than for resale or use in production for manufacturing – Basically, if you're into production and manufacturing, then you're not the consumer. Consumer means the one who is acquiring the goods, that is, who is purchasing the goods for some amount of the money and also using that service and becomes the owner of the good.

❖ WHY WE NEED TO PROTECT THE CONSUMER?

– Previously when this consumer act was not there what used to happen to a consumers Health was victimise the sellers used to take advantage of customer they used to charge for more price than the price should be there for a particular product then if the consumer used to ask for to lessen the price the seller used to never take it they would never allow the price to be reduced and there used to be certain kind of defect in the goods and if The consumer or the buyer wanted to replace the goods the seller didn't allow and then if you're going to a shop also the buyer wants to see the goods the seller would never allow the same it was a kind of victimisation of the consumer which led to this act of consumer protection act 1986 where consumer protected and consumer have every right to select to choose those particular goods and services which that person is interested and also satisfied if they are purchasing the goods so that is why this consumer Protection act came.

Reasons for enacting the act

- Collective Bargaining
  Sellers lobby; keeping price high- Previously, the sellers used to come together and they used to set the price, leading to a kind of monopoly. Consumers have the right to go and bargain for the same.
- Multiple laws
  Indian Contract Act; Sale of Goods Act; Essential Commodities Act Indian contract act was their sale of goods of the act was their essential commodity act all these things the consumer had to go through to take a seller or to sue the seller for certain kind of problem the seller must have done to the consumer now there is one law called consumer protection act anything happens to the consumer and he is now sure that which act to approach and go to the court and get whatever is needed.
- Hurdles in litigation
  Going to regular court; expensive and time-consuming
  A certain kind of litigation means if there is certain kind of people or not understanding each other there is certain kind of differences taking a person to court becomes a very big problem there are so many cases Who is going to hear you but in case of protection act what happened this since the Case in the consumer protection act so it is handled by a separate board of people legally and the process is much less time consuming and is also cheaper than the court, because if you're going to court you have to give money to the lawyer and the time goes on extending that is why previously buyers used to never get the sellers for any kind of mistake but nowadays because of the consumer protection act sellers can be taken to the court and the process is very simple and is not time-consuming.

- Remedy
  Punishment in the form of punitive and deterrent measure
  So, this is more or less like a remedy to the consumer who is being victimized.

CONCEPT OF CONSUMER PROTECTION

- Consumer protection means safeguarding the interest and rights of consumers. In other words, it refers to the measures adopted for the protection of consumer from unscrupulous and unethical malpractices by a company and to provide them speedy redressal of their grievances. Consumer protection aims in protecting the rights and interest of the consumer. Malpractices by the sellers and business are taken care of by the Consumer Protection Act.

CONSUMER PROTECTION ACT

- The Consumer Protection Act of 1986 was enacted for better protection of the interests of consumers.
- The provision of the act came into force with effect from 15 April 1987.
- Consumer Protection Act imposes strict liability on a manufacturer in case of supply of defective goods by him and a service provided in case of deficiency in rendering of its services.

HISTORY OF THE CONSUMER PROTECTION ACT

- The act was passed in Lok Sabha on 9 December 1986, Rajya Sabha passed it on 10 December 1986, was assented by the President of India on 24 December 1986, and was published in the Gazette of India on 26 December 1986. Finally, it came into effect from 1 July 1987.

FEATURES OF THE CONSUMER PROTECTION ACT

- It applies to all goods services and unfair trade practices unless specially exempted by the Central government.
- It covers all the sectors whether private, public, or co-operative.
- It provides for the establishment of consumer protection councils at the central, state, and district levels to promote and protect the rights of consumers and three-tier quasi-judicial machinery to deal with consumer grievances and disputes.

OBJECTIVES

- To protect the consumer from abuse by the seller or the service provider. If there are any kind of malpractices or problems regarding the quality, quantity, pricing, etc., or if the seller is not behaving properly with the consumer, then the consumer is protected in the Consumer Protection Act.
- To provide a venue where a consumer can go for their grievance redressal.
- To ensure the better quality of living by improving the quality of consumer products and services.

IMPORTANCE OF CONSUMER PROTECTION ACT

Importance from consumer's point of view:

1. **Unorganized consumer** - In developing countries like India, consumers are not organized. There are very few consumer organizations that are working to protect the interest of consumers. Consumer protection provides power and rights to these organizations as these organizations can file a case on behalf of the customer. The Consumer Protection Act protects the right of the consumers from unnecessary harassment of the seller and these organizations fight on behalf of the consumer.

2. **Consumer ignorance** - I just want to mention why the consumer act is better than going to a court is for regarding goods and services is here The person is harassed and it is not necessary to be going to the court and complaining any organisation dealing with this rights can go ahead and file a case on behalf of the consumer. This protection spread awareness so that consumer can know about the various redressal agencies most of the consumer doesn't know the rights what are rights they should be getting through protecting consumer act, we are educating these kind of consumers and giving them a fair idea regarding the redressal agencies to which the consumer should be approaching in case of any problem.

3. **Widespread exploitation of consumers** - Consumers are exploited when businessmen use various unfair trade practices to cheatto increase their profits. Consumer protection provides safeguards to consumers from such exploitation.

Importance from the consumer point of view

- **Businessmen use society's resources** - They earn profit by supplying goods and services to the members of society. They must use their resources for the benefit of consumers. Many businessmen are focused on only profit but through the Customer Protection Act, businessmen are also educated and are responsible to carry out their businesses in a way that would be beneficial for the society.
- **Social responsibilities** - A businessman has social obligations towards customers. It is the responsibility of the businessmen to provide quality goods at reasonable prices. Consumer protection guides businessmen to provide social responsibilities.
- **Government intervention** - If businessmen want to avoid the intervention of the government, then they should not indulge in unfair trade practices. Businessmen should voluntarily be involved in the activities that protect the interest of consumers.
- **The consumer is the purpose of business** - The basic purpose of the business is to create more and more consumers and retain them and businessmen can create more customers only by satisfying the customers and protecting the interest of consumers. The main purpose of business is to earn a profit and the second most important purpose is to attract more customers. If the businessmen are involved in fair trade practices, it would definitely attract more customers.

SCOPE OF THE CONSUMER PROTECTION ACT

- Requirements to performance, composition, content, design, construction, finishing, packaging of consumer products – All products and services comes under the preview of the consumer protection act. Performance of the company, composition of the product, content, design, contents of the packaging, etc., come under the scope of the Consumer Protection Act. The Consumer Protection Act ensures best quality, price, content, and design.
- Requirements as to kind, class, grade, dimensions, weights, material - Consumer Protection Act compels the sellers to ensure good quality of the raw material and consistent weight of the packaged material.

- Requirements as to the methods of sampling, tests, and codes used to check the quality of the products - Consumer Protection Act also takes care of how the sampling is done, which testing approaches are used, which tools are used, how is the quality is all checked, whether quality check is stringent, etc.
- Requirements as to precautions in storage transporting and packaging - Consumer Protection Act also takes care of how the goods are sampled, packaged, stored, and transported.
- Requirements that a consumer product be marked with or accompanied by clear and adequate, safety warnings or instructions

NEEDS OF THE CONSUMER PROTECTION ACT

The necessity of adopting measures to protect the interest of consumers arises mainly due to the helpless position of consumers.

- **Social responsibility**- it is the moral responsibility of the business to serve the interest of consumers. Keeping in line with this principle, it is the duty of producers and traders to provide the right quality and quantity of goods at a fair price to the consumers: it is the social responsibility of the business to provide goods and services at the right quality and should be consumer-friendly and the pricing factor should be good enough.
- **Increasing awareness**- The consumers are becoming more mature and conscious of their rights against the malpractices by the business. There are many consumer organisations and associations that are making an effort to build consumer awareness: increasing awareness regarding the product, the rights, malpractices of the seller. Malpractices that the seller is doing to the consumer and what are the rights the consumer should be having are increasing awareness.
- **Consumer satisfaction**- father of the nation Mahatma Gandhi had once given a call to manufacturers and traders to *"treat your consumers as God"*. Consumer satisfaction is the key to success in business. Hence, businessmen should take every step to serve the interest of consumers by providing them quality goods and services at a reasonable price: when good quality is given fair price, services are given excellent then the consumer satisfaction

increases. Mahatma Gandhi said treat your consumers like God, We are treating a consumer as God then One consumer can bring another hundred consumers. This method, all the companies are following nowadays, you should be taking care of the consumer. The consumer should be coming first whatever the consumer wants in terms of pricing. You should be making sure that we are trying to give them whatever they are asking for at the same time there should be a quality product and the pricing factor should be reasonable. Due to globalisation and liberalisation what happened is that the market is open and the consumer can get anything from anywhere, if you are not giving quality products then you cannot sustain in the business. Consumers will get its product but the business cannot sustain and many consumers will go away.

- **Survival and growth of the business-** The business has to serve consumer interest for its survival and growth. On account of globalisation and increased competition, any business organisation which indulges in malpractices or fails to provide improved services to their ultimate consumer shall find it difficult to continue: Because of globalisation market is open and any good can go anywhere and any good and services can come anywhere and we don't need to be feeling proud that you know we are the only one who is providing goods and services if it is an automobile industry or a food or chocolate or baking or clothes anything and everything can go anywhere, in order to survive and maintain the position these kinds of unpredicted environment and in terms of competitors quality product and reasonable price has to be the main Motto of the business.

- **Principle of trusteeship-** resources are supplied by the society. They are merely the trustees of the resources and, therefore, they should use such resources effectively for the benefit of the society, which includes the consumers: The society merely other trustees of the resources and therefore They should use such resources effectively for the benefit of the society. Business, company anything that you are starting is for the society and it belongs to the society and it should be society friendly so whatever goods and services we are providing we are acting on the behalf of the society and the available resources should be effectively used and benefit for the society and the consumer.

❖ RIGHTS OF THE CONSUMER

1. Right to safety - To be protected against marketing of goods or the provision of services that are hazardous to health and life: if we are purchasing certain goods and services which are dangerous but we need it. For example, a gas cylinder that is dangerous in itself because if it burst it would be killing people, the building is also blown because of the gas cylinder bursting but we have to use that but the safety mention and precaution have to be taken but being consumer we Hardly know regarding the safety measure so the product and the services which are hazardous to health and nature so it is the right of the consumer to know regarding the safety measures of the product they are using and this education should be provided by the seller.

2. Right to information - To be protected against dishonest or misleading advertising or labeling and the right to be given the facts and information needed to make an informed choice: any kind of advertise or dishonesty is going on this kind of information regarding the ads and dishonesty of the seller in terms of pricing The consumer has every right to ask for the information. When you are using a telephone, Electricity you are paying the electricity bill and telephone bill you are paying the property tax previously what you paid why you paid what is the actual amount you should be paying if being the consumer you go and ask the property tax department or the telephone department or the electricity department they used to never tell but now due to the consumer protection act each Service Provider And the seller is bound with the law to give the consumer right information regarding the questions of a particular service the consumer is asking. For example, i am paying the monthly electricity bill of Rs.2000 if today I go and ask the electricity office why I am paying so much so they are bound to show you why you are paying, cannot say that we are not supposed to show you, and this is the kind of right to information which every consumer should be knowing regarding the same and should be utilising that right to gather information before you make payment.

3. Right to choice - To choose products at a competitive price with the assurance of satisfactory quality: competitive market every

consumer has the right to select goods and services from a variety of goods and services of the same quality and same pricing factor.

4. Right to representation: To express consumer interest in the making and execution of government policies. Whenever the government is making a policy regarding the consumer, the consumer has every right to suggest the policies of the government. For example, being a faculty if I feel the government should be giving a bonus during Diwali without fail to the faculty and I can request the government to make this policy sometimes we do get a bonus but sometimes we don't. If we go and approach the government if the government thinks it is necessary then the government will improve that.

5. Right to seek redress: To be compensated for misrepresentation, shoddy goods or unsatisfactory services: if the quality of the goods is not good And if you are a consumer and you had to purchase a steel water bottle but instead of steel one you are given a plastic bottle you wanted steel but you got plastic and this is the misrepresentation, the of the plastic bottle is not good The pricing factor is high and for this kind of things you can get compensation for the bad quality products.

6. Right to consumer education: To acquire the knowledge and skills necessary to be an informed customer: you can acquire knowledge regarding the goods and services so that consumer education is mandatory and you have the right to get that no one will stop you from getting that education regarding the goods and services.

7. Right to basic needs: To guarantee survival, adequate food, clothing, shelter, healthcare, education, and sanitation- the consumer has got the right to basic needs in terms of food, clothing, healthcare, education, sanitation, survival all these things are the basic rights, and consumer protection also helps you in doing that.

8. Right to health environment: To live and work in an environment which is neither threatening nor dangerous and which permits a life of dignity and well-being- being a consumer being the citizen of India has the right to a healthy environment wherever you are staying you should get a healthy environment wherever you are working you should be getting a healthy environment it is the basic right of the citizen of India and consumer protection also tries to help you in that.

❖ CONSUMER RESPONSIBILITY

1. Consumers must exercise their right - The consumer must select the product according to his preference. He must file a complaint if he is not satisfied with the quality of the product: all the rights which I have to explain to you like the right to safety, right to help, right to redress, all these rights are of the rights of a citizen of India and the consumer should exercise these rights.

2. Consumers must be cautious - The consumer should not blindly believe the words of the seller. He must insist on getting full information on quality, quantity, utility price, etc.: whatever the seller is saying it is not necessary that he is telling you the facts he might have some other ulterior motive maybe for example I have gone to the market and I met my friend who is a housing agent and she tells me I have a very good property it's a one-bedroom flat if you want you can start with your business and you just have to pay me Rs. 50 lakhs and it's very very good property the price will be going high henceforth, many people are waiting in the line to take that offer so I came to know that my friend is telling me the truth so I should be finding out the facts and figures before I make a choice this is the responsibility of the consumer the only seller is not the one who should be giving you the fact you being the consumer you have got every right and responsibility to find out of fact regarding any goods and services.

3. Consumers must be quality conscious - Consumers themselves can stop compromising the quality of the product. While purchasing the goods or services, consumers must look for quality marks such as ISI mark, Agmark, ISO mark, Wool mark etc.: you should be knowing the exact quality you should be quality conscious when you're purchasing any goods and services you should be saying the mark like the ISI mark, Agmark, ISO, wool mark all these marks give you a guarantee that this product I have gone through a stringent quality check and they are of good quality so being a consumer you should be well educated regarding, seeing the quality in case of Tetra pack juice, milk You should be saying whether that it is saying tetra pack or not, is it properly sealed or not whether the bottle is puffed or not. The seller gives you any kind of goods assuming the buyer should be knowing what you should be looking at before buying or purchasing a particular product.

4. Consumers must insist on cash memo - To file a complaint, the consumer needs evidence of purchase, and the cash memo is the evidence or proof that the consumer has paid for the good or service: being a consumer you should be insisting on getting a cash memo. Students, you must know why there is a need for a cash memo. For getting a cash memo and if a certain thing goes wrong with the goods you can go and exchange or take the seller to the court but without the cash memo sometimes the seller also cannot understand whether you are taking the goods or services. A cash memo is a proof that selling has been done and the seller cannot make black money out of that because without a cash memo it's proof The quantity of goods has been sold without a cash memo a seller can always put forward a different quantity different number to evade the tapping of tax. always insist on getting a cash memo.

5. Consumers must file complaints about the redressal of genuine grievances - The consumer must file a complaint even for a small loss. This awareness among the consumer will make the seller more conscious to supply quality product: whenever there is a problem in quality whether it is for one product or two product, or 1000 products doesn't mean that the product is small or the purchase a small but if you are getting a bad product means we should be going ahead with the complaint. If you are always complaining then what happens is the seller would try to give you goods and services which are of good quality.

THREE-TIER CONSUMER GRIEVANCES MACHINERY UNDER THE CONSUMER PROTECTION ACT, 1986, AND THEIR JURISDICTION

Forum means a group or a body that consist of members and these members are the ones who have got and who are experienced in Consumer Protection Act and they would be listening to the case and give solutions or advice for the same.

1. District Forum - It consists of a president and two other members. The president can be a retired or working Judge of the district court. They were appointed by the State Government in 1986, and had jurisdiction to entertain complaints where the value of goods and services did not exceed the limit of

Rs. 5 lakh which is now raised to Rs. 20 lakh. The agency sends the goods for testing in the lab. If the aggrieved party is not satisfied by the judgment of the district forum, then they can file an appeal in state commission within 30 days by depositing Rs. 25000 or 50% of the penalty amount, whichever is less: there are three members out of which one is the President and other two members would be helping the President. Since this is regarding any kind of law consumer protection act law is involved in so that the person who is the President should be a judge who knows the law in and out and the president can be retired or a working judge who is working in district court. The district-level person who would be heading the district forum the President should be appointed by the state government. Any cases regarding rent, salary, seller not providing quality goods and services all these cases if it is within rs20 lakh then this case would be taken to the district forum. Suppose a case has come to the court regarding a car and it is worth Rs. 20 lakh means the value of the car is Rs. 20 lakh and the car was provided to the person and the car has affected the consumer can go to the court and wants to fight for the same in The district forum. Once a complaint is filed the process is- You're not happy you need to go to the office of the district forum there you need to file a case, Fill the form giving every detail and mentioning the amount and mentioning the type of case you are fighting for and The party's name like who is fighting against who (The buyer's name and the seller's name) and it would be deposited there and the price that you have to pay the registration charges is very less it might be 1000rs, maybe 500rs. Once the cases file comes to the district forum within 30 days the district forum would be sending a notice to both the parties and would be asking you to be present in front of the court. You are present there would be a hearing, if one party is present and another one is not present doesn't mean that the court cannot make the decision they can make the decision. Once the case is filed and it comes in front of the district forum, parties are present, goods would be sent to a separate place for checking regarding whether the complaint is correct or not and then after that, the decision would be taken. During this period, The decision has been taken that the seller should be providing another fresh car to the buyer because the car was not of good quality but if the seller is not happy the seller can appeal to the state commission which is the higher of District Forum And should be done within 30 days and have to deposit Rs.25,000 or 50% of penalty amount and then can take this case to the state commission and then the case would go to state commission and the state forum will take care of that.

2. State Forum - It consists of a president and two other members. The President must be a retired or working judge of the High Court. They all were appointed by the State Government in 1986, and had jurisdiction to entertain complaints when the value of goods and services exceeded the limit of Rs. 5 lakh, which is now raised to Rs.1 crore. The state commission sent the goods for testing in a lab if required. If the upset party is not satisfied with the judgment then they can file an appeal in national commission within 30 days by depositing Rs. 3500 or 50% of the penalty amount, whichever is less

3. National Forum - It consists of a president and four members one of whom shall be women. They were appointed by the Central Government in 1986, and had jurisdiction to entertain complaints where the value of goods or services exceeds the limit of Rs. 20 lakh, which is now raised to Rs.1 crore. If the aggrieved party is not satisfied with the judgment, then they can file a complaint in Supreme Court within 30 days.: The number of members consists of the president and also out of four other members one of them should be a woman. The members are appointed by the central government. Previously it shouldn't be exceeding Rs.20 lakh but now if the case exceeds Rs.1 Crore then the case would be in front of the national forum. In this case, the same process as the notice would be sent to the person and the person should be present and the same things happened in the 30 days, The suggestion and judgement are given. If the person is not happy with the judgement The party can file a complaint in the Supreme Court which is the highest court in the country within 30 days of the judgement.

Indian Case Laws

1. Corporate Bodies can be sued under the Consumer Protection Act (CPA)

Karnataka Power Transmission Corporation (KPTC) v Ashok Iron Works Private Limited

How the factual matter of the case arose

The case dates back to the last century, when in 1991, Ashok Iron Works, a private company that manufactures iron applied for obtaining electricity from the state's power generation company – the Karnataka Power Transmission Corporation (hereinafter KTPC) for commencing its iron production. However, despite paying charges and obtaining confirmation for the supply of 1500 KVA energy in February 1991, the actual supply did not begin until ten months later, in November 1991. This delay led to incurring of losses by the private company. This prompted a complaint to the Belgaum Consumer Dispute Forum and later Karnataka High Court, under the Consumer Protection Act 1986 for the delay in supply of electricity.

Legal Arguments by KPTC

- **Commercial supply not covered under the act** – The major argument relied on by the power generation company KTPC was that the complaint was not maintainable since the Consumer Protection Act 1986 excludes commercial supply of goods. The applicant company was engaged in manufacturing of iron, and hence, intended to use the electricity for commercial consumption, which is excluded under the act.
- **A private company is not a consumer** – The other argument by KTPC was that the complaint is not maintainable because the complainant is not a 'person' under Section 2(1)(m) of the Act, 1986. This section defines who can be included as a consumer, and because it didn't contain "a company incorporated under Companies Act" – the applicant company is not a consumer.

Supreme Court Ruling in the case

- "**Includes – is an inclusive definition**" – Supreme Court relied on the ruling in Dilworth v. Commissioner of Stamps, where Lord Watson said that the word "include" is very generally used in interpretation clauses in order to enlarge the meaning of words or phrases occurring in the body of the statute; It may be equivalent to "mean and include". The court also relied on other acts such as the General Clauses Act that includes a private company within the purview of the definition of a "person". Hence, Ashok Iron Works Private Company was held to be a person.

- **Supply doesn't mean sale** – The Supreme Court relied on another case – Southern Petrochemical Industries, where it was held that supply is not equivalent to a sale. Therefore, the supply of electricity by the KPTC to a consumer would be covered under Section 2(1)(o) being 'service' and if the supply of electrical energy to a consumer is not provided in time as is agreed upon, then under Section (2)(1)(g), there may be a case for deficiency in service. Thus, the clause stating "supply" of goods for commercial purpose would not apply.

Thus, the court allowed the complaint on the two grounds that the applicant – Ashok Iron Works Private Limited, can sue as a person, and that supply of electricity, if found deficient can be a fit ground for claiming compensation. The Supreme Court sent the case back to District Forum for retrial on these grounds.

2. Medical services fall within the scope of the Consumer Protection Act (CPA)

Indian Medical Association v V.P. Shantha and others

The factual background of the case

The cases arise as a writ petition was filed by the Indian Medical Association seeking the Supreme Court to declare that the Consumer Protection Act (hereinafter "Act") doesn't apply to the medical profession.

Questions involved in the case –

1. Whether a medical practitioner can be regarded as rendering 'service' under the Consumer Protection Act, 1986?
2. If a medical service is rendered for free, will it be covered under the Act?

Arguments by Indian Medical Association –

Reliance on cases which state that such medical service by a government healthcare system is not a "service" – It has been held that the payment of direct or indirect taxes by the public does not constitute "constitute "consideration" paid for hiring the services rendered in the Government hospitals. It has also been held that contribution made by a Government employee in the Central Government Health Scheme or such other similar Scheme does not make him a "consumer" within the meaning of the Act.

Medical professionals are governed by a separate Code of Medical Ethics –

medical practitioners are governed by the provisions of the Indian Medical Council Act, 1956 and the Code of Medical Ethics made by the Medical Council of India. In the matter of professional liability, professions differ from other occupations for the reason that professions operate in spheres where success cannot be achieved in every case and very often success or failure depends upon factors beyond the professional man's control. Thus, since medical negligence can be dealt with by medical experts in their own jurisdiction, the Consumer Protection Act shouldn't apply.

There is no expert in medical science in the Consumer Courts –

The Consumer Protection mechanism provides that there must be experts in accountancy, law, economics, industry etc, but doesn't mention "medical science", therefore, the act intended to exclude medical profession from its ambit.

Reasoning of the final verdict – Medical professionals are covered under the Consumer Protection Act

- The medical practitioner and a patient carries within it a certain degree of mutual confidence and trust and, therefore, the services rendered by the medical practitioner can be regarded as services of personal nature, but it is not a contract (such as that between a buyer and seller) and hence, the exclusionary word "contract of personal service" would not apply. Thus, the receiver of the medical help is a consumer.

- The Court held that District, State and National Consumer Fora can summon experts in the field of medicine, examine evidence and generally act to protect the interest of consumers. Thus, there is no legal bar or deficiency in examining medical profession cases by consumer courts.

- Doctors and hospitals who render service without any charge whatsoever to every person availing the service would not fall within the ambit of "service".

- In a government hospital, where services are provided free of charge – the Consumer Protection act would not apply. If however, there are paying customers and well as service being provided for free to the poor, it shall be covered as a service under the act.

- If the insurance policy company pays for the treatment, it is on behalf of the customer, and hence, it will be covered under the Act.

3. Medical services should be rendered in accordance with the law

(Dr.) Arvind Shah vs Kamlaben Kushwaha

The factual background of the case

The case arises as a result of the death of complainant Kamlaben Kushwaha's 20-year-old son due to medical negligence by the petitioner doctor. The mother alleged that the medicines prescribed had no relation to the ailment – malaria, whereas the actual cause of death was said to be pulmonary oedema. The doctor alleged that he did not diagnose the deceased for malaria, as pathological tests are necessary to establish that conclusively, and no such report was made available to him. While the State Commission found the doctor guilty of medical negligence and awarded a compensation of 5 lac rupees with interest at 9%, the case was appealed by the doctor in the National Commission.

Basic question that the National Commission sought to answer –

– If and in what circumstance can a doctor be held guilty of medical negligence
– Appropriate compensation for a case of medical negligence

Reasoning and Decision of the National Commission – Failure to write a prescription gives rise to guilt under medical negligence

- The National Commission places reliance on the codes, ethics and practices of the medical professionals regulatory bodies and notes that every doctor while treating a patient, even outpatients, is under a responsibility to record basic health parameters such as blood pressure, temperature, pulse rate etc. This is provided under guidelines of the Medical Council of India as well.

- This record must also include brief summary of the symptoms, past illnesses. This is a primary duty of disclosure owed by the physician to the patient. Thus, failure to record such details constitutes medical negligence.

- The national commission also highlighted that the doctor is guilty for deficiency in service, due to his failure to record the patient's conditions and issue a medical prescription.

- The national commission also notes the denial of the doctor of having written the prescription served as evidence in the first place, but later accepts treating the patient. This conduct, in the language of the commission, does not reflect professional conduct worthy of a medical practitioner.

- Considering the socio-economic conditions in India, it is necessary to nurture doctor-patient relationships based on trust. Having a ready prescription also helps the patient consult another doctor, in case the initially prescribed line of curative medicine does not work. Similarly, it helps the medical practitioner establish that due care was taken according to prescribed standards in the field of medicine.

- The Commission noted that while the doctor is indisputably held guilty of medical negligence by not issuing a proper prescription, there is no material available on record to conclusively establish the negligence of the doctor with the cause of death. The medicines prescribed were not related to the established cause of death – pulmonary oedema. As a result, the amount of damages ordered by the State Commission were reduced by the National Commission to Rs. 2.5 lacs.

4. Medical services should be rendered in accordance with the law

Poonam Verma v. Ashwin Patel

The factual background of the case

In this case, the respondent doctor, Ashwin Patel, was trained in homoeopathy for four years and started his private practice. The appellant Poonam Verma, approached the Supreme court for compensation for her deceased husband, who was administered allopathic drugs for viral fever, and later typhoid fever by the homoeopathy doctor. Her husband passed away within eight days of the treatment.

Questions before the court

- Whether the appellant's husband is a consumer, who can avail damages for negligence in service?
- Whether the conduct of the respondent doctor is negligent, and there is a breach of duty of care?
- Determining the amount of damages to the deceased's wife

The reasoning of the court – Prescription of Allopathic drugs by a homoeopathy doctor amounts to negligence

– Deceased was a consumer of medical services – The Court relied on the reasoning in the classic case Indian Medical Association v. BP Shantha, and held that the Consumer Protection Act is applicable to medical professionals, including hospitals and private practitioners. Thus, the deceased was a "consumer" of the medical services.

- Determinants of negligent conduct by a doctor – The Court relied on a case to hold that a doctor, when consulted by a patient, owes him certain duties, namely, (a) a duty of care in deciding whether to undertake the case; (b) a duty of care in deciding what treatment to give; and (c) a duty of care in the administration of that treatment. A breach of any of these duties gives a cause of action for negligence to the patient.

- The National Consumer Forum held that the doctor was negligent in administering strong antibiotics to Pramod Verma initially for the treatment of Viral Fever and subsequently for Typhoid Fever without confirming the diagnosis by Blood Test or Urine Examination.

- **Registration to practice bars Homeopathy practitioners from Allopathy** – The Court placed reliance on provisions of the Indian Medical Council Act, 1956 and Maharashtra Medical Council Act, which state that a person cannot practice medicine in any state unless he possesses requisite qualification and is enrolled as a Medical Practitioner. The definition of medical practitioner does not include Ayurveda, Unani, Homeopathy, or Biochemic System of medicines.

- Further, the certificate of registration issued to such homeopathy practitioners states that it entitles them to practice in "Homeopathy Only". Thus, in accordance with established legal cases, rules of medical negligence, evidence in the form of prescriptions, the court reiterated the principle – *Sic Utere tuo ut alienum non loedas*– a person is held liable at law for the consequences of his negligence and held the doctor guilty of active negligence.

- **Compensation and Costs** – The Court decided a compensation of ₹ 3 lacs while considering the last drawn salary of the deceased and the number of dependents. Legal costs in the case were also reimbursed, and the Court directed the Medical Council of India to initiate appropriate proceedings against the action of the homeopathy doctor.

5. Educational institutions must refund any extra fee paid

Sehgal School of Competition v Dalbir Singh

The factual background of the case

In this landmark judgement concerning educational institutions that dates back to the year 2005, a student was asked to deposit lump sum fees of ₹18,734 as fees for coaching for medical entrance examinations for the next two years. This was deposited by the student in two complete instalments within the first six months of classes. However, the student realised later that the quality of the coaching institute was substandard, and therefore sought a refund for the remaining period, which was refused by the coaching institute.

Questions before the court

- Can a student seek a refund of fees paid to a coaching class for the remaining period of classes that are yet to be held?
- In case of a refusal to refund fee, can a claim for mental agony for pressing legal charges to be sought?

The reasoning of the Commission – Upholding student's right to be refunded for remaining classes

- **Clauses prohibiting refund of fees are unfair** – The Commission notes that educational institutes or coaching centre that charge a lump sum fees for the whole duration or should refund the fees if service is deficient in the quality of coaching etc. Any clause saying that fees once paid shall not be refunded is unconscionable and unfair and therefore not enforceable. This view was maintained by District and State Forums as well as in appeal by the National Commission.
- **Quashing respondent's argument on the reservation of seat** – The respondent coaching centre argued before the commission that the student had withdrawn voluntarily and, therefore, there exists no deficiency of service. They submitted records that showed good results of the institute and alleged that it was wrong to observe that their coaching was not up to the mark. To justify taking the entire fees of two years lump sump, it was stated that the conditions imposed by the coaching required non-transferability of the seat, and therefore no refund of the fee was possible under any circumstance. The court dismissed this argument and further quoted UGC guidelines that mention that even if a student has not attended even a single class, an amount of ₹1000 may be deducted and proportionate charges for hostel fees, etc, and the balance amount has to be refunded in its entirety. On blocking of the seat, the Commission advised that a reserve list of candidates may be maintained, and waitlisted candidates may be given the opportunity to apply for the seat.

- **Additional compensation** – In the order by State Consumer Forum, it was mentioned that not just the balance amount of fee, but also a higher compensation for legal costs as well as the pain that the student had to undertake, could be availed in such cases.

6. Sympathy should not influence compensation.

Nizam Institute of Medical Sciences v Prasanth S. Dhananka & Ors

Factual Background of the case

This consumer case arises out of a complaint of medical negligence where a 20-year-old engineering student was admitted to the Nizam Institute of Medical Sciences (NIMS) after he complained of chest pain. Several tests and X rays were done that revealed a tumor, however, it could not be ascertained whether the tumor was malignant or not, therefore, the patient was advised to undergo surgical removal of the same. After the surgery, the patient developed acute paraplegia with a complete loss of control over the lower limbs and some other related complications that led to urinary tract infections, bedsores, etc. The family of the patient held NIMS vicariously liable and the State of Andhra Pradesh statutorily liable (being a government hospital) for the negligence of the doctors concerned. Allegations were primarily leveled against a doctor, Dr. P.V. Satyanarayana for negligence before, during, and after the operation.

Arguments by the patient's family

- The father of the patient, since he was an engineering student, had pleaded with doctors to let him finish his education first before undergoing the operation as there was no emergency or immediate danger to life
- There were no pre-operative tests conducted
- Operating on the tumor that had neurological implications, there was no neurosurgeon present
- Consent was taken only for the tumor excision, however, the doctors removed not just the tumor but also surrounding ribs, tumor mass, and destroyed blood vessels that led to the condition of paraplegia (paralysis).

Supreme Court verdict

Consent by the patient – The Court trashed the argument by the hospital that since the patient was not conscious – implied consent to operate is assumed to avoid a second additional operation.

Negligence by a medical professional – The Court looked at various cases of medical negligence and held that as long as a doctor follows a practice acceptable to the medical profession, he cannot be held liable for negligence merely because a better alternative course or method of treatment was also available. This also includes a scenario where just because a more skilled doctor would not have chosen to follow a practice or procedure which the accused followed. The conduct needs to be judged based on the day of the operation, and not on trial. However, based on the evidence, in this case, gross negligence is made out in part of the doctors.

Compensation – "Balance between multiple parties while awarding compensation"

- While holding the doctors of NIMS liable, the court considers the following – compensation for i) present burden of medical expenses, ii) prospective burden of expenses, iii) loss of future earnings, iv) pain, suffering, loss of amenities and enjoyment of life and shortening of life expectancy and v) damages/compensation for father, mother, brother and maternal uncle of the patient who will now be wheelchair-bound for the rest of his life.
- Under multiple heads cumulatively, the court awarded damages worth ₹ 1 crore. However, the court also rejected some amounts claimed by the patient as unjust – such as ₹2 crores in a deposit form, to be withdrawn if a future medical development allows his condition to improve.
- The Supreme Court mentions that the award of compensation is a balance between many parties and interests, and sympathy for the patient must not come in way of awarding a fair and adequate compensation.

7. Discovery rule for medical negligence.

V.N.Shrikhande v. Anita Sena Fernandes

Factual Background of the case

This consumer case is decided by the Supreme Court of India on appeal from the orders of the National Consumer Disputes Redressal

Commission. The case involves the petitioner – Anita Sena, who was a nurse by profession. She underwent a stone removal surgery from her gall bladder but claimed that she continued to experience pain. For nine years, she had a gauge left in her abdomen by the surgeon who operated on her. This required a second surgery, and sufferance for many years – therefore, charges for negligence and compensation of Rs.50 lakhs was demanded by the petitioner.

The Essential question before the court:

Whether a petitioner can still approach the court for a deficiency in service after nine years and would it be barred by limitation?

Principles applied by the court:

When can a court accept the consumer case – The court lists that the matter must satisfy certain essentials. The petitioner should fall within the definition of 'consumer' as defined in the act and there must be a 'defect' or 'deficiency in service', and the complaint should have been filed within the prescribed period of limitation, only then it can direct that the complaint may be proceeded with.

The Discovery Rule of limitation – Limitation is a legal concept that puts a restriction on one's ability to approach the court after a period of delay. This has been introduced to keep a check on frivolous cases, and act as a disincentive for people have not been mindful of enforcing their rights. It also insulates defendants from defending very old claims. In medical cases, the court states the regular limitation period under the act must not apply. It refers to an American case, where a surgical sponge left behind in a patient's body was discovered after ten long and painful years. It held that where a foreign object has negligently been left in the patient's body, the limitation period will not begin to run until the patient could have reasonably discovered the malpractice.

Application of these to the present case – Rejecting the case on limitation and evidentiary grounds

The Court while highlighting the Discovery Rule categorically says that it is not applicable in the present case due to the below-mentioned reasons.

- Since the petitioner was a nurse working in a hospital, it was reasonably expected of her to have contacted the appellant and apprised him about her pain and agony and sought his advice. Neither did the petitioner contact her operating surgeon, nor any other doctor of the hospital she was employed in, in these nine years.
- During the discovery of gauze in her abdomen, the operating surgeon would have taken appropriate action for extracting the same without requiring the respondent to pay for it.
- Any person of ordinary prudence, who may have suffered pain and discomfort after surgery would have consulted the concerned surgeon or any other competent doctor and sought his advice but the petitioner-nurse did nothing except taking some pain killers. Thus, her long silence militates against the claim for compensation and hence, the complaint was dismissed.

8. Both parents and minor can claim for compensation under the Consumer Protection Act

Spring meadows hospital v. Harjot Ahluwalia

The Factual Background of the case

This landmark case arises out of a complaint against Spring Meadows Hospital, where the minor child – Harjot Ahluwalia was admitted by his parents. The child was diagnosed with typhoid and was injected a solution by a nurse after which his condition deteriorated. He was shifted to an auto respiratory ICU at AIIMS, where it was found that due to the injection administered, his brain got damaged and he would only live in a vegetative state for life. The parents of the child approached the court for a case of medical negligence and demanded compensation, on behalf of the child.

The Essential question before the court

- Can parents of the child, being the consumer, approach the court for availing compensation?
- Can the court award compensation to the parents for mental agony?

Arguments by the nurse and the hospital

- There was no medical negligence as the nurse was professionally qualified
- The solution of the injection administered was already being given in the oral form, hence the nurse did not do any test for injection.
- The nurse did not exercise independent decision, was only acting as per directions of the pediatrician.
  The hospital also argues that compensation cannot be claimed twice, by both the child and his parents.
- The hospital also sought refuge in the fact that after the child was declared vegetative by AIIMS, they volunteered to offer medical services without charge to the parents.

The court while making a case for gross negligence quashed these arguments and held the hospital responsible, for the medical college of the nurse had no affiliation, the injection overdose had led to the child's brain damage and there was no resident doctor present.

The reasoning of the court

- **Definition of consumer wide enough to cover the beneficiary:** When a young child is taken to a hospital by his/her parents and the child is treated by the doctor, the parents would come within the definition of the consumer having hired the services, and the young child would also become a "consumer" under the inclusive definition.
- **Compensation can justifiably be claimed by both parents as well as the child:** The court states that the child is justified in seeking compensation for the recurring medical expenses, equipment, etc, for the vegetative state he is rendered in. The parents are also, as beneficiaries entitled to seek compensation for the pain, acute mental agony and lifelong care that they'd be required to give to the child. As a result, the court upheld the compensation of Rs.17.5 lakhs awarded by the National Commission, which was also the highest amount ever awarded until the case was decided in 1997.

9. Imposition of penalty for frivolous consumer claims

Sapient Corporation Employees Provident Fund Trust v HDFC & Ors.

Factual Background of the case

This case arises as a result of a complaint of an alleged wrongful debit from a bank account. The complainant trust – Sapient Corporation Employees Provident Fund Trust maintained an account with the respondent HDFC Bank. The bank received instructions from the Employee Provident Fund Organisation (EPFO) that mentioned order of payment of ₹1.47 crores against the trust, and that no other payments from the trust's account be made until EPFO's liability is settled by the trust. The trust, however, issued an instruction to the bank not to debit any amount until further communication as they wanted to seek a stay order. However, in payment of the statutory due to EPFO, the bank, after giving due time, debit the account with an amount of ₹1.47 crores. The trust has challenged this as a deficiency in service and demanded the amount debited along with interest, damages, and legal expenses.

Essential Question before the National Commission

- Whether the bank committed any default by paying an amount payable as a statutory due decided by a judicial order?
- Can a bank be held guilty for deficiency in service for paying a rightful due?

Court – No deficiency in service for releasing an amount due on court order

No negligence or deficiency in service by HDFC Bank – The Commission dismissed the argument of the complainant that without any authority or mandate, debiting the amount due to EPFO of ₹1.4 crores is a deficiency in service. An action in compliance with the direction of a statutory authority such as EPFO cannot be said to be willful negligence or deficiency in service. The bank also informed the trust, as its customer, and gave them due time. Hence, the action is legal and proper.

Frivolous consumer cases are to be penalized – As per Section 26 of the Consumer Act, any consumer fora under the act has the power to dismiss a complaint made frivolously or one that is vexatious or unnecessary. Further, the court notices that the trust has already won the appeal from EPFO orders at the Appellate stage, whereby they would receive the entire amount with interest. Therefore, the case is without any merit and no remedy is made. For this false litigation, the court imposed a penalty of ₹25,000 on the complainant trust that would be paid to the HDFC Bank.

10. Compensation to the complainants for frivolous appeals.

Delhi Development Authority v D.C. Sharma

Factual Background of the case

In this case, DC Sharma (respondent), a government servant paid an initial amount for allotment of a plot of ₹ 5 lacs in 1997, by the Delhi Development Authority (hereinafter called DDA). He requested extra time for the instalment payment as he wished to avail loan facility from his office. Meanwhile, it was realised that the plot allotted to him through a draw of lots had already been allotted to another person, two years before the draw of lots. Due to this negligence of the DDA, the respondent approached the District forum, that dismissed the case. Subsequently, the state Consumer forum was approached that passed an order in favour of the respondent.

Order of the State Commission

The state commission in its order held the state responsible, for DDA is a government entity. It directed DDA to allot an alternative plot of the same kind or pay the escalated price of ₹30 lacs. The DDA relies on a frivolous argument that the case is liable to be dismissed since the respondent did not pay the instalment and therefore, his application stood rejected. Whereas, in reality, the allotted plot number has already been assigned to someone back in 1995 and the DDA took no steps to correct its own error in the allotment.

Order of the National Commission

Government departments such as DDA harassing genuine buyers in technical pleas – The National Commission criticised the conduct of DDA by stating that Governments and public authorities should not adopt the practice of relying upon technical pleas for the purpose of defeating legitimate claims of citizens and do what is fair and just to the citizens. It was well within the capacity of the DDA to remedy this error and take corrective action. On the contrary, it kept the condoning its own mistake by shifting the blame on the respondent.

Punitive damages for pursuing a frivolous case – While upholding the order of the State Commission, The national commission imposed costs of ₹2 lacs as well as punitive damages of ₹5 lac rupees on the DDA and asked them to recover the amount from erring officials who pursued the case for eighteen years. This long delay led to harassment of the respondent and filing of meritless appeals in various courts. This has not just added to litigation costs but also wasted time of several courts as well as the public ex-chequers money.

If you like to file a consumer complaint then click on the link below to get in touch with our team.

Intellectual Property Rights Act (India), 1972

Today's topic of discussion is Intellectual Property Rights (IPR).

MEANING - Intellectual Property (IP) refers to several distinct types of creations of mind for which a set of exclusive rights are recognized and the corresponding fields of laws.

IP is based on your intellectuality, certain kinds of talent, like you love to compose music, some people love to write books, some like to write scripts, and some want to invent new things. These kinds of innovations and inventions should be protected, so others don't copy them. To protect them, the government has come out with intellectual property rights, where all the people who are inventing for the betterment of the society are given a right and recognition to protect them from anyone else copying their work without their permission.

❖ TYPES OF IPR

1. TRADEMARK
2. PATENT
3. INDUSTRIAL DESIGN RIGHTS
4. TRADE SECRETS
5. COPYRIGHT

PATENT - For every invention, you get an IPR. For patent rights, you need to have an improved mechanism or a newly purchased feature. For example- if you see a canon camera it has different features, a movie camera has different features, one company cannot copy features of a canon company and add them to its features. If the company wants to copy a feature from a canon company, it has to approach the canon company and get permission from the canon company, without getting permission if you include the features, it will be legally incorrect and you can be sued for the same. For improved mechanisms, we can get a patent right. For the Design part, outer configuration design you can get a patent right. The brand name cannon is also patented and intellectual property rights are given. So no one can copy it. You might have observed that no two companies have the same name. If you are having the same name also, something would be different there. These kinds of rights are patent rights. For example- In a CD player you can get a patent right for the outer cover design, the music played. Like sa re ga ma pa, has added music from the 60s, 70s, all popular tracks. It has also come with radio where all old songs are there if I want to copy them, I cannot copy these same features if you are copying music, scripts, stories, dialogues from movies, like in movies if you are copying the same dialogue for another movie for that you need to take permission from the owner. All these things come under copyrights.

Different types of the design part, mechanism, technology will be coming under patent rights

The brand name would be registered under the trademark. If you see a Maruti, BMW, reliance, all these companies have different brand names, and they are registered under trademark, so no second company can copy your name, if someone is copying without the owner's permission or knowledge, then he will be sued by law.

There is a certain regime for Indian IPR.

1. It meets international obligations while safeguarding national interests- The copyright, trademark, the patent is at the international level, at the same time the national level is taken care of, it is important because, for ex- I love music and I am composing a piece of music is of international levels like jazz music, Rap or rock music, it is of international standards, but that international standard goes straight to the international market, without coming to India or any benefit to India. This is incorrect because I belong to India and whatever my discovery

would first be in my national then taken forward in the international market, it can be exposed to the foreign world but before that, it should be a national interest. As covid-19 is going on and if any Indian company is coming out with a vaccination that is good enough to contain covid -19 but it would be of international standards but if it is not helping India, it is not correct. It should be of national interest while having an international obligation, it should be modern, at par with the time, moving ahead with the time. Everything should be of national interest, meeting the international standards and according to the need of the hour.

There are certain legislative measures, the rules and regulations that ought to be followed, for which certain acts have been established.

❖ THE PATENTS ACT, 1970

PRODUCT PATENT - Under this act, the product is coming, which product you are coming out with, if you are inventing water bottle, which is having a 3 layer of copper coating, a layer of steel, with a silver coating, so this would be a unique type of bottle, good for health also. As you have discovered the product should be patented, the patent act is for the product, every product, bottle, CD, Cars, bikes any kind of product will come under the product patent, and the product is patented

PATENT TERM - A patent stays for 20 years after which it can be renewed.

PUBLIC HEALTH SAFEGUARDS - The product to be patented must be in favor of public health, not against it.

❖ THE TRADEMARKS ACT, 1999

SERVICE MARKS COLLECTIVE MARKS - Trademarks are for brand names, service marks, symbols, signs for a company. If in a merged company, both component companies have different logos, it is referred to as collective mark.

TERM - Previously, a trademark was provided for 7 years, which was later extended to 10 years.

THE DESIGN ACT, 2000

The Design Act started in 2000. It relates to the features and designs of the product.

THE COPYRIGHT ACT, 1957

This is to protect your music, stories, books, and dialogues.

THE BIODIVERSITY ACT, 2001

Protection of the environment, how well we can protect the environment, how we can control the climate, how we would be taking care of tree plantation, controlling soil erosion, how to clean reserves, how we can make the land more fertile, all these come under the Biodiversity Act, 2001.

THE LAYOUTS AND THE INTEGRATED CIRCUITS ACTS

The circuits within your mobiles, within radio, TV, laptops, or others through which technological instruments are coming to life are also protected.

INDUSTRIAL DESIGNS

ELECTRICAL JUG - The protection you receive is only for the appearance of the article and not how it works. If you have made an electrical jug and when you switch it then the jug comes to power and water gets boils through electricity, in industrial design, the appearance of electrical jug would be having a right, no two people can have a similar-looking jug, but the working part can be copied because in industrial design we are not protecting how it works. integrated circuits will be protected.

Design registration is intended to protect designs that have an industrial or commercial use - Any kind of industrial or commercial design will be registered, if it is beneficial to the society.

Duration of protection is initially for 10 years and extendable for another term of 5 years.

Design of stamps, labels, tokens, cards, cartoons, or parts of the article are not sold separately. A feasible copy is one in which some changes have been made.

TRADEMARKS

A trade is any sign that can distinguish the goods of one trader from those of others. The sign includes words, logos, pictures, or a combination of these. Trademarks are the signs that are separate from others. For example, shape, color, logo, and other features.

TO REGISTER A TRADEMARK THE MARK MUST BE DISTINCTIVE

When you are making a logo, and going for a trademark, it should be distinct, clear, easily differentiable. It should not be deceptive, contrary to law or morality, or identical or similar to any earlier marks for same or similar goods.

A TRADEMARK IS USED AS A MARKETING TOOL SO THAT CUSTOMERS CAN RECOGNIZE THE PRODUCT OF A PARTICULAR TRADER - It is also for a marketing thing so you can distinguish between one product and another and the customer can easily recognize. For ex- If you take a Samsung mobile and Vivo mobile, both of the features are different, customers can differentiate the logo of Samsung and Vivo, the features, size, the colour would be different in the case of both companies.

HOW TO SELECT A TRADEMARK?

1. A word letter or any combination thereof, which is simple in design
2. If it is a word, it should be easy to speak, spell, and remember
3. The ideal word for the trademark is an invented or a coined word
4. Words that are laudatory or directly describe the character or quality of the goods should not be adopted
5. Geographical names connected with the reputation or the quality of the goods for which registration is sought are all trademarkable Trademark is regarding a small, original, easy to speak and spell, and related to geographical names.
   WHAT IS GIR?
   Geographical indication restriction (GIR) is an indicator used to identify agricultural, natural, or manufactured goods originating from a definite territory in India.
   It must have a special quality or characteristics or reputation based on climatic or production characteristics unique to the

geographical location. For example, silk sarees, Banarasi silk sarees, Kanchipuram silk sarees, etc.

Any association of person, producers, organization established by or under the law can apply to represent and protect the interests of producers. GIR can be registered by those people belonging to a particular area or into manufacturing these kinds of products. At the same time, they can apply for GIR rights.

The registration of geographical indicators is 10 years- You can register once and you can have the registration for 10 years, and after that, you can renew.

Renewal is possible for a further period of 10 years - You can extend your registration for more than 10 years, but for this, you need to take permission by applying for the renewal.

A trademark is a sign that is used in a course of trade and it distinguishes goods and services of one enterprise from those of others

❖ LAW OF PATENTS

1. *PROTECTION PART*
2. *ENFORCEMENT PART*

1. *PROTECTION PART-*
- CRITERIA FOR PATENTABILITY - It should be new and useful for the public. It should also be non-obvious and available everywhere.
- *CAPABLE OF INDUSTRIAL APPLICATIONS* - The product to be patented should be easy to design and manufacture.
- PATENT ACT SPECIFIES - *What are not considered as Inventions?* the things that are not inventions, patent rights can specify. For ex- I have invented a Thermos, it is already there if I change the colour of the bottle and said this is my new invention, that is but obvious and is already there, what new have I added to that, if a new feature is not there then I will not get the right.

What are not patentable inventions? The patents that are not beneficial for the people, the society, or the country cannot be patentable inventions. For example, pistols, ammunition, guns, etc.

2. ENFORCEMENT PART-
    *   OPPOSITION PROCEEDINGS- when people say, this invention is my invention and you have copied this, these situations are opposed, how should you be taking care of this, should be looked after.
    *   LICENSING PROVISIONS- The process of getting the license, while getting a driving license certain procedures need to be followed to get driving licenses.
    *   INFRINGEMENTS SUITS PROVISIONS- If someone is copying my invention, what are the things I need to do to protect my rights.

WHAT DOES PATENT SYSTEM DO?

1. ENCOURAGES RESEARCH - Patent encourages research. If you come out with a new invention, such as goods, services, design, or medicine, it would be patented.
2. INDUCES AN INVESTOR TO DISCLOSE HIS INVENTIONS - Suppose an inventor had invented a medicine that is beneficial for COVID-19, he will be getting the right to disclose it and encourages the inventor to disclose that invention.
3. PROVIDES INDUCEMENT FOR CAPITAL INVESTMENT – Through patent, the government will give you the option for investment, where other people can help you with the invention. For example, in Ahmedabad, some people came out with an organic sanitizer spray that sanitizes the full body; the government supported this initiative by providing support and patent rights.
4. ENCOURAGES TECHNOLOGICAL DEVELOPMENT - It is required to have the new Technological development. To be on par with the world every country should have good technology. India is technologically powerful, and I feel proud to say that. Any technological development should be encouraged and given patent rights, and you are sure that no one can copy your invention.
5. ENCOURAGES ESTABLISHMENT OF NEW COMPANIES - Any kind of new company can be established through these patents.

ADVANTAGES OF A PATENT TO THE PUBLIC

1. KNOWLEDGE OF INVENTION ADDS TO THE SCIENTIFIC BACKGROUND FORMING BASE FOR FURTHER RESEARCH - Knowledge about inventions to the public. For example- the plasma treatment for COVID-19, this research is further continuing. This research would be a breakthrough for covid-19 if India would be the first to prove that through plasma treatment Covid-19 will be treated. Different parts of the world will also be benefited. A doctor from New York is trying. But India took the first step, Kerala and Telangana are also going for plasma treatment. If they succeed it will be a breakthrough and beneficial for the public.

2. REASONABLE ASSURANCE FOR COMMERCIALIZATION - In India, hydroxide sulphate is provided to different parts of the world, it is a commercial process. India is manufacturing and the world wants it, so it is for the commercial process. The patent right is with India not to the world.

3. PATENT OPEN FOR THE PUBLIC TO USE - After its term expires or when it ceases to be in force, the public can give their input with respect to your invention.

INVENTION

The invention is a successful technical solution to a technical problem - If there is a problem and you're providing a solution to the problem, then it is a new invention.

To be granted a patent, an invention must be new, non-obvious, and has industrial application – An invention should have a patent and should be new.

DIFFERENT WAYS OF DEALING WITH AN INVENTION

1. Make it public for free use by the public (like publishing in the journal)
2. Work, the invention is in secrecy without it (like coca-cola) their invention is not a secret. Everyone knows which ingredients they are using. Patenting Composition

3. Work- The invention openly without patenting it (directly put in the market)- certain works are directly put in the market without being patented or having a patent right. Suppose you are good at making chocolates and started with the chocolate brand, you are giving it for free, or you can patent it so that no one can copy, but people can use it. You can do without patent rights and give them to the public. This way you can deal with your inventions.

PATENTS

A patent is a monopoly right.

The inventor will be deciding the fate of the patent. Monopoly means whole and sole right. It is granted for any kind of invention, like food, services, medicine, etc.

It is given to the person who has invented it or to the assignee who is assigned by the inventor. It is given for a limited period and it is valid only within the country of grant.

WHY DO YOU NEED PATENT INFORMATION?

Patent information is important to understand what resources you need, how much money you need, and what raw materials would you require.

80% Not published anywhere.

FIRST PUBLICATION: Inventions disclosed in patent well before being published in any other type of document.

Invention	Patent published	the first publication in any Form
Punched card	1988.	1914
Television.	1932	1928
Jet engine	1936.	1946

When you are working on a journal or research, which is published, it will be online for that also you need to have patent information.

Expired patent - The patent rights that are already expired, can be used by the public and there is no need to pay.

To avoid redundant research, use of technology given in patent specification as a stepping stone: There is so much research done on artificial intelligence and it is a topic everywhere. People are mesmerised by artificial intelligence. AI is linked to every sector, Marketing, HR, finance, airlines, every sector. There is much research on it and still, there is a Scope for further research. If you know the patent right, the research doesn't stop there, if a person has made an AI report on how it is beneficial HR in terms of Talent management, there are other scopes for predictive analytics, future study where medical and financial Fields are benefited, how the share market will be benefited through artificial intelligence. This can only be known when I know how much research is done and what I should be doing further.

Patents not only for major technological breakthroughs

It is not only for technological breakthroughs it is also for an individual for a company and can get patent rights.

Individuals or companies do not recognize the true market value of a particular invention - If it is not a breakthrough, then the company doesn't understand the value of a small thing.

For example- Anti Theft device for motor cars- is a small thing for the company, but it is an important breakthrough for the people who are using the car and you can catch the thief easily. So this is a breakthrough for the public but not for the company and for this the patent right is required so that no one can copy the invention.

Also, the pen which has a camera and can record. All these things are small, but it helps a lot to individual Company doesn't think that it is a big thing but it is beneficial for the public and it does have a patent right. Patent rights are not only for major things but also for small things. A small thing like how you can save your petrol or how you can water your plants, like 50 plants in five minutes. These things are small but for individuals, it can be a breakthrough. The small things are not valuable for big companies but it is very beneficial for society and individuals.

For patents, it is not necessary to have a great invention. Small inventions are also eligible for a patent right, if it is beneficial for the society.

PROTECTING OF INTELLECTUAL PROPERTY IN INDIA

(PATENTS, DESIGN, TRADEMARKS and COPYRIGHTS)

Ministry of commerce and industry   Ministry of human resource
                                        development
Department of industrial policy and promotion   Dept. of
                                                   education
Controller general of patent, design & trademark   copyright office
Patent office   Trademark Registry   Registration of copyrights
         GIR
SrJoint controller   Joint registrar of
of patents and designs   trademarks

Ministry of Commerce and Industries is concerned with industrial production and manufacturing. Human resource development is related to offices and education.

1. Ministry of Commerce and Industries
    Department of industrial policy and promotion takes care of the industrial aspect, under that is controller general taking care of patent, designs and trademarks, patent office who would be giving you the patent right and this office is under Sr. joint controller of patents and designs. GIR is geographical Indication restrictions. Under the Trademark registry, the joint registrar will give the trademark rights.
2. The Minister of Human Resource Development comprises the Department of Education that looks after the educational system. The copyright office handles the registration of copyrights.

What are the problems of IPR?

1. PIRACY – It refers to creating a cheaper and fake version. Many actors crib or complain that before their movie comes out people have already seen it on their laptop or computer. Such privacy issues are not protected, making it a very difficult and common situation under IPR.
2. FREE CULTURE MOVEMENT - Intellectual monopoly consist of harming health and benefiting concentrated interest and progress. For example, diet coke is harmful to health, but is still

patented. Certain products which can be harmful to health, like diet coke. It is a patent right, monopoly, but in reality diet, coke is harmful to health. Keto diet and different diets are not good for long term goals, it will make you weak. So many drinks, products have come into the market that people don't want to go for butter instead they choose Nutrilite. Ghee is the best substitute in place of butter and Nutrilite, people think it is beneficial but in the long run, it is harmful. The intellectual policy introduces new products and society thinks it good but in the long run it is not benefiting. It is benefiting concentrated interest, through intellectual property many people have been benefited. Musicians have come out with remix versions of old songs, personally when I hear old songs of Kishor Kumar, mhd. Rafi or lata Mangeshkar, Asha Bhosle Ji, it is very touchy and I feel good. But in the remix version, they have put a modern touch and tune to it but it doesn't have the same feel, it might be catchy. These kinds of things are benefiting concentrated interest, the original songs sung by people present and others taking the songs and recreating the Remixes version are only getting benefit but the original people aren't benefited. Sometimes the song is good but not every time. The people used and copied are benefited not the original singers.

If you are inventing something, make sure you are getting a patent and IPR.

INDIAN CASE LAWS

Recent landmark judgments regarding intellectual property

1. Bajaj Electricals Limited vs. Gourav Bajaj & Anr.

Facts: The Plaintiff was a part of the renowned Bajaj industry conglomerate, and had electrical stores of the same brand name. The Defendant owned 2 electrical stores and used the name 'Bajaj' as a part of his store names and also had a website for the same. Besides this, the Defendant used the expression "Powered by: BAJAJ" in the course of his trade. The Plaintiff established their right over the name by proving that 'Bajaj' had been legally granted the status of a well-known trademark, and thus the Defendant had no right to use it. It was further contended that the use of the above stated expression by the Defendant was a clear attempt to deceive the public by suggesting that the Plaintiff sponsored/ endorsed the Defendant's stores. Thus the Plaintiff filed a suit for an injunction against the infringing act by the Defendant.

Held: The Bombay High Court pondered the question as to whether the present case came under the defense of use of personal name. They held that such defense was not valid as the Plaintiff had adequately proved the mala fide intention of the Defendant behind the adoption of the name 'Bajaj' in the course of trade. The Court passed an interim injunction against the use of the trademark in the store names as well as the domain name of the Defendant.

2. Marico Limited vs. Abhijeet Bhansali

Facts: The Defendant herein was a social media influencer, who also operated a YouTube channel of his own. In a video posted on the channel, the Defendant made denigrating comments about Parachute Coconut Oil, which is the Plaintiff Company's product. The Plaintiff Company had earned immense goodwill in the market owing to the good quality of their goods and were vigilant regarding the disparaging comments being made about their product, as well as the use of their trademark 'Parachute'. The use of the trademarked name violated the exclusive right conferred to the Plaintiff as the proprietor of the trademark, which amounted to infringement. Thus they approached the Bombay High Court seeking an injunction against the Defendant.

Held: The Court relied on the Trademarks Act, 1999 and in a clear interpretation of Section 29 of the Act, held that the Defendant was guilty of infringing the trademark of the Plaintiff by using it without prior authorization in his video. Hence, an interim injunction was passed against the Defendant along with an order for the removal of the impugned video.

3. Sameer Wadekar & Anr. vs. Netflix Entertainment Services Pvt. Ltd & Ors.

Facts: The present suit was instituted upon the basis of an allegation that the Defendant had copied the literary work of the Plaintiff and converted the same into a web series without his consent, thereby infringing his copyright. The main contention raised by the Plaintiff was that there were several similarities between his work and the web series, and that he had previously shared his work with an individual who was a known associate of the Defendant. Hence he claimed copyright infringement and sought an injunction against the release of the web series.

Held: The Bombay High Court scrutinized both the works, and concluded that the similarities were not sufficient to declare the web series as a copy of the literary work of the Plaintiff. The similarities that arose were merely related to the concept, and no infringement could be claimed for the same. It also held that the mere fact that the Plaintiff had shared his work with an associate of the Defendant was not enough to establish a prima facie case of copyright infringement. Thus the application for injunction was dismissed and the release of the web series was permitted.

4. Star India Pvt. Ltd. vs. Moviestrunk.com & Ors.

Facts: The Plaintiff herein was a film production and distribution company, whereas the Defendants operated several online streaming websites. The present suit was filed against the illegal streaming of one of the Plaintiff's films on the Defendants' websites, which amounted to copyright infringement. The Plaintiff thus approached the Delhi High Court seeking relief against the infringement.

Held: The Court recognized the right of the Plaintiff granted by the Copyright Act, 1957 over the exclusive exploitation and distribution of their copyrighted content. There was a clear case of infringement against the Defendants who had made the film available to the public without the knowledge and consent of the Plaintiff. Hence the Court granted an injunction and also awarded suitable damages.

5. International Society for Krishna Consciousness (ISKCON) vs. Iskcon Apparel Pvt. Ltd & Ors.

Facts: The present suit was filed before the Bombay High Court for alleged trademark infringement and passing off. The Plaintiff contended that by selling garments under the name of 'Iskcon', the Defendant was infringing their trademark and attempting to pass off his brand as being associated with the Plaintiff group. The Plaintiff also sought to get their mark declared as a well-known trademark.

<u>*Held:*</u> The Court declared that in the present scenario, a clear case of trademark infringement had been established, and hence ordered the Defendants to refrain using the Plaintiff's mark. It was also concluded that the Plaintiff's mark satisfied all the statutory requirements of a well-known trademark, and thus the Court declared it as such.

The Information Technology Act (IT Act), 2000

This act was established in the year 2000 and is one of the important laws related to Indian cyber laws. Cyber law relates to the cybercrimes. It was passed in the Indian Parliament in 2000 and consists of 13 chapters and 4 schedules. This law helps in promote business through the internet. Nowadays, we are getting to know cyber laws, since a large number of people are doing their business online, there is an online business setup and it is carried out through the internet. Privacy protection is very important, and, at the same time, the crimes are happening because the business is being done through the internet. Hence, Technology Act has come into existence.

Due to increased crime in cyberspace, the Indian government understood the problems of internet users, and for safeguarding the interest of internet users, this act was made. Cybercrime has increased recently. Previously, we used to go to the shop and select the dress or select furniture, that is, the transaction was physical. Nowadays, people don't have time, with a click of a button through the internet, we can select a dress, furniture, books, food, and each and everything else. When the market is open and the internet is open, anyone can click and get information. Previously when you wanted money, you had to physically go to the bank, and then, withdraw. Nowadays, through a click of a button, we are going online and transferring the money. There has been an increase in cybercrime. Along with good people, bad people are also there, waiting for an opportunity to hack your account and business information, or pass on the important aspect, material, or information regarding one country to another country. Since there is a rise in cybercrimes there is a need for an appropriate action.

❖ OBJECTIVES OF THE IT ACT

1. It is the objective of the IT Act 2000 to give legal recognition to any transaction which is done in an electronic way or through the use of the internet - Any kind of transaction in terms of money or a business document from one county to another, or a business set up outside India, if there is a requirement of certain kind of document or making passport or visa. All these documents are sent through E-media, that is, electronic media. All these transactions made should have legal recognition. If you are signing a document and sending it to my business partner, and if my signature is not legal or recognised, then the transaction will not take place. To have the recognition and legal backing, the objective of IT act is to give legal recognition through the internet.

2. To give legal recognition to digital signature for accepting any requirement via computer - If I am signing something and there is a need for my signature to carry on any business, for example, I might be having business in the USA, and since I am not available in the USA, but my company requires a signature to be made by me and sent it to them, it can be done through a digital signature and my signature will be there in the digital mode and can be sent and has legal recognition. My signature in digital mode is well acceptable and business can be carried on that basis.

3. To provide facility of online filing of documents related to school admission or a registration in employment exchange - While taking admission, because of Covid-19 too, admissions are happening online, no need of going physically. Filling the documents related to the admission process and admission is done and this is legally correct.

4. Accordingly to the I.T. Act 2000, any company can store their data in electronic storage - Storing and pilling the documents that are easy to store in the computer through electronic storage.

5. To stop computer crime and protect the privacy of internet users - Computer crime related to hacking, copying important documents, copying important information, etc. these are all private things and they should be protected.

6. To give legal recognition for keeping books of accounts by bankers and other companies in electronic form - In a bank, so many accounts and transactions are occurring nowadays, as the internet has become better, and there are so many facilities, instead of piling up the data and books and books, it is better to keep all this data safe on the internet. To make all this data safe, it is important to protect this data.

7. To give more power to IPO, RBI, and Indian evidence act for restricting electronic crime – All the currencies and the coins, whatever money-related objects are coming or whatever is available in India, it is only done and controlled by the Reserve Bank of India. And these people should be getting more power and any kind of crime happening, such as a fake note being circulated in the country. Who does this crime? People do this crime. And RBI should be given the power to control these fake notes, since this is a crime and it should be stopped.

❖ SCOPE

1. Every electronic information is under the scope of the IT Act, 2000, but following electronic transactions are not under the IT Act, 2000 – Any type of electronic information, like bank accounts, business (if a company is having an online meeting), books, each and everything – All these things are under the scope of the IT Act, 2000.

2. IT Act, 2000, is not applicable on the attestation of creating trust via electronic way; physical attestation is a must - Attestation means when you're submitting documents for admission in a college, like they say a photograph or a document should be attested by the attested officer. The signatory power like principal or vice-principal who is the head of the organisation. This is an attestation, which involves a seal and is not under the act, so it is not applicable. Attestation act is not under the IT act, as you need to be present physically.

3. Making a will of anybody - For this, physical attestation by two witnesses is must. Suppose my family is having a business and my dad feels like making a will in case he dies, to specify how will the property be divided between his children. This process should be the physical process. it cannot be done through the internet or e-media.

4. A contract of sale of any immovable property - A whole building, like the Leaning Tower of Pisa, the Ganga river, if you are going to make a contract, these are all immovable properties that you cannot simply pick up. So, all these things cannot be under the scope of the IT Act because the problematic property is immovable.

5. Attestation for giving power of attorney of property - It is not possible via electronic record. The attorney is giving a ride to another person on behalf of you and that person can take care of the property. This situation doesn't come under the IT Act, 2000, as it is taken care of physically and not electronically.

Chapters of the IT Act, 2000

- Chapter Two
  Any contract that is done by a subscriber, if he signs the electronic agreement by digital signature, will be valid. Suppose an agreement for house rent is to be made between me and my friend, but when the contract was made I was not in India, I was in Australia. But the deal can be made if I simply take out the softcopy of the agreement, do the digital signature and send it across. Then, it will be valid.

- Chapter Three
  This chapter explains the details that all electronic records of government are acceptable unless any other law has any rules regarding written or printed record. Any kind of government records in term of in terms of government business, transactions, or properties, is under the IT Act, 2000, but if someone says that it cannot come under the IT Act then it will be spared and it will not come under the IT Act.

- Chapter Four
  It deals with receipts or acknowledgement of any electronic record. Every electronic record that has any proof is called receipt and it should be in the hand of who records the electronic way. It involves any kind of receipt or acknowledgement. Say, you have taken admission in MIT college and it was online and you have a receipt of 1 lakh against the admission. It is an acknowledgement of henceforth that you have got an admission in MIT College and you are a student of MIT College. If this kind of acknowledgement is coming through electronic media, it comes under the purview of the IT Act, 2000.

- Chapter Five

  This chapter powers an organization to secure the electronic records and digital signatures. These can be secured by applying any new verification system. When you have a digital record or a digital signature or an electronic record, then it is the responsibility of the company to secure it in any way it feels necessary. There is no fixed way to secure it.

- Chapter Six

  This chapter states that the Government of India will appoint a controller of certifying authorities and he will control all activities of certifying authorities. "Certifying authority is the authority who issues digital signature certificate". There should be a controller who should be controlling every process. In this chapter, we are talking about the appointment of certifying authority. He is the person who gives and who has the authority to certify that a digital signature is a legal one. Certification regarding digital signature will be given by the authority that is appointed by the government and this will hold true for any kind of document or business transaction that takes place.

- Chapter Seven

  In this chapter, powers and duties of certifying authority are given. Certifying authority will issue a digital signature certificate after getting Rs. 25,000. If it is against public interest, then certifying authority can suspend the digital signature certificate. To have a digital signature, you must pay Rs. 25,000 to the certifying authority and once the person gets the money, then the certifying authority will give you the digital certificate that contains your digital signature, which is legally recognized. But, if it is against the public interest, then the certificate would be suspended.

- Chapter Eight

  This chapter tells about the duties of a subscriber regarding a digital signature certificate. It is the duty of the subscriber to accept all information and digital signature certificate that, within his knowledge, is true. In this chapter, it gives information to the person who has applied for a digital signature. If I am a subscriber and opting for a digital signature, it is mandatory for me to fulfill all the terms and conditions of the authority and that whatever information I am providing should be true.

- Chapter Nine

  If anybody or a group of body damages the computer, computer system, or the computer networks by electronic hacking, then they are responsible to pay a penalty of up to Rs. 1 crore. For judgment on this, the government can appoint an adjudicating officer. So, let's say someone is hacking a computer. Nowadays, there are many ethical hackers, and ethical hacking is good for business. But there is some unethical hacking too, which is used by terrorists to access the essential documents from the computer of India or any other country. Some essential documents that are relevant and vital from a country point of view as well as competitive are using documents from another company. If these documents would leak, then it would be very harmful to the company. This kind of thing is known as unethical hacking. Nowadays, many people are also hacking accounts and it is unethical hacking. If someone is hacking, unethically through computers and computer networks by electronic hacking and if they are found out, then they have to pay a penalty of Rs.1,00,00,000. To give this judgment and punish them, the government appoints adjudicating officers who will take care of this and give the relevant punishment.

- Chapter Ten

  Under this chapter, a cyber-regulation appellate tribunal was established. It can solve cases related to orders of adjudicating officer. The adjudicating officer is already appointed to curse the unethical hackers. The pending cases will be taken care of by the appellate, which is again appointed by the government

- Chapter Eleven

  For controlling cybercrime, the government can appoint cyber regulation advisory committee that will check all the cybercrime. If anyone is found responsible for a cybercrime, they would be responsible for paying Rs. 2 lakhs or can get up to three years imprisonment or both. Such penalties are applicable for any kind of cybercrime, like the morphing of a picture to degrade a person's reputation and image, hacking the account of a person to steal important documents from someone's computer, etc.

- Chapter Twelve

  Police officers also have the power to investigate dangerous cybercrimes under IPC Section 1860, Indian Evidence Act, 1872,

RBI Act, 1934, and IT Act, 2000. These are especially applicable for dangerous cybercrimes, like a person is being threatened by murder, some terrorist attack has been planned, a terrorist has entered the country, or some important information or documents have been taken away from the intelligence system and given away to another country.

The IT Act, till chapter 12, deals with various types of cybercrimes and how people can be protected from them. It has extended all the powers from the police to individual powers for the protection of business privacy and all the important personal documents.

ADVANTAGES OF THE IT ACT, 2000

1. Helpful in promoting e-commerce (electronic commerce or electronic business) - Nowadays people don't want to go to a shop themselves and purchase anything, and if you want to set up a business, it is not vital for you to have a physical place to show the people. If you see, big companies like Myntra and Amazon are doing business through electronic media. It is online business and the advantage is that you don't need to have more people, you just need a computer and a server with the business and the most important thing is that the customer can go online and check and select from the choices available and even the business is easier through the click of a button The business is done and the transaction takes place at the same time. The goods are delivered in a few days. These are the advantages of carrying a business through electronic media and helps in promoting e-commerce.

2. Enhance the corporate business - Suppose while doing the business a customer is facing some problem. Like, say, if I have a mobile shop and one customer is not happy with their mobile or wants to go for a recharge, instead of the customer coming to my shop I can always help the customer online. First, the customer has to pay online. Once I provide the service, I will send the receipt online. I will not send any person physically to collect the cash or give him the receipt. What the customer wants we can know easily through emails. Any business document or a signature required can be attained online. So, the corporate business has enhanced. Through e-commerce business, the customer can be taken care of easily and

the information regarding any future product or the future plan by the company can be easily given to the consumer.

3. High plenty for cybercrime - If a cybercrime is taking place, like hacking, there is a penalty of Rs.1 crore. If any person is found indulging in any kind of cybercrime, like documents stealing or hacking an account, then there is a penalty of Rs. 2 lakh and prison for three years.

4. Filling exams form - Colleges forms, school forms, admission forms, business formalities or any online lecture, for all these, filing of form online can save up a lot of time and money.

SHORTCOMINGS OF THE IT ACT, 2000

1. Infringement of copyright has not been influenced by this law - Now, students. You already know everything about copyright. Suppose if I am writing a book, it is my private property and no one has the right to copy my book without my knowledge. So, what I will do is, I will apply to the government and I will get a copyright for my book so no one can copy it. If someone is infringing the copyright and is copying certain things from my book without my knowledge, despite my having the copyright, then such activities do not come under the IT Act, 2000.

2. No protection for the domain name - The domain name is the address of the website. And they are a private entity. If, suppose, I have a website named Professor Reena Lenka's website and if someone is copying my name, it is totally against the law, but it doesn't come under the protection of the IT Act, 2000. It won't be a criminal offence but it will be a civil offence.

3. Act is not applicable on the power of attorney, trusts, and will - This act is not for any attorney, trust, or will. An attorney means that you are giving them the power to look after your business so that this online thing cannot happen, and for this, sometimes, physical presence is required. Trust will come under the purview of the IT Act, 2000.

4. Act is silent in matters of taxation - Any kind of tax, taxation on luxury item, taxation on business, taxation on travel, and taxation in restaurants, all of these cannot come under the IT Act, 2000.

5. No provision of payment for stamp duty on electronic documents - Any kind of documents must be legal. Suppose you have joined a

company as an HR and if you've given an offer letter and in that offer letter there is a stamp of the company. For example, if, say, you join Reliance. Then, the stamp of Reliance would've come on the offer letter and this stamp duty makes it legal and proves that you are employed by Reliance, and if something unfavorable happens in the future, then Reliance can be taken to the court. The stamp duty cannot be an electronic; it has to be physical, so it doesn't come under the IT Act, 2000.

INDIAN CASE LAWS

Section 66-A, Information Technology Act, 2000: Cases

1. Sajeesh Krishnan v. State of Kerala (Kerala High Court, Decided on June 5, 2012)

Petition before High Court for release of passport seized by investigating agency during arrest

In the case of Sajeesh Krishnan v. State of Kerala (Decided on June 5, 2012), a petition was filed before the Kerala High Court for release of passport seized at the time of arrest from the custody of the investigating agency. The Court accordingly passed an order for release of the passport of the petitioner.

The Court, while deciding the case, briefly mentioned the facts of the case which were relevant to the petition. It stated that the "gist of the accusation is that the accused pursuant to a criminal conspiracy hatched by them made attempts to extort money by black mailing a Minister of the State and for that purpose they have forged some CD as if it contained statements purported to have been made by the Minister." The Court also noted the provisions under which the accused was charged. They are Sections 66-A(b) and 66D of the Information Technology Act, 2000 along with a host of sections under the Indian Penal Code, 1860 (120B – Criminal Conspiracy, 419 – Cheating by personation, 511- Punishment for attempting to commit offences punishable with imprisonment for life or other imprisonment, 420 – Cheating and dishonestly inducing delivery of property, 468 – Forgery for purpose of cheating, 469 – Forgery for purpose of harming and 201 – Causing disappearance of evidence of offence, or giving false information to screen offender read with 34 of Indian Penal Code, 1860)

2. Nikhil Chacko Sam v. State of Kerala (Kerala High Court, Decided on July 9, 2012)

Order of the Kerala High Court on issuing of the summons to the petitioner

In another case, the Kerala High Court while passing an order with respect to summons issued to the accused, also mentioned the charge sheet laid by the police against the accused in its order. The accused was charged under section 66-A, ITA. The brief facts which can be extracted from the order of the Court read: "that the complainant and the accused (petitioner) were together at Chennai. It is stated that on 04.09.2009, the petitioner has transmitted photos of the de facto complainant and another person depicting them in bad light through internet and thus the petitioner has committed the offence as mentioned above."

3. J.R. Gangwani and Another v. State of Haryana and Others (Punjab and Haryana High Court, Decided on October 15, 2012)

Petition for quashing of criminal proceedings under section 482 of the Criminal Procedure Code, 1973

In the Punjab and Haryana High Court, an application for quashing of criminal proceeding draws attention to a complaint which was filed under Section 66-A(c). This complaint was filed under Section 66-A(c) on the ground of sending e-mails under assumed e-mail addresses to customers of the Company which contained material which maligned the name of the Company which was to be sold as per the orders of the Company Law Board. The Complainant in the case received the e-mails which were redirected from the customers. According to the accused and the petitioner in the current hearing, the e-mail was not directed to the complainant or the company as is required under Section 66-A (c).

The High Court held that, "the petitioners are sending these messages to the purchasers of cranes from the company and those purchasers cannot be considered to be the possible buyers of the company. Sending of such e-mails, therefore, is not promoting the sale of the company which is the purpose of the advertisement given in the Economic Times. Such advertisements are, therefore, for the purpose of causing annoyance or inconvenience to the company or to deceive or mislead the addressee about the origin of such messages. These facts, therefore, clearly bring the acts of the petitioners within the purview of section 66A(c) of the Act."

4. Mohammad Amjad v. Sharad Sagar Singh and Ors. (Criminal Revision no. 72/2011 filed before the Court of Sh. Vinay Kumar Khana Additional Sessions Judge – 04 South East: Saket Courts Delhi)

Revision petition against the order of the metropolitan magistrate

In a revision petition came up before the Additional Sessions Judge on the grounds that the metropolitan magistrate has dismissed a criminal complaint under Section 156(3) of the Criminal Procedure Code without discussing the ingredients of section 295-A, IPC and 66-A, IT Act.

In this case, the judge observed that,"...section 66A of Information Technology Act (IT Act) does not refer at all to any 'group' or 'class' of people. The only requirement of Section 66A IT Act is that the message which is communicated is grossly offensive in nature or has menacing character." He also observed that the previous order "not at all considered the allegations from this angle and the applicability of Section 66A Information Technology Act, 2000 to the factual matrix of the instant case."